AS GOOD AS NEW

A GUIDE TO RENOVATING THE EXTERIOR OF YOUR OLDER HOUSE

Prepared by Paul J. Jakubovich, preservation consultant for

The City of Milwaukee, Wisconsin

John O. Norquist, Mayor

ACKNOWLEDGEMENTS

As Good As New was published in July, 1993 by the Department of City Development of the City of Milwaukee, John O. Norquist, Mayor.

Author:
Paul Jakubovich
Preservation Consultant
with assistance from Carlen Hatala
and Les Vollmert

Original Artwork and Photographs:
Paul Jakubovich

Cover Design
Dennis Zuber

❖ ❖ ❖

Graphic Design and Pre-Press Production:
General Graphics Corp.
Milwaukee, WI

Word Processing
Linda Wallner

❖ ❖ ❖

Printing:
A to Z Printing Company, Inc.
Wauwatosa, WI

Many people have assisted the project staff during the preparation of **As Good As New,** and their help is gratefully acknowledged. The following people made significant contributions to the production of **As Good As New:**

Abatron, Inc.

Mayra Donnell, Donnell's Clapboard Mill

Al Emmons, Jr., Creative Construction, Inc.

Bud Endries, Creative Changes

Richard Gifford, Advance Photo Service

David La Haye, Videographer, Dept. of City Development, City of Milwaukee

Lee Hanks, Forest Products Technologist, Eastern Region, U.S. Forest Service

John S. Lindstedt, President, Artistic Plating Co.

Ernst and Wayne S. Pretschold, Pretschold-Milwaukee Awning Corp.

Ruth Ruege, Rare Books Librarian, Milwaukee Public Library

Virginia Schwartz, Coordinator of Humanities, Milwaukee Public Library

Gary Serwatt, William Pietsch Co.

Judith A. Simonsen, Curator of Research Collection, Milwaukee County Historical Society

Keith Stankewicz, National Paint and Wallpaper Co.

State Historical Society of Wisconsin

John Tadych, American Building Restoration

Frank van der Hoogt, Enterprise Art Glass Works, Inc.

The project **As Good As New** has been funded with the assistance of a grant-in-aid from the National Park Service, U.S. Department of the Interior, under provisions of the National Historic Preservation Act of 1966, as amended. Historic Preservation grants-in-aid are administered in Wisconsin in conjunction with the National Register of Historic Places program by the Division of Historic Preservation of the State Historical Society of Wisconsin. The contents and opinions contained in this publication do not necessarily reflect the views or policies of the National Park Service, the State Historical Society of Wisconsin or the City of Milwaukee.

This book may be ordered from:
Department of City Development,
Historic Preservation Planning Staff,
P.O. Box 324,
Milwaukee, WI 53201-0324.
(414) 286-5707

City
of
Milwaukee

Published By
The Department of City Development
July 1993

Second Printing December 1999

Cover Photo: The Sanford Kane House, 1841 N. Prospect Avenue.   *Title Page Photo: The transom at the George P. Miller House, 1060 E. Juneau Avenue.*

AS GOOD AS NEW

A Guide to Renovating the Exterior of Your Older House

TABLE OF CONTENTS

INTRODUCTION

INTRODUCTION

INTRODUCTION

INTRODUCTION

INTRODUCTION

INTRODUCTION

INTRODUCTION

INTRODUCTION

INTRODUCTION

INTRODUCTION

This book is intended to assist property owners to properly rehabilitate the exteriors of older houses in Milwaukee. It includes information on the designs, materials and construction methods that are needed to undertake a successful rehabilitation today. A successful rehabilitation is one in which the distinctive original exterior features of your house are treated appropriately. The intent is not to require complete restoration, but rather to ensure that, as a house is repaired and updated, the original character is not obscured by unsympathetic alterations. Too often the history of an older house unfolds as a series of well-intentioned, but hapless, remodelings and insensitive "modernizations" that have gradually eroded the beauty and intrinsic value of a house. Milwaukee has lost almost as much of its valuable architectural heritage to bad remodelings as it has to demolition.

Today, intact historic architectural character is a marketable asset in Milwaukee's older neighborhoods. In fact, many people will pay more for an old house that has retained its original exterior features than they will for a "modernized" older house that has been sided and stripped of its porches, ornate trim and original windows. This book is conceived as a guide to help you make well-informed design decisions in the hope that the architectural integrity and old world craftsmanship of Milwaukee's houses will no longer be needlessly lost in the name of improvement. ∎

Milwaukee County Historical Society

A Milwaukee duplex at 2021-23 N. 28th street as it looked in 1907 when it retained its original architectural detailing.

2021-23 N. 28th street as it looks today stripped of its architectural character by successive insensitive remodelings.

Previous Page: A Street Scene in the North Point North Historic District

GETTING STARTED

GETTING STARTED

GETTING STARTED

GETTING STARTED

GETTING STARTED

GETTING STARTED

GETTING STARTED

GETTING STARTED

GETTING STARTED

GETTING STARTED

THEY DON'T MAKE HOUSES LIKE THEY USED TO

So you have an old house that needs to be fixed-up and you are not quite sure where to start. Perhaps your first thought is to tear off all that old paint encrusted wood trim and give the house the streamlined, clean, modern lines of the new houses that are being built in the suburbs. After all, if a new suburban house costing well over $100,000 doesn't have large windows, a generous front porch, wood trim around the windows and doors or fancy trim at the eaves, can these features really be all that good? On the other hand, perhaps you like the way older houses look, but have been told that it is impossible to get old features repaired or replicated, that certain traditional building materials are not available today or that preserving a house's character costs so much more than conventional remodeling that it is a luxury strictly for the rich.

The interior of an architectural salvage warehouse where old house parts are sold as antiques.

Salvage One, Chicago

Our purpose in writing this book is to show you that you can rehabilitate your house in a way that will bring out its best features without costing a fortune. We want you to know that the craftsmanship and unique features commonly found on older houses are intrinsically valuable and worth keeping in the same way that antique furniture is valuable today. In fact, it is a sad comment on the growing appreciation for handcrafted old house parts that a brisk illicit business has developed in stealing architectural features off old houses for resale as "architectural antiques." Once limited largely to fireplace mantels and stained glass, today dealers are marketing exterior pieces such as original front doors, ornamental exterior panels, eaves brackets, porch railings, and porch columns removed from old houses. The fact is that the craftsmanship, materials and design features of days gone by can seldom be matched today and to destroy such features is to throw away part of the value of your old house. The original style of your house also contributes to the value of your entire neighborhood and for this reason it should be preserved as a neighborly gesture for the benefit of all. By carefully maintaining your house's remaining historic features and, perhaps, restoring things that have been lost or have deteriorated, you will be preserving and enhancing its value for years to come. You may also be saving yourself a great deal of money, since it often costs just as much or more money to do an inappropriate remodeling as it does to do a sensitive rehabilitation.

When planning the work, it is important to keep the following points in mind.

1. You <u>can</u> make your house comfortable, safe, convenient and energy efficient without eliminating what is old and valuable. For example, old windows can be made energy efficient without changing their appearance from the exterior.

2. Although you can express your personal taste in your home by the colors, wallpapers, and furnishings you choose, you should resist the temptation to alter the stylistic character of the exterior of your house to reflect your taste by, for example, trying to make your Victorian house look "colonial" on the outside by removing the porch and installing a fake Georgian door.

3. Try to think of your old house as a single unit with no removable parts. Every change you make chips away at the integrity of your house. The cumulative effect of lots of small changes such as blocking down original window openings to accept smaller, stock-sized windows, or substituting wrought-iron for original wooden porch posts is a loss of character, and, in today's old house real estate market, often a loss of resale value as well.

WHAT DO THE TERMS RESTORE, REMODEL AND REHABILITATE MEAN

Although these three terms are often used interchangeable today, they actually mean very different things. The word "restore" means to return a building to its original appearance by stripping away later additions and authentically returning it to the way it looked at some particular time in its early history. This treatment is usually reserved for museum structures, such as the Pabst Mansion, because of the expense of meticulously restoring or replacing old materials and features exactly the way they originally were.

"Remodel" often means the opposite of restore. It is frequently the process of stripping away a house's original features so that it will have a new architectural character completely unlike its original look. The goal of a successful remodeling is often to make the building's original appearance unrecognizable. Typical remodeling activities would include removing an original porch, installing siding over the original siding and all of the trim, replacing the windows with new windows unlike the original ones in size and appearance and making additions that are out of character with the original building.

"Rehabilitate" means to take steps to return a structure to a state of good repair and update it to accommodate modern life styles and standards of comfort and efficiency. Rehabilitation includes aspects of restoration: retaining and repairing original features; renovation: incorporating new elements such as updated electrical circuitry, heating plants or skylights; and remodeling: totally changing an original feature, such as the reconstruction of an old kitchen or bath or the installation of a backyard deck and the conversion of a rear window to a set of French doors to provide access to it. The important thing to remember about proper rehabilitation is that it preserves the old structural and decorative features that give a house its style by using modern elements sparingly and only in a manner that is sympathetic to the original design. Proper rehabilitation is what this book is about.

WHAT TO DO BEFORE YOU START

Most successful rehabilitation projects, even seemingly minor ones, involve three distinct phases: research; planning and design; and hiring a contractor and beginning construction. Short-cutting any one of these phases or doing them out of order can result in a less than satisfactory finished project. Doing rehabilitation work on a house is a serious, time consuming and expensive business and should be approached with the same care and forethought that you would put into buying a car, planning a long vacation trip or making a major financial investment. Time and effort spent up front before the first nail is hammered or board is cut will reap rewards by saving money, avoiding delay, and minimizing frustration later.

One of the first things you should do is to become familiar with your house and its

Milwaukee County Historical Society

2597 N. Oakland Avenue as it originally looked.

A 1991 view of the same building as remodeled shows the cumulative result of numerous small but insensitive changes that have robbed the building of its historic character.

architectural style. Go outside and look at your house, note especially its materials, shape, and decorative features. Each house, no matter how modest, has features that give it its architectural style. Among the most important of these are: the building materials; the front door and front porch; the windows and their decorative trim; and the roof shape and cornice. It is the way these features are put together that gives a house its special character and defines its style. The next chapter, "Architectural Styles of Milwaukee's Houses," provides information that will help you determine the style of your house.

In the process of getting familiar with your house's architectural style, you may become interested in researching your house's history. Finding out when a house was built, who the architect was, and who first lived there is enjoyable, detective-like work that can usually be done by the homeowner. It can produce some pleasant surprises and increase your interest in the property. During a thorough research process, a wealth of details about the history of a house and its occupants can be uncovered that can be used to guide the planning and design of a rehabilitation. Doing research will also heighten your awareness of the time period during which your house was constructed. This can be very helpful when trying to select materials and fittings that are historically appropriate for the house.

The history of an older building is developed by piecing together bits of information from a variety of sources that include, but are not limited to, the following: original building permits, City tax roll records, Milwaukee Sentinel newspaper articles indexed by subject from 1848-1890, plans filed at the

Wisconsin Architectural Archive, Milwaukee City Directories, Milwaukee County Deeds, old fire insurance maps, and historic photos. Before you start researching the house yourself, you should call the City of Milwaukee

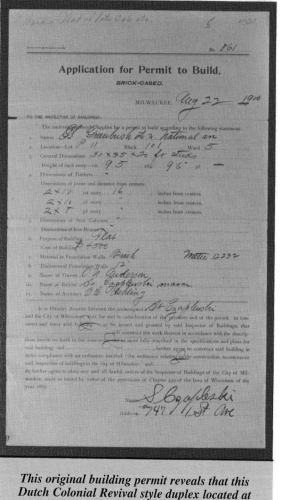

This original building permit reveals that this Dutch Colonial Revival style duplex located at 806-808 S. 4th Street was built in 1900 at a cost of $4500 to the designs of local architect Otto C. Uehling for O. N. Anderson.

Historic Preservation Commission to see what information they already have on file.

806-808 S. 4th Street today.

Finding the construction date of a house is of prime importance so that the rehabilitation work can accurately reflect the period in which the house was built. If the Historic Preservation Commission does not have information on your house, you should start by looking for the original building permit. If the house was built after the city started issuing building permits in 1888, there is a good chance that the original permit will still be on file with the City's Department of Building Inspection (Municipal Building, 10th Floor, 841 North Broadway). An original permit typically lists the original owner, architect (if any), builder, type of foundation, overall dimensions, estimated cost, and the type of exterior wall construction. Although not all buildings will have an original permit on file, most will have at least some permits for later repairs that document changes to the building or the construction of outbuildings such as a barn or garage.

A researcher often has to interpret and expand on small pieces of information to explain and date the apparent changes to a building over the years. It is not unusual for seemingly small interior work recorded in a permit to coincide with undocumented, significant exterior changes to the building as well. A plumbing permit for a new bathtub and sink, for example, may pinpoint the date of other alterations done as part of a general campaign to bring a house up to date.

If an original permit does not exist, there are other options for determining the age of a building, but the process is more complicated and sometimes only an approximate construction date can be determined. If you fail to find an original building permit, as would be the case with most buildings built before 1888, the next step would be to research old City tax records at the Milwaukee Central Public Library, 814 West Wisconsin Avenue. You must have an exact legal description of the property and its ward number in order to track the property in the tax rolls from year to year. Although tax rolls usually make no specific mention of buildings, there is a dollar value given for both the "Real Estate," which

means the value of the land only, and for "Improvements," which generally refers to the value of buildings. The first year that significant taxable "Improvements" appear on the tax role often indicates the date that the first major building was erected on a property. Tax roll research, especially interpreting a change in value, can become very complicated and confusing, and you may need the assistance of someone experienced in this type of work to help you.

Another research method for determining a construction date is using a combination of information from Milwaukee City Directories, insurance atlases, and property deeds. Milwaukee City Directories, published annually since 1847, almost without interruption, list alphabetically by surname the names, addresses and occupations of all city residents. Property deeds are filed at the Milwaukee County Courthouse, 901 North Ninth Street, for all property in Milwaukee County. Each time a property is sold, a new deed is recorded. Deeds generally do not make specific mention of the dates buildings were constructed on them, but the sales value of the property, which is recorded on each deed, can be an indicator when a significant improvement, such as a house, was built on the property. In general, deed research is valuable because it provides the names of all of the owners of a property. The home addresses of the owners and their occupations can be tracked year by year through the listings in the city directories to pinpoint or confirm the dates and location where a person lived. Often the construction date of a house may coincide with the first year that an owner appears in the city directory at that address. If no owner is listed as living on a property at a certain

date, it may indicate that the land was vacant. It is up to the expertise of the researcher to determine whether an existing building could have been constructed at the date indicated by the research. Deed and city directory research usually has to be used in conjunction with tax roll research to pinpoint the construction date of a building.

Insurance atlases, which are books of maps of the city showing the outlines of buildings, were published regularly from 1876 into the later 1950s. These are useful in combination with deed research, the tax rolls, and city directories to pinpoint the approximate construction date of a house. For example, if a house does not appear in the 1876 atlas, but does appear in the 1882 atlas, it can be concluded that it was built between 1876 and 1882, thus narrowing the time period that must be researched. Insurance atlases can be found at the Central Library and at the County Historical Society Library, 910 N. Old World Third Street. Care must be taken in using these atlases because some editions were updated in subsequent years by pasting little patches of paper showing the outlines of new buildings that had been built over the original pages. Since the paste-overs are not dated, it is impossible to know when a building on a paste-over in an updated atlas was built.

The two major photo collections accessible to the public which feature historic Milwaukee architecture are at the Local History Room of the Milwaukee Central Public Library and the Milwaukee County Historical Society. The chances of finding historic photos of your old house in one of the collections are actually very small. Most historic house photos are still owned privately in small private collections or kept in family photo albums. Researching the public photo collections, however, can be very valuable in terms of learning more about historic architectural styles and details in Milwaukee, and you might just get lucky and find an old view of your house.

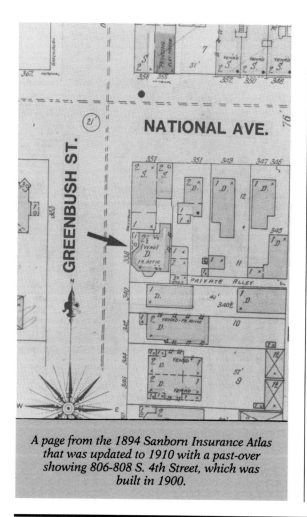

A page from the 1894 Sanborn Insurance Atlas that was updated to 1910 with a past-over showing 806-808 S. 4th Street, which was built in 1900.

The Wisconsin Architectural Archive located at the Milwaukee Central Public Library is a repository for many old architectural drawings. Although the collection mostly contains architectural drawings for large, expensive homes, churches, commercial, and institutional buildings, there are some drawings of more modest Milwaukee homes that can serve as references for recreating architectural detail on similar houses. The drawings are mostly catalogued by the architect's name.

Finally, if you are interested in learning more about the life of a former occupant of your house, you could consult the following published histories of Milwaukee which contain biographies of many of the city's early shopkeepers, tradesworkers, business leaders and professionals. Because of the similarity of the titles of these books, most historians refer to them by the names of their editors.

History of Milwaukee (1881) Frank A. Flower, ed., Chicago: Western Historical Publishing Co.

History of Milwaukee: From Its First Settlement to the Year 1895 (ca. 1896) Howard Louis Conard, ed., Chicago: American Biographical Publishing Co.

Memoirs of Milwaukee County (1909) Jerome A. Watrous, ed. Madison, WI: Western Historical Association.

History of Milwaukee City and County (1922) William George Bruce, ed. Milwaukee: S. J. Clarke Publishing Co.

History of Milwaukee, Wisconsin (1931) John B. Gregory, ed. Milwaukee: S. J. Clarke Publishing Co.

If the previous owner of your house is not mentioned in the published histories, you may be able to glean at least some information by consulting the Milwaukee City Directories, published almost without interruption since 1847, which list the names and occupations of all city residents. Some of the earlier city directories also record the date of death of a householder, if it occurred during the year of publication.

PLANNING THE REHAB

Careful planning is vital to a successful rehabilitation. Before any actual work begins, it is important to establish a master plan for the project. Before you order any materials or enter into any contracts with tradesmen, you need to sit down and think through what you want to change, why you need to do it, and in what chronological order the work should proceed. In deciding what needs to be done, you need to create a prioritized list of activities with essential maintenance items, such as roofing, at the top of the list and amenities, such as a new patio or deck, further down the list. You must do the basics first by addressing life and safety hazards such as faulty electrical or heating systems as your highest priority, followed in order by weatherproofing (repairing or replacing the roof, gutters, flashings, siding, paint, windows or drainage), and then tackling plumbing, dry-rot, and long-term foundation problems. After you have addressed these needs, you can go on to restore damaged or missing architectural features or perhaps remodel a kitchen or bathroom or add amenities such as a new room.

When planning the rehabilitation of an old house, homeowners are typically faced with the need to make judgments about which features are salvageable or should be saved and which are expendable. It is a common pitfall to remove too much historic building material that is still perfectly sound or could have been repaired and saved, often at a lower cost than installing the new and usually lesser-quality materials available today. Far too much of our architectural heritage has been ripped out of older buildings and consigned to the dumpster because it was thought to be irreparable. When too much original material is torn out, the cost of the job is needlessly increased, leaving little money for recreating missing details in the original style or adding amenities. Contractors, who are not familiar with restoration techniques or the value of older materials, are often too quick to judge material as "unsalvageable." Remember that it is easy and cheap to rip things out of a building, but it is very difficult and expensive to put new things in. So do not allow yourself to get carried away when you start demolishing old work, because if you do, you will pay for it later. Always try to work with and save original material when possible. This is done for sound economic as well as historic reasons. Of course not all old work is good, but generally if the design of an architectural detail is consistent with the style of the house and the workmanship and the inherent quality of the material is good, it should probably be saved.

After you have decided on a master work plan for your rehabilitation, you need to decide what you can do yourself and what you need to hire a professional to do. Although there is quite a bit of work you can do yourself with a little practice, enough time, and the proper tools, there are some jobs that you should probably contract out. Electrical and plumbing work are usually best left to professionals because of the complexity of the codes and the legal requirement to have at least electrical work done by a licensed electrician. In general, you should probably hire a professional when the task requires technical skills you lack and cannot readily learn; the task requires equipment you do not have, cannot rent or is highly complex or dangerous to operate; the building codes are so complex you cannot understand them; the quality of your workmanship is so poor that the resulting work is likely to detract from the appearance or structural integrity of your house; you need to have the work done within a short time; your time is worth more than what it would cost to hire the work out; and whenever you find yourself involved in a task and realize that you just don't know what you are doing.

On your average residential rehab project, there is quite a bit of work you can do yourself and, for economic reasons, may, in fact, have to do yourself. Although do-it-yourself jobs can be satisfying and cost-saving to a homeowner, you should keep in mind that learning a rehabilitation trade skill from scratch takes time and practice and early experiments with a new skill do not always produce professional-looking results. In general, rehabilitation work is time-consuming even for professionals, so be honest with yourself about the amount of time you can devote to a project. You can probably safely tackle tasks that require meticulous attention and extraordinary sensitivity to architectural features; that utilize skills or equipment you are familiar with or would like to learn; and that are time consuming, but do not require much skill, such as stripping paint from woodwork. If you are serious about doing considerable amounts of rehabilitation work yourself, you are going to have to be equally serious about the tools you buy or rent to get the job done. Do not be fooled into thinking that you can make reproduction moldings, doors and balusters yourself, unless you have a considerable assemblage of professional-grade machinery and tools as well as the skill to use them. Remember that 100 years ago much of the wooden millwork seen on old houses was produced in factories by skilled workers using heavy machinery that would be considered sophisticated even by today's standards.

Sturdy, heavy-duty ladders are essential for rehabilitation work and steel frame scaffolding is also almost indispensable for many exterior and interior projects. It is much easier to work from a scaffold than it is to spend many backbreaking hours standing on a narrow ladder rung. Purchasing a few sections of scaffolding is a good investment if your project is lengthy, but scaffolding can also be rented by the day, week or month.

It is also advisable to purchase quality, contractor-grade small power tools, such as a drill, router, circular saw, or cordless driver/drill because you will be subjecting them to the same uses and conditions encountered by professional contractors. Professional power tools have a greater initial cost than homeowner grade tools, but they last much longer, produce better quality work, and get the job done faster to reduce operator fatigue. One common pitfall among amateur rehabbers is failing to keep the cutting edges of chisels, planes, and saw blades in sharp condition. Dull tools are difficult to work with, can be unsafe to the user, and produce poor quality work. Some homeowners have bought special tools and other equipment and then sold them when the work was finished to recoup some of the cost of the project. Fortunately, many of the tools you will need to rehabilitate your house can be rented at a low cost from one of the city's tool loan centers, which are listed in the government section of the telephone directory under City of Milwaukee.

SELECTING A CONTRACTOR

Inevitably, professional help will have to be hired to complete part or all of some rehabilitation projects. Hiring the right architect or contractor is a skill in itself. The Yellow Pages of the telephone directory contain literally pages of listings of contractors, but figuring out which one is right for you will require considerable detective work. It is very important not to skimp on this task, since hiring the wrong contractor can turn your rehabilitation into a costly nightmare. Start by getting recommendations from friends, relatives, neighbors or even strangers who have had good rehabilitation work done on their houses similar to what you want to do. Go look at completed jobs and, if possible, talk to the clients to see how they felt about their working relationship with the contractor. Was the contractor reliable about appearing for work and staying on the job until it was completed? Did he or she abide by their estimates? Was the contractor generally honest? Of course, you should talk to the contractor yourself to determine if he or she will be easy to work with. Most contractors have their own way of doing

things, so make sure their way will be sensitive to respecting the historic fabric and architectural character of your house and that they understand that you are not looking for a standard "remodeling" job. Above all, do not settle for the response, "You can't get that kind of work today." In recent years, there has been a veritable renaissance in the manufacture of traditional building materials and a

significant increase in the number of restoration-conscious tradeworkers. Rehabbers and contractors today do not have to rely mainly on architectural salvage dealers for old house parts as was the case fifteen years ago. The list of companies that make building products designed for the restoration and reproduction housing market has grown tremendously over the past several years. In 1976, there were

Scaffolding makes working on big projects much easier.

reportedly only 205 companies nationwide whose products could be considered historically styled. By 1991, that list had grown to nearly 3,000 companies and continues to expand rapidly. You may have to catalog shop by mail for some architectural items, but in the old days, Milwaukee builders, architects and homeowners did the very same thing to get unique architectural features for their houses.

Once you have narrowed your search to a few candidates, check to make sure the contractor has an established business. Consumer fraud in the home-improvement business is one of the biggest rackets in the United States. Fly-by-night contractors abound. Check to see if the contractor has an office, preferably with at least one staff member, and how long he or she has been in business. Check with the Better Business Bureau for registered complaints. Check to see if the contractor is licensed, insured and bonded. Although hiring a licensed contractor does not assure you of getting the right person for your job, at least it is another indication that your candidate may be a serious professional with a reputation to protect.

When you are fairly comfortable with your field of candidates, get competitive bids in writing from at least three different contractors on the same set of plans or written specifications. Tell each exactly what work you want done and the quality of the materials you expect. Have the contractor indicate when he expects to start the work and how long it will take. If a contractor suggests adding work beyond what you have asked for, have him give you a separate price for that. Once the bids are in, discard any that seem excessively low or excessively high. Keeping in mind that the low bid may not be the best one to go with, decide among those in the mid-range based upon the contractor's reputation, the quality of similar work he has done in the past, his reliability, and your impression of how well the two of you would get along. Bear in mind when reviewing the bids, that good contractors cannot work cheap because a contractor's labor rate must take into account overhead costs such as the insurance, tools, and trucks that contractors must maintain in order to stay in business. Contractors who submit very low bids often do not carry insurance, have poor quality or inadequate equipment, and may not be familiar with restoration work. Also, good contractors are often busy and you may have to wait for them to have an opening on their schedules to start your job.

Once you have selected a contractor, define your mutual obligations in a written contract referenced to a detailed set of plans or specifications describing the work. Most contractors will submit their bid on a contract form that you accept merely by signing and returning with a downpayment. Before you sign such a form, you need to be sure that the work described in the bid is exactly what you want done. If the contract language for the scope-of-work is too vague, you should meet with the contractor and arrive at a written agreement that specifies exactly what is to be done and what materials are to be used.

Remember that communication is the key to a good homeowner-contractor relationship. Because most contractors are not designers or architects, they require precise instructions in the form of a detailed contract which may include drawings, old photographs, written specifications, and a provision for verbal directions. Too often homeowners make the mistake of leaving pivotal decisions regarding design and materials up to the contractor, and later complain about not getting what they wanted. Contractors are not clairvoyant, and you must communicate to them exactly what you want.

For that reason, it is very important for the homeowner to be able to recognize accurate and appropriate historic design, even if an architect or other professional designer is hired to do the actual rehabilitation design work. Familiarize yourself with the characteristics of the architectural style of your house. Look for architectural details that may be missing from your house by looking at other houses of the same style. It is important to pay special attention to the small details that contribute so much to an authentic appearance such as the precise dimensions of the lumber and the quality of the original materials. A common mistake among well-intentioned rehabbers today is mixing different historic architectural styles or improperly interpreting them to create a falsely historic appearance by trying to make a house look older than it is, such as making a Victorian house look Colonial or a Craftsman house look Victorian. The result is often a hodge-podge which is neither historic nor aesthetically pleasing.

Carpenters of years ago were familiar with the architectural styles of their times and could often independently design and build architectural details, such as a porch, to match the style of the house. Most carpenters today do not have that ability and are not familiar enough with historic building styles to design new features that will fit in with the architecture of an old building. Nevertheless, if they are skilled and capable of following architectural plans, they should be able to replicate a period design properly drawn up by a designer or perhaps even duplicate a feature by using another similar feature as a model. If you are uncertain about whether or not the design of your rehabilitation is appropriate to the period and style of your house, you can contact the staff of the Milwaukee Historic Preservation Commission to arrange for a review by the architects on the staff. Although they cannot design a rehab for you, they can review plans prepared by others and render an opinion as to whether or not the work is appropriate in design and suggest changes. There is no charge for this service.

Once the job starts, you need to be understanding of the contractor's problems. Rehabilitation is a nerve-wracking business fraught with difficulties ranging from bad weather, workers or subcontractors who don't show up at the appointed time, materials that arrive late, and the little surprises sometimes encountered in working with old buildings because of quirks in old-time construction practices or hidden problems. A little sympathy and understanding on your part will probably go a lot further toward ensuring a successful job than perpetual nagging or accusation. Above all, stay calm and keep your sense of humor. Recognize at the outset that some things are going to go wrong, the work will take longer than expected and will cost more than you originally thought. ∎

Milwaukee Public Library

Even years ago things could go wrong, as this photo of a southside Milwaukee house under construction in the early 1900s illustrates.

HISTORIC ARCHITECTURAL STYLES IN MILWAUKEE

HISTORIC ARCHITECTURAL STYLES IN MILWAUKEE

HISTORIC ARCHITECTURAL STYLES IN MILWAUKEE

HISTORIC ARCHITECTURAL STYLES IN MILWAUKEE

HISTORIC ARCHITECTURAL STYLES IN MILWAUKEE

INTRODUCTION

This chapter describes the architectural styles that are most prevalent in Milwaukee. Architectural styles that are represented by only a few buildings in Milwaukee are not described. "Style" in architecture is a convenient classification system used to identify a building and place it in a historic context. Style is determined by the assemblage of architectural details, features, and building forms that were used at a particular period of time to give a building a certain look or recognizable character. Some of these styles were a reflection of deep philosophical beliefs or social movements, while others appear to have been more the product of changing fashion. The particular names used to describe the various styles in this book are those commonly used today by architectural historians.

The following architectural descriptions are meant to serve as a general guide in identifying the style of your house. Since the way a building looks is the result of many factors and influences, "pure" examples of a particular style are rare. Sometimes only the basic form, roof type, or a few decorative details are all that can be used to ascribe a style to a particular structure. Sometimes elements of two or more styles can be represented in a single building, since styles tend to overlap. For example, Queen Anne characteristics can be found in many of the houses built in the Colonial Revival style in the 1890s and early 1900s. In general, expensive, architect-designed houses were conceived more often in one unifying style while less costly houses often randomly mixed features of different architectural styles in the same building.

Being able to identify the predominant architectural style of a house is very important when planning a rehabilitation. Familiarity with style will help determine what missing details to replace and what types of materials are most appropriate to use in repair work. The illustrations are intended to serve as helpful guides in identifying the various versions of a particular style. If you need help to identify the architectural style of your house, you should contact the staff of the Milwaukee Historic Preservation Commission. ∎

ITALIANATE

Sixteenth century palazzo designs of the Italian Renaissance and the country homes of rural Tuscany provided the architectural vocabulary for a popular residential style of the mid-nineteenth century. The "Italianate" was in vogue for residential construction in Milwaukee between about 1850 and 1880.

The influence of the earlier Federal and Greek Revival styles can be seen in the flat surfaces, cubic form, and formal symmetry of some early examples, while towers, cupolas, irregular plans, and surface richness characterize later examples. Many of the Italianate houses in Milwaukee have low hip or shallow pitched gabled roofs, round or segmentally arched windows, and a variety of ornamental details including brackets at the wide overhanging eaves, carved window enframements, and chamfered square posts on the porches.

In Milwaukee the Italianate style reflected an era of growing affluence when not only the rich, but also those of middle income, could afford to dress up their residences with applied architectural ornament. Architects and builders alike had access to pattern books as well as to publications highlighting new and historic architecture and utilized these sources to detail their buildings. High style, architect-designed houses featured costly carved ornament handcrafted by local craftsmen. Rich-looking, but economically-constructed, carpenter-built houses were also prevalent in this era due to the widespread availability of mass-produced, machine-made, scroll-sawn, and laminated wood ornament. Such factory-produced ornament was available through local lumber yards and from mail order catalogues.

Italianate houses constructed of local cream color brick were similar in design and composition to their frame counterparts, but took on a special character from the uniformity of their pale yellow brick walls. Window surrounds were frequently constructed of projecting brick. Lintels were sometimes of carved stone, although wood and metal hoods were more common. Limestone was often used to clad the foundation, and brick quoins were sometimes applied to accent the corners.

The Italianate Style came into vogue in the later 1850s and enjoyed its heyday in the 1870s when the city's first great fortunes were being made. Although there once were numerous imposing Italianate mansions and villas in Milwaukee, especially in the Central Business District, and along North Prospect and West Wisconsin Avenues, most have been razed. The style is represented today mostly by the numerous more modest Italianate houses found primarily in the Yankee Hill, Lower East Side, Walker's Point, and near West Side neighborhoods. ∎

845 N. 11th Street (c. 1870).

1810 N. Palmer Street (1868)

ITALIANATE STYLE HOUSES

1119 N. Marshall Street (1874)

1024-26 E. State Street (1875)

VICTORIAN GOTHIC

An interest in medievalism coupled with the popularization of Italian Gothic architecture by the writings of Englishman John Ruskin resulted in what is today called the Victorian Gothic style. The style evolved in England during the 1850s and 1860s and is distinguished by its flamboyant use of polychromy, surface texture, picturesque massing, and bold, heavy ornamentation concentrated on the upper portions of the building. The Victorian Gothic style enjoyed its heyday in the United States during the 1870s and early 1880s. The style was introduced to Milwaukee in the 1870s and remained popular through the early 1880s. It was locally often referred to as the "New American Pointed Style."

A more complex style than the earlier Gothic Revival of the pre-Civil War era, the Victorian Gothic can be identified by a number of characteristic elements: steeply-pitched gable roofs, a profusion of dormers and gables, strong contrasts in scale between small elements and large ones, heavy hood molds, pointed arches and tall, vertical proportions. In contrast to the earlier, lighter and more curvilinear ornament of the Gothic Revival era, Victorian Gothic ornament is often very angular and has a heavy, pseudo-structural look to it. In masonry houses, the light color of the local cream colored brick and the buff color of the local limestone made dramatic polychromatic effects somewhat difficult to achieve, but rich patterned effects were attempted anyway by using stone belt courses or bands of brick laid either in soldier courses or on edge in a sawtooth pattern. Some of the masonry houses built of the local cream brick are known to have been originally stained or painted a dark red color in order to contrast the brick walls with the stone trim. Roofs were very important to the overall decorative scheme and often the wood or slate roofs would incorporate patterns of brightly colored and decoratively shaped shingles to achieve the desired effect. Entire wood-shingled roofs are known to have been painted or stained in rich colors to coordinate with the colors of the rest of the house, while for very costly houses, rare red and green slate was imported and laid in patterns.

The Victorian Gothic was once an extremely popular style in Milwaukee, utilized on every type of house from the worker's cottage to the large mansion. Although most of the once numerous and strikingly opulent mansions have been razed, many of the middleclass houses and modest cottage examples still stand. Unfortunately, most have lost their decorative bargeboards and window hoods. They are still often recognizable by their steeply-pitched roofs, pointed-arched windows, and relentlessly vertical proportions and rectilinear character. Extant examples can be found in the West Side, Brewer's Hill, Walker's Point, Bay View, and the Lower East Side neighborhoods. ∎

1201 N. Prospect Avenue (1874)

1535 N. Marshall Street (1876)

VICTORIAN GOTHIC STYLE HOUSES

3130 W. Wells Street (1878)

1321 N. 21st Street (c. 1880)

QUEEN ANNE

The Queen Anne was probably the most creative, inventive, and exuberant of the nineteenth century architectural styles. It was popular from the 1880s through about 1905 during which time the style evolved from a picturesque confection of shingles, brackets, and spindles into the later so-called "Free-Classic" phase which exhibited more restraint in overall form and applied ornamentation in favor of bold geometric massing.

The Queen Anne style traced its origins to the late 1860's work of English architect Richard Norman Shaw. Although misnamed after England's Queen Anne, who reigned from 1702 to 1714, the style was actually a reinterpretation of the earlier, rural medieval manor houses of fifteenth, sixteenth, and seventeenth century England. Shaw's designs were extensively published and came to be much admired in the United States. Popular Boston architect H. H. Richardson, who based his early works on Shaw, further advanced the development of the style in the United States in the 1870s. It was the Philadelphia Centennial Exposition of 1876, however, that really popularized the new style. The two half-timbered buildings erected by the British government at the Exposition were much praised and touted as modern structures that could easily be adapted to the residential architecture of this country. Since the Tudor architecture that served as the inspiration for the English Queen Anne style was perceived as being an ancestor of America's Colonial architecture, the style was readily accepted by a populace that was beginning to feel nostalgic about its own Colonial past. Like their counterparts throughout the rest of the country, Milwaukee architects became skillful at designing Queen Anne style buildings beginning in the early 1880s and kept it up until just past the turn of the century. The popular demand for this fresh, new, highly original and highly livable house type was tremendous.

The early phases of the Queen Anne style celebrated the use of a variety of building materials. Shingles, clapboard, brick, stone, terra cotta, and stucco were popular and sometimes all were combined on the same house. Irregular floor plans, picturesque massing, and variety in color and texture were also emphasized. A profusion of chimney stacks, dormers, and gables added to the complexity of the roof profiles. Bay windows, oriels, balconies, and sweeping verandahs disguised the boxy character of the house giving it a rambling, picturesque look. A great variety of window shapes, types and sizes was commonly used on a single house and beveled, etched and colored glass panes were popular for glazing. Chimneys became significant elements of the design and were often paneled or inset with raised brick, terra cotta or stone ornaments and dramatically corbelled at the top.

The free classic phase of the style in the 1890s was inspired by the classical architecture of the 1893 Columbian Exposition in Chicago. In residential design this was manifested by houses that had simpler, less picturesque profiles. These houses had a "smoother" appearance because fewer different materials and less pattern were utilized on the exterior. Classical detail replaced the exotic carved decorations, turned spindles, and oriental fretwork motifs that had been popular earlier. Conically-roofed, round corner towers, which began to appear by the late 1880s, reached the zenith of their popularity in the mid-1890s and are particularly characteristic of the free classic phase. In Milwaukee, the Queen Anne style is represented by both frame and masonry houses ranging in scale from large mansions to small worker's cottages. The Queen Anne coincided with one of the city's greatest periods of growth and was one of the most widely-built residential styles in Milwaukee. Large numbers of Queen Anne houses in a great variety of configurations survive in the Lower East Side, West Side, Walker's Point, Near South Side, Brewer's Hill, and Bay View neighborhoods. ∎

1841 N. Prospect Avenue (1881)

2378-80 N. First Street (1885)

1119 E. Knapp Street (c. 1885)

822 N. 26th Street (c. 1890)

QUEEN ANNE STYLE HOUSES

1646 S. 28th Street (c. 1885)

2577 S. Superior Street (1889)

851 N. 29th Street (1891)

937 N. 33rd Street (1897)

COLONIAL REVIVAL

Although for most of our young country's history American's had looked to Europe as a source for architectural style, in the 1880s America's tastemakers developed an interest in the stylistic possibilities of our own Colonial heritage. This interest was heightened by the Centennial Exposition in Philadelphia in 1876 which helped to foster an awareness of American history. Seventeenth and eighteenth century housing types, particularly Georgian examples, were viewed as distinctly American and complemented the country's renewed patriotic fervor and nostalgia for simpler times. Part of this interest contributed to the development of the Queen Anne style, while another aesthetic track evolved into what is termed the Colonial Revival. Rather than directly copying actual eighteenth century buildings, architects working in the Colonial Revival style freely adapted decorative elements and general characteristics of Colonial buildings to suit the expansive Victorian lifestyle. Like elsewhere in the country, this style was popular in Milwaukee from the mid-1890s through World War I. An increasing interest in more accurate copies of early American buildings lead to the emergence of the Georgian Revival style just before World War I.

Colonial Revival houses were most frequently constructed of wood, but they could also be built of brick. When brick was used, it was frequently imported red brick from out-of-state manufacturers rather than the local, cream color variety. Colonial Revival houses were often much larger in scale than real eighteenth century houses. The houses were generally rectangular in shape with a hip, gable, or gambrel roof and large dormers. Bay windows are common. Large front porches, or verandahs, retained their popularity, even though they were not found on real Colonial residences. Classical, two-story porticos were used on large, expensive houses while one-story porches with Classical columns, either plain or fluted, were used on more modest houses. Six-, nine- or twelve-over-one double-hung sash windows were common. Classical eighteenth-century features such as Palladian windows, cameo windows, traceried fan lights, sidelights, pilasters, quoins, broken pediments, dentils, modillions, and swags were all used to create the desired decorative effect. Examples of Colonial Revival houses can be found in the Upper East Side, West Side, Near South Side, and Bay View neighborhoods. ■

2828 N. Shepard Ave. (1897)

2112 N. Lake Drive (1906)

COLONIAL REVIVAL STYLE EXAMPLES

953 N. 33rd Street (1895)

1038 S. 26th Street (1899)

AMERICAN FOURSQUARE

One of the most common early twentieth century housing types found throughout the country is the American Foursquare. This style appealed to the changing tastes of the post-Victorian era when simplicity in form and economy in building were desired features. These plain boxy houses were considered to be the functional "modern" style dwellings of their period and were very popular with middleclass homeowners in much the same way that the ranch house and the split level would be in the 1950s and 1960s. The American Foursquare enjoyed its greatest popularity from about 1905 through the early 1920s.

The American Foursquare can be easily identified by its boxy, two-story, rectangular shape crowned by a hipped roof with broad, overhanging eaves. A large dormer is frequently incorporated into the front roof slope. This basic shape offered the most house for the money. One-story porches are generally found extending completely across the facade, supported by plain columns or square posts. Rather than fancy turned balusters or ornamental spindles, handrails were usually comprised of square pickets or of flat slats which were sometimes pierced with simple, geometric shapes. Windows are often grouped and are rectangular in shape with simple framing and one-over-one sash or eight-over-one sash. The walls of the Foursquare are generally plain with the upper and lower stories often clad in different materials. Clapboard or brick with wood shingles or either brick with stucco or stucco with wood shingles were common combinations. Depending upon the client's taste, the Foursquare could be the essence of simplicity or could be dressed up with detailing in the Colonial Revival, Craftsman, or Prairie Styles. American Foursquare houses can be found today throughout the city. ∎

3046 N. Hackett Avenue (1910)

3132 W. McKinley Boulevard (1907)

AMERICAN FOURSQUARE STYLE HOUSES

2013 N. Hi-Mount Boulevard (1913)

3000 N. Maryland Avenue (1910)

ARTS AND CRAFTS

The revivals and reinterpretations of England's late medieval and early renaissance architecture provided American architects with much inspiration throughout the nineteenth and early twentieth centuries. Many elements of English architecture were manifested in the Victorian Gothic and Queen Anne styles, for example. It also led to the evolution of the Arts and Crafts movement. A philosophy of life and social order as well as a style, the Arts and Crafts philosophy was popularized by the dynamic English aesthetician and designer William Morris (1837-1896). Morris was a prolific writer, designer, printer, weaver, manufacturer, and social theorist who espoused a return to hand craftsmanship. Revolted by the vulgarity of machine-made products and by the degradation of life brought about by industrialization, Morris sought to bring his concept of morality to the field of design. Convinced that great art could not be produced by unhappy men, Morris advocated the use of traditional materials and craftsmanship in the manner of the Medieval trade guilds where the craftsman would also be the designer of his own work. Morris' romantic vision was in reality more of a retreat from the industrial world of his age than a vigorous attempt to reform the world around him. His ideals spawned a number of cooperative guild communities in which craftsmen lived in rural communal villages and produced handmade articles. Elbert Hubbard's Roycroft Community in East Aurora, New York was one American manifestation of this movement. The Arts and Crafts primarily was a decorative movement that produced furnishings with simple, sturdy, rectilinear forms and wallpaper and textile designs based on natural plant forms. Although not an architect himself, Morris inspired a number of British architects such as Charles Voysey and M. H. Baillie Scott, who in turn influenced American design. True to its celebration of the individual craftsman and the simple life, Arts and Crafts architecture expressed itself most noticeably in the design of residential structures. It drew its inspiration primarily from the simple vernacular English yeoman farmer's house of the Middle Ages and emphasized geometric form and smooth surfaces rather than texture and applied ornament. Houses influenced by the Arts and Crafts movement were very popular in Milwaukee from the late 1890s through World War I, after which time, the style fell out of favor.

Arts and Crafts style houses have an appealing cottage-like quality even when large in size. They are sturdy in appearance, most often two and a half stories in height, irregularly massed and feature multiple, steep gables. In Milwaukee most examples are constructed in a combination of brick, wood shingles, and stucco. It is common to find many houses with brick lower stories and stucco or shingled upper stories. The wood shingles are square cut and not shaped in decorative patterns like the shingling on Queen Anne houses. Red or brown were the preferred colors for brick. The second story sometimes projects slightly over the first and is supported by simple corbels. Windows are cottage-like, of varying sizes, and are multi-paned. Upper story windows were often sheltered by small hoods or pent roofs. Chimneys are prominent, but have plain tops instead of the dramatic corbelling typical of Queen Anne houses.

In Milwaukee, this English style was immensely popular and was practiced by many local architects. As a result, Milwaukee has a large inventory of Arts and Crafts style houses, and they can be found in the Upper East Side, Yankee Hill, Bay View, and West Side neighborhoods, as well as elsewhere throughout the city in areas developed between 1900 and 1915. ∎

825 N. 33rd Street (1908)

3010 N. Summit Avenue (1908)

ARTS AND CRAFTS STYLE HOUSES

1223 S. 28th Street (1915)

2976 N. Cramer Street (1909)

CRAFTSMAN STYLE/ BUNGALOW

The size and diversity of the city's inventory of Craftsman-style houses is one of the great architectural strengths of Milwaukee. Popular not only in Milwaukee, but throughout the United States from about 1905 to 1930, the Craftsman style's most notable innovation, the bungalow, was not merely a housing type, but the physical embodiment of a lifestyle captured in wood, stucco, stone, and brick. Unlike many earlier styles which trickled down to the middle and working classes from the architecture of the well-to-do, the Craftsman style, especially as manifested in the construction of bungalows, began as a middleclass phenomenon. Robert Winter in **The California Bungalow** states that the Craftsman bungalow "provided psychic fulfillment of the American Dream." It epitomized upward mobility when that was an expected, if not always attained, feature of American life. The Craftsman mode in general was also hailed as an honest architectural style for the average working man. The houses were simple yet artistic, and artistic was equated with respectable. They were considered to be modern in that they were compact, efficient, and informal with many built-in conveniences. The bungalow, in particular, was considered to be an ideal family home and a stepping stone on the way up to a more substantial house for the industrious family.

Craftsman design had a broad-based appeal. Words like cozy, homey, comfortable, snug, honest, and picturesque were frequently used to describe the Craftsman house and its interior in the early twentieth century. In many ways the Craftsman home symbolically represented, and actually provided, a retreat from the hectic outside world and the wearing side effects of industrialization and technology. Most examples of the style were built away from city centers in burgeoning tract suburbs where the distance from work required the use of an automobile, ironically the one product of modern technology that, more than any other, helped to create the hectic pace of daily life and rapid change in the American lifestyle from which people wanted to retreat.

The Craftsman style was most often manifested in the construction of the new house type it introduced, the bungalow. The term bungalow had its roots in the Bengali word bangala, sometimes bangla, bungales or banggolos, a term used to describe a part of India, as well as the native buildings of that region. By the eighteenth century, Europeans in the region had adapted the native house type to their own purposes and the word came to refer to a one-story building with a porch or verandah and wide, overhanging eaves. The English, in particular, combined elements of indigenous building types with aspects of the English cottage and the British army tent. Eventually, "bungalow" became the standardized spelling in the early nineteenth century and came to mean a simple one-story dwelling with a wide porch. From the very beginning, the bungalow was considered to be suitable for use as a retreat, a non-urban structure symbolic of a return to a simpler life. Bungalows were built by the English for Colonial administrators throughout the British Empire and were later adapted as second homes, seacoast cottages, or rural retreats in England where the name imparted an exotic character.

As far as can be determined, the term "bungalow" first appeared in reference to an American building in the **American Architect and Building News** in 1880 in a discussion of a Cape Cod summer house. A second reference appears in A. W. Brunner's **Cottages or Hints on Economical Building** (1884) where again the bungalow is associated with a vacation retreat. The bungalow evolved into its currently recognizable form in Southern California. By the early years of this century, the bungalow was being heavily promoted throughout the U.S. as a model house type in many popular broadly-read publications including **The Craftsman, Ladies Home Journal**, and **House Beautiful**. There was even a **Bungalow Magazine** published between 1909 and 1918. Many bungalow house plan books were published by contractors and builders across the country. One such local publication is a catalogue published by builder-contractor Harry Mewes, now in the collection of the Milwaukee County Historical Society.

Of all the various publications that promoted the bungalow, **The Craftsman** was probably the most significant. **The Craftsman**, a monthly magazine published between 1901 and 1916, promoted the philosophy of editor Gustav Stickley, a Wisconsin-born designer and the leader of the Craftsman movement in America. Articles stressed the ideal of a democratic and functional architecture based on the integration of natural materials and forms, handmade decorative arts, and naturalistic garden design. At the center of the Craftsman philosophy was a concern for "home" and domestic life. **The Craftsman** encouraged the improvement of all aspects of domestic design, offering articles or advertisements for such items as "bungalow furniture" and wickerware, earthenware, table-runners, and hammered-copper bookends made by the Roycrofters of East Aurora, New York. Stickley and his followers were indebted to William Morris and the late nineteenth century English Arts and Crafts tradition for the philosophy of a high standard of craftsmanship, and of design derived from natural forms intended to counter the machine-oriented industrial order.

Milwaukee followed the national trend and witnessed an extraordinary boom in bungalow construction from about 1905 through the 1920s. Great numbers were built both individually and in speculative tracts in newly platted neighborhoods on the city's west, north, northwest, south, and southwest sides. Bungalows were also built on vacant sites scattered throughout older neighborhoods. In the 1920s, bungalows, and the casual lifestyle they epitomized, gradually became unfashionable as tastes increasingly favored period revival styles such as Dutch Colonial, Georgian, and Tudor.

Although the classic bungalow, as first developed in California, was only one story in height, most of those built in Milwaukee were a story and a half with an attic that had one finished room at the front of the house. The true bungalow is characterized by a broad, low gabled roof with the gable end sometimes fronting the street and sometimes oriented to the side. Gabled and shed dormers are common roof features. The jerkinhead gable was also frequently used. An open porch extended across the front of the house and was supported by massive, square, tapered posts set on brick, rusticated concrete block, or fieldstone-veneered piers. These types of tapering boxy supports are referred to as elephantine posts. If a balustrade is present, the individual balusters consist of flat boards often alternating with square pickets and sometimes pierced with simple, geometric or floral shapes. On front-gabled bungalows the porch sometimes is gabled. On side-gable varieties, the porch roof is generally an extension of the front roof slope. Rafter ends are almost always exposed at the eaves. Chimneys are of simple shouldered construction most often executed in brown tapestry brick or red brick. Craftsman style houses were built of combinations of brick, stucco, wood shingles, and clapboard. Clapboard varieties are the most common and usually have shingled gables and dormers, although stucco was very popular. Local variations on the style are almost endless. In addition to bungalows, many two-story houses with Craftsman design features and two-and-a-half story Craftsman style duplexes were also built.

Although often mass-produced in speculative tracts, many Milwaukee Craftsman houses and bungalows, nevertheless, exhibit remarkably good workmanship and the use of the high quality materials that were advocated by the spokesmen of the movement. Although at first all bungalows had a Craftsman appearance, in the 1920s the trend to historic period design resulted in bungalows being built that were dressed up with tile roofs and Mediterranean features, while others incorporated a hip roof, arched doorway, and half-timbering and were called "English bungalows." By the 1920s, a type of porchless bungalow with a projecting glazed sunroom and open terrace on the front became very popular.

Craftsman style houses and bungalows can be found today throughout the entire city of Milwaukee. Scattered examples are located in the older nineteenth century neighborhoods while entire blocks of bungalows can be found on the city's north and northwest sides, south and southwest sides, and in the Bay View neighborhood. ∎

2177 S. 11th Street (1913)

1929 N. 51st Street (1915)

2651 S. Shore Drive (1917)

CRAFTSMAN STYLE HOUSES AND BUNGALOWS

2959 N. 48th Street (1922)

2979 S. Clement Avenue (1929)

2565 N. Humboldt Blvd. (1922)

Tudor: 2517 N. 47th Street (1923)

Arts & Crafts: 2173 N. 53rd Street (1921)

Mediterranean: 2951 N. 49th Street (1924)

PERIOD REVIVAL STYLE BUNGALOW INFLUENCED HOUSES

Tudor: 2551 N. 47th Street (1922)

Mission: 2456 N. Grant Boulevard (1924)

Mediterranean: 2779 S. Humboldt Park Court (1927)

PRAIRIE STYLE

The Prairie Style was a distinctively American style that originated in Chicago at the turn of the century. Its chief spokesman, proponent, and leader was Frank Lloyd Wright. Wright's vision caused him to originate a type of house he said echoed the Midwest prairie with its rolling plains and open expanses. Architects who worked for Wright, as well as associates who shared his vision of a unique style, constituted a group that came to be called the Prairie School. Since the movement was headquartered in Chicago, a large number of the residential projects were carried out in the nearby suburbs, especially Oak Park, as well as in adjacent Midwest states. Numerous architectural publications, as well as popular periodicals, including the **Ladies Home Journal** spread images of the Prairie Style across this country and abroad. From these sources architects and builders across America were able to utilize details and incorporate elements of the style into their own repertoire in order to keep up with the latest architectural fashions.

In contrast to most other houses of its time, the Prairie house is characterized by long, low, horizontal masses. Low pitched hip or gabled roofs extend dramatically beyond the side walls and appear to hover over and shelter the spaces below. The Prairie house was generally designed with a central mass from which wings, terraces, porches, and balconies radiate in a irregular, asymmetrical fashion. Walls can be sheathed in stucco, brick, or a combination of these two materials. The favored brick is the long, narrow, Roman brick, usually brown in color, whose horizontality was further emphasized by mortar joints raked horizontally. Rather than double-hung sash, Prairie Style architects preferred casement windows grouped in horizontal bands across the facade. They were often glazed with leaded glass set in geometric designs. The bands of windows were often recessed on the second story, wrapped around corners, and butted right up against the soffit, which added greatly to the effect that the roof hovers or floats above the building. On stucco houses, wooden lintels, sills, and window frames were generally extended to create a flat board horizontal banding or gridwork across the facade. On brick houses, this banding is achieved with stone belt courses. Entrances are often placed on the side of the house, in inobtrusive locations on the front, or below an overhanging terrace or balcony, giving the impression of being "hidden" or protected. Chimneys are simple and massive in size and generally project through the roof in a rectangular, slablike fashion. Urns and built-in planters encouraged the planting of vines and other vegetation to help integrate the house into its setting. Despite allusions to the open Prairie and the natural integration of the house to its site, most Prairie houses in Milwaukee were built on narrow urban lots, necessitating designs that were more compact and less sprawling than Wright's classic masterpieces.

Several Milwaukee architects practiced in the Prairie style between 1905 and 1920. A few examples were executed in stucco with nearly-flat, low-pitched roofs, but most were built of brown or tan tapestry brick with hip roofs, widely-projecting eaves, battered walls, stone banding enframing groups of windows, and prominent central entrances often sheltered by shallow arched hoods or deep front porches. Milwaukee has a considerable number of Prairie Style houses and duplexes, most of which are clustered on the city's Upper East Side, on the West Side, and in suburban Shorewood and Wauwatosa. ∎

904 S. 30th Street (1919)

2906 E. Linnwood Avenue (1909)

726 N. 31st Street (1911)

PRAIRIE STYLE HOUSES

2360 N. Terrace Avenue (1915)

2430 E. Newberry Boulevard (1922)

2420 N. Terrace Avenue (1916)

DUTCH COLONIAL REVIVAL

The Dutch Colonial Revival, like the Colonial Revival, evolved out of the revival of interest in America's Colonial past. The name is something of a misnomer, however, since the style's most distinctive feature, the gambrel roof, did not originate with the Dutch. The gambrel or double-pitched roof began appearing in America in the early eighteenth century and is thought to have been introduced into New England and the Mid-Atlantic colonies by English settlers. The gambrel roof enabled houses to have a full attic story and also to use shorter rafters in its roof construction, eliminating the need to cut and haul a large number of long, massive timbers up to the top of a house to construct the roof. In the Dutch settlements of the Hudson Valley where the gambrel roof was adopted by the practical Dutch colonists, early roofs of this type had very short upper slopes with long lower slopes that terminated at the end of the roof with no overhang. Later examples in New Jersey feature an exaggerated bell cast profile to the gambrel with wide overhanging eaves.

The Dutch Colonial house, a two-story house distinguished by its gambrel roofed second story, began appearing in the 1890s and was popular through the 1920s. Early examples have an exaggerated verticality with steeply pitched roofs that appear in three basic forms, front gable, side gable, and cross-gabled with the gable often being the chief design element of the facade. On early twentieth century side-gabled Dutch Colonials, the large expanse of roof is interrupted by two or more gabled dormers, sometimes having balustraded false balconies cut into the roof. On these early examples, the front slope of the gambrel roof sometimes flattens out to cover a porch that extends across the entire front. Dutch Colonials were built of a variety of materials including brick, clapboard, stucco, and stone.

After flagging in popularity in the second decade of the twentieth century, the Dutch Colonial style experienced a resurgence in the 1920s, and hundreds of examples were built in Milwaukee. The 1920s Dutch Colonials are less Victorian in appearance than their predecessors with the emphasis placed on symmetrical facades that usually do not have a porch across the front. The most common type of these later Dutch Colonials is the side-gabled gambrel with a single, large shed roof dormer extending across nearly the entire length of the roof. The front gabled type was far less popular than it had been at the turn of the century. When built with the gable end facing the street, the Dutch Colonial often had long, shed roof dormers on either side of the roof. The front gable Dutch was a popular configuration for duplexes. On the side-gabled examples, the entrance is situated at the center of the facade and flanked on either side by groupings of two or three rectangular sash. The eave overhang is minimal, and the entry is sheltered by a small, gabled hood, porch, or pergola. A typical feature of the postwar Dutch-Colonials is the enclosed sun room attached to one side of the house, which is sometimes balanced by an open terrace or porch on the opposite side of the house. Examples of the Dutch Colonial style can be found throughout the city and in the adjacent suburbs of Shorewood and Wauwatosa. ∎

3209 N. Shepard Avenue (1899)

2556 N. Sherman Boulevard (1921)

DUTCH COLONIAL REVIVAL STYLE HOUSES

2009 N. 59th Street (1926)

3494 N. Humboldt Boulevard (1927)

GEORGIAN REVIVAL

The Georgian Revival grew out of the late nineteenth century fascination with America's past that spawned the Colonial Revival style. The Georgian Revival was a more literal and exact interpretation of eighteenth century architecture than the preceding Colonial Revival, which tended to graft Colonial features onto Victorian house types. The original Georgian style buildings that were constructed in this country in the eighteenth century were named after England's first three King Georges. The Georgian style was an English adaptation and reinterpretation of the works of sixteenth century Italian architects, especially Andrea Palladio, who had, in turn, freely adapted forms from Classical Roman buildings to create a new architecture during the Italian Renaissance. The style was popularized by influential English architects, such as Sir Christopher Wren, and widely disseminated both in England and her colonies, including America, through numerous patternbooks, handbooks, and architectural treatises. Because of the lack of trained architects in America, Colonial builders and contractors relied heavily on these illustrated texts to create the most up-to-date houses possible in England's remote North American colonies.

Georgian architecture is characterized by symmetry, hipped roofs, double-hung, multi-paned windows, geometric proportions and applied Classical ornament. The corners of a building might be emphasized by the use of quoins or pilasters but the central entrance is the principle architectural feature of a Georgian house and is emphasized by the use of enframing pilasters and a pediment or architrave. Unlike most architectural styles, authentic Georgian houses usually do not have a porch at the entrance; rather, the door is left fully exposed to view and is uncovered. A pediment was frequently incorporated into the hip roof above the entrance for decorative purposes as well. Palladian windows, composed of a large arched window flanked by narrow flat head double-hung sash, were also frequently used, most often above the central front entrance. Windows were generally glazed with six-over-six or nine-over-nine sash. Regularly spaced gabled dormers may accent the steep roof as do prominent chimneys. Belt courses frequently divide the first from the second stories on brick houses. Modillioned cornices are common.

The use of the term "Georgian" to describe America's eighteenth century Palladian-inspired buildings first came into use around the turn-of-the-century, and the term "Georgian Revival" was coined to describe the renewed interest in that style that took place between the late 1890s and the 1930s. The prominent East Coast architectural firm of McKim, Mead and White did much to popularize the revival in the late nineteenth century and the first examples of the style were being constructed in Milwaukee by the early 1900s. Most were constructed of red brick with white-painted trim, but scattered frame examples can also be found. These early Georgian Revival houses were built at the same time that examples of late Queen Anne, Colonial Revival, Tudor Revival, Foursquare, Craftsman, Prairie, and Arts and Crafts houses were going up, illustrating the wide range of styles prevalent in the first decades of the twentieth century.

The Georgian Revival was in many respects a reaction against what were thought to be the frivolous, gaudy, attention-getting excesses of the Queen Anne style. The Georgian Revival style came to be synonymous with conservative "good taste," and the symmetrical, ordered facades bespoke refinement, stability, sobriety, and permanence. As in earlier stylistic shifts, Milwaukee's well-to-do were the first to embrace the Georgian Revival, and many abandoned their fussy Victorian houses to build in the new style in the North Point and Upper East Side neighborhoods prior to World War I. For those who chose not to move, remodeling an outdated residence in the Georgian Revival style was common. By the 1920s, more modest examples were being constructed to house the middle class throughout the city. The Georgian Revival has remained a popular style down to the present. ■

2135 N. Lake Drive (1911)

2851 N. Grant Boulevard (1918)

GEORGIAN REVIVAL STYLE HOUSES

1325 S. Layton Boulevard (1924)

2933 E. Newport Avenue (1930)

TUDOR REVIVAL

The Tudor Revival is the general name applied to a phase of later nineteenth and twentieth century English inspired architectural design that incorporates elements from Tudor, Elizabethan, Jacobean, and English vernacular buildings from the late fifteenth, sixteenth and early seventeenth centuries. This era was a time of great architectural change as traditional medieval English building forms were becoming influenced by Italian, Flemish, and French Renaissance design. In the nineteenth century, newly affluent Americans and Britons developed a fondness for the architecture of this era because of its associations with old money and the landed English gentry and because the irregular forms and unique details of the Tudor era allowed for more picturesque design possibilities and more display of hand craftsmanship than the rigidly symmetrical and formal buildings of the eighteenth century. The sprawling nature of the Tudor house also lent itself to the expansive Victorian and Edwardian lifestyles. British architects, such as Richard Norman Shaw, successfully synthesized the romantic architecture of the Tudor manor house with the needs of Late Victorian upper-class life to create picturesque suburban and country houses evocative of the age of Henry VIII and Queen Elizabeth I. Such structures were irregular in shape and massing and incorporated stone, brick and half-timbering with numerous chimneys, gables, battlements, and stone-mullioned windows.

In America between the 1890s and the 1920s, the English-style manor house underwent reinterpretation as the freewheeling late Victorian version of the Tudor style was distilled into a more historically and archaeologically accurate copying of actual Tudor examples. Architects and patrons made a concerted effort to copy specific elements from historic structures and to use "correct" materials, sometimes to the point of actually importing building materials from England to ensure an authentic appearance. Sometimes whole portions of historic English buildings would be shipped over to the United States and incorporated into a new structure.

Like many of the architectural styles that came before it, the Tudor Revival was first fashionable among America's well-to-do and then filtered down to the middle classes in the 1920s. Unlike their estate-sized counterparts, however, the middle class Tudors rarely copied a specific historic building, but rather utilized generic Tudor features and materials to convey the quaintness and charm of Elizabethan England. "Charm" in fact was the key word used to sell the Tudor style to the middle class; virtually every article about the Tudor Revival that appeared in popular periodicals during the 1920s emphasized its "charm." Time has not diminished its appeal, and in new suburban tracts across the country, Tudor style houses are still being built.

In Milwaukee, the Tudor Revival was popular from the late 1890s through the 1930s. The earliest examples were built along Prospect Avenue and in the North Point area. Large, rambling, Tudor houses were built along the shores of Lake Michigan and on the most expensive boulevards. Smaller examples were constructed in newly-platted neighborhoods on the city's East, North, West, and South sides and in such suburban communities as Shorewood and Wauwatosa. By the 1920s, the Tudor Revival had become the preferred architectural style of Milwaukee's elite. The Great Depression put a halt to most residential construction in Milwaukee, and only a few large examples of the style were built in the 1930s. Greatly simplified versions of the Tudor Revival, frequently executed in local Lannon stone, were built in the later 1930s, 1940s and early 1950s, but the popularity of the style was soon eclipsed by the ranch house.

The Tudor Revival is characterized by asymmetrical design and massing and a steeply pitched gable roof, frequently interrupted by gabled dormers. Milwaukee examples are generally two and a half stories high. Wood shingles, tile or slate were the preferred roofing material. Most of the Milwaukee Tudors were constructed of brick, often with cut stone trim around windows, doors, and at the corners. Some of the most costly houses are sheathed entirely in local Lannon stone or imported stone. It is also common to find Milwaukee Tudors sheathed with brick on the first story while the second story and gables are half-timbered. Windows are most often rectangular in shape and grouped in bands of two or three units, but they are glazed with a wide variety of sash types. Most commonly seen are diamond-paned leaded casement windows, six-over-one leaded sash, or diamond-paned leaded upper sash over plain lower sash. On occasion, round headed windows are used, especially to illuminate a story-and-a-half "great room" or living room. Chimneys are large and extend dramatically above the rooftop and often have terra cotta chimney pots. Tudor Revival doors are generally round headed or set in a Tudor arch. They are often massive in appearance and are made of oak, with small observation windows and elaborate strapwork hinges. ∎

1537 N. Prospect Avenue (1901)

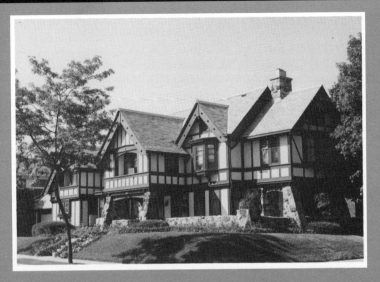

2924 E. Linnwood Avenue (1905)

TUDOR REVIVAL STYLE HOUSES

5924 W. Washington Boulevard (1926)

3237 N. 51st Boulevard (1933)

MEDITERRANEAN REVIVAL

The Mediterranean Revival, Mission, and Spanish Colonial Revival styles are terms applied to buildings incorporating elements of Spanish, Italian Renaissance and Baroque architecture. These buildings often incorporate Moorish features as well. The late nineteenth century interest in America's Colonial past took different forms in different parts of the country. On the East Coast, the architectural legacy of our Colonial past consisted of seventeenth and eighteenth century buildings based on English prototypes. In California, Florida, and the Southwest, however, the extant Colonial buildings consisted of Spanish mission churches, haciendas, and other structures inspired by the architecture of Spain, but adapted to the conditions and materials of the New World. By the 1890s, architects in the southern and western states began exploring these indigenous forms to create a new regional style. In the early twentieth century, this new Spanish style was widely publicized in architectural periodicals and gained new adherents across the country, even in cold northern climates where it was not indigenous.

The Mission Revival Style, the earliest manifestation of interest in Mediterranean architecture, was based on the adobe churches built by Spanish missionaries in California and in the Southwest. It is characterized by simple, smooth-plastered stucco walls, unframed arched openings, and low-pitched red tile hip roofs. Arcades, recessed porches, as well as wooden balconies are common. Shaped parapets and gables are often incorporated into the roofline, and they are frequently pierced with ornamental windows or quatrefoil openings.

Very little exterior ornament is used, but, if present, it consists of cast concrete or terra cotta molded into Baroque-inspired sculptural designs.

Growing interest in the decorative possibilities of Spanish-derived architecture led to the development of the Spanish Colonial Revival style, which was popular from just after the turn of the century through the 1920s. Unlike the Mission Style, the Spanish Colonial Revival was inspired by the opulent buildings constructed in Spain and Mexico during the Baroque and Moorish periods. These structures were more highly ornamented and picturesque than the Mission Revival Style structures. Like the Mission Revival Style, the Spanish Colonial Revival is typified by stucco walls, but the stucco is often textured rather than smooth. Red barrel tile covered, low pitched roofs are also common. The most distinguishing feature of the Spanish Colonial Revival Style is its abundant use of applied ornament. Carved wood, plaster, cast stone, and terra-cotta ornament based on Spanish Baroque or sixteenth century Spanish-Moorish design (Platteresque) is concentrated around doors and window openings and along the frieze below the eaves. Window openings in a variety of sizes and shapes are asymmetrically placed. Narrow round headed windows are often grouped in threes with twisted columns separating each sash. Balconies and window grilles (rejas) are frequently applied to the exterior.

The Mediterranean Revival was a third evocation of this country's fascination with Spanish, Spanish Colonial, and Italian architecture. An amalgam of many influences, the Mediterranean Revival sought to capture the more picturesque and evocative elements of the Spanish and Italian heritage and often combined elements of Moorish-influenced design with details from Italian villas and vernacular structures. While only a few scattered examples of Spanish Colonial Revival and Mission Revival style structures were constructed in Milwaukee, a great many Mediterranean Revival houses were built throughout the city.

Many of the basic features of the Mediterranean Revival resemble those of the Mission and Spanish Colonial Revival styles including the use of low-pitched tile roofs, arched doorways, and wrought iron balconies. Most Mediterranean Style houses built in Milwaukee were constructed of brown tapestry brick or Lannon stone rather than stucco. Stone trim was often incorporated around windows and doors and at corners. Red or green roofs of clay tile are a standard feature of the style locally. Most houses tend to be rectangular in shape with symmetrical facades, although some houses are L-shaped with the entrance located at the intersection of the two wings. Rectangular and round-headed windows are often used on the same house. Recessed entrances are framed by pilasters, irregularly-shaped cut stone pieces, or by architraves. The round-headed windows tend to be narrow and grouped into threes, framed by pilasters or twisted columns. Duplexes and bungalows also received Mediterranean touches, often as simple as incorporating a hip roof with a few round-headed windows, a round-headed door and perhaps a small iron flower balcony. Mediterranean Revival houses built between 1915 and 1930 can be found on the city's Upper East Side and in the Bay View, West Side, and South Side neighborhoods. ∎

2819 E. Bradford Avenue (1912)

5306 W. Garfield Avenue (1926)

MEDITERRANEAN REVIVAL STYLE HOUSES

3301 W. Highland Boulevard (1926)

5102 W. Washington Boulevard (1928)

MILWAUKEE DUPLEX

The term duplex, as it is used in Milwaukee, describes a two-family dwelling in which the flats are stacked one on top of another rather than side by side as in a doublehouse. Although precise documentation is lacking, it appears that duplex construction began in the 1880s and became the city's most popular housing type in the 1890s. Most of the very early duplexes appear to have been simple, rectangular structures with the gable end facing the street and a single entrance off to one side opening to a small hall leading to a first floor flat and a stairway to an upper flat. This type of duplex is nearly extinct today. It was very soon after the duplex building type appeared in Milwaukee that the more functional arrangement of providing each unit with its own outside front door became the norm.

Duplex construction experienced a boom after the turn of the century and construction peaked between 1904 and 1916. Duplexes were built in virtually every neighborhood of the city. Between 1910 and 1914, duplexes constituted over 60 percent of the housing units constructed, far outnumbering single-family houses. By 1930, the city had some 25,209 duplexes compared with 56,139 single family residences. The surge of duplex construction coincided with a boom in Milwaukee's population and the growth of large, prosperous, working and middle classes. The duplex was an economical solution to home ownership; it provided the homeowner with rental income to help pay the mortgage, and it fit well onto narrow urban lots. It also provided tenant families with many of the amenities of a single-family house that were unavailable in an apartment building, including more rooms, a private entrance, attic and basement storage, a yard, and being part of a family neighborhood.

The Milwaukee duplex underwent a continuous evolution in design, but a few basic building types emerged that were dressed up in the latest design features as architectural styles changed over the decades. The front gabled duplex form was the model for most of the duplexes built. During the 1880s, a small recessed upper porch appeared above the first floor entrance porch so that upstairs residents could also have a private outdoor front porch. In another variation, the upper flat received its own first floor front porch and private entrance, generally on the opposite side of the facade from the front porch and entrance to the first floor flat. Variations on this arrangement can be seen throughout the city, dressed up with Queen Anne or Colonial Revival details and sometimes with towers or turrets. The large front gable at the attic story was often ornamented with patterned or plain shingles, mouldings, pedimented windows, or a Palladian window. Frequently the roof was cross-gabled with large gables on the side elevations as well, and these gables were often ornamented, too, especially when the duplex was located on a corner lot. By the turn of the century, the front gabled duplex had developed a full porch across the front with the two entrances paired at one side of the facade, although many examples of the type with widely separated entrances continued to be built. The upper flat had access to an open deck on the porch roof. Duplexes during this period often featured Tudor, Arts and Crafts or Craftsman details such as stucco cladding, half-timbering, shingled upper stories or exposed rafter tails at the eaves.

By 1910 duplex design began to exhibit a great deal of variety in composition. While front gables were still constructed, side-gabled varieties became popular. The porch no longer necessarily extended across the entire front, but was often shortened to just shelter the side-by-side entrances. Brick and brick with stucco were popular materials at this time, while the designs continued to exhibit English and Craftsman details.

After World War I, duplex design encompassed a variety of styles including the Mediterranean Revival, Tudor Revival, Craftsman, and Prairie styles. By far the most common type of duplex to be built in the 1920s, the "generic" duplex of its era, was the two-and-a-half story hip roofed Craftsman variety. This duplex type generally had a shingled upper story and clapboard lower story with hip roofed dormers on each slope of the roof. Two porch types were common: the long porch extending completely across the front or a small porch just big enough to shelter the entrances. Porch piers were often of brick or rusticated concrete block and topped with simple battered box posts.

Like all building activity, duplex construction tapered off during the Great Depression, but revived after World War II, although not at anywhere near the number of units built in the early part of the century. Examples of duplexes can be found throughout the city. ■

*1838-40 N. Warren Street
(late 1880s)*

*2472-74 N. Murray Avenue
(1891)*

931-33 N. 33rd Street (1897)

1143-45 N. 21st Street (1918)

MILWAUKEE DUPLEXES

*2100-02 N. Newhall Avenue
(1897)*

*1733-35 N. 48th Street
(1915)*

*3245-47 N. Humboldt Boulevard
(1926)*

POLISH FLAT

Polish flat is a term used to describe a unique architectural manifestation of immigrant culture in Milwaukee. Polish flats, as their name indicates, were built almost exclusively by immigrant Poles in their neighborhoods on the South Side, in the Riverwest area, and just north of Brady Street on the Lower East Side. Home ownership was a cultural imperative to the Poles, and, as soon as economically possible after their arrival in Milwaukee, it was customary for them to purchase, build, or move to a vacant lot a small, one-story or story-and-a-half frame cottage. These houses were the typical, mass-produced workers' cottages of the period and featured modest Victorian Gothic or Queen Anne details on the front, if they had any detailing at all. They were generally front-gabled structures and were often originally built on a cedar post foundation. As families expanded, newly-arrived relatives needed a place to stay, or the family just needed some rental income, the Poles would improve their residences by lifting-up their existing wooden house in its entirety and building a ground level or partially sunken basement apartment out of wood, brick or concrete block under it. These walk-in basements had street level windows and their own door to the outside, usually on the front under the stoop to the upper unit, but sometimes at the side of the house. Steep wooden steps would then be built up to a small wooden porch at the entrance to the upper unit.

To date, it has not been determined if this local phenomenon correlates with building practices in Poland or if it represents an adaptation to local conditions. Raised flats of similar appearance are located in Chicago, also a city with a large Polish population, but it is not known if they were built in the Polish quarters of other American cities. The construction of Polish flats mostly occurred during the 1890s and the first decade of this century and had pretty much ended by World War I. Polish flats can be found in the greatest concentration north of Brady Street on the Lower East Side and on the South Side where some streets, like South Fifth Place, feature entire blocks of them. ∎

2646-48 N. Fratney Street (c. 1880; c. 1900)

2449-49A S. 14th Street (1893)

2488-90 N. Bartlett Avenue (1901)

1435 W. Arthur Street (1906)

POLISH FLATS

WOOD, SIDING & TRIM

WOOD, SIDING & TRIM

WOOD, SIDING & TRIM

WOOD, SIDING & TRIM

WOOD, SIDING & TRIM

WOOD, SIDING & TRIM

Restoring wood siding and trim can be a challenge, but is well worth the effort. Beneath the modern substitute siding covering many older houses in Milwaukee, restorers are discovering architectural bonanzas of well-preserved, original wooden siding, carefully cut trim boards, and elegant, decorative sidewall shingling. In many cases, not only is the wood craftsmanship worth preserving, but often even the wood itself is almost irreplaceable and overlooked as an important part of the building's history. Modern siding and trim materials made of aluminum, vinyl, or steel cannot match the beauty of wood, nor its wide range of decorative and color possibilities. According to the rehabilitation standards for historic buildings established by the U.S. Department of the Interior, deteriorated architectural features, such as siding and trim, should be repaired rather than replaced whenever possible. In the event replacement is necessary, the new material should match the material being replaced in composition, design, color, texture, and other visual qualities. In the case of wood siding, this means it is best to replace wood with wood.

WOOD

An appreciation of old, wood-sided houses has to begin with some knowledge of the uniqueness of the wood that was used to build them. Most houses in Milwaukee built before World War I contain lumber taken from what were some of the world's largest and finest stands of white pine timber. In the nineteenth century, vast primeval pine forests stretched across the northern regions of Wisconsin, Michigan, and Minnesota. Those centuries-old pine forests were harvested during the last half of the nineteenth and early twentieth centuries to build much of Milwaukee and other cities throughout the midwestern and northeastern United States. The white pine trees that grew in those forests were majestic giants that often measured six feet in diameter at the base and stood about 180 feet high, although heights of up to 250 feet were not uncommon. One tree alone could yield enough lumber to construct three spacious Victorian houses.

The trees in these mature, naturally established forests are referred to as "old growth." The majority of the old growth white pine trees were between 300 and 400 years old when they were cut, while some rare supergiants that were reportedly eight feet in diameter at the base, were probably much older. In contrast, the pine timber harvested today for construction lumber is usually no more than 40 years old and yields saw logs only about 24 inches in diameter. The old growth white pine lumber was an outstanding building material

A northern Wisconsin lumber camp about 1890.

Milwaukee Public Museum

that was strong, yet light in weight, easily workable, and relatively resistant to decay. In those ancient forests, the typical tree grew without a single branch in its first 100 feet, and, as a result, its logs yielded clear or knot-free lumber of the highest quality. White pine was used for virtually every part of a building including the structural framing, siding, trim, doors, windows, and shingles.

By about 1920, old growth white pine was nearly extinct in the Great Lakes states because of unrestricted harvesting, forest fires, and the clearing of some forests for farm land. Southern yellow pine, which grows primarily in the South and South Atlantic states, is the common construction lumber used today throughout most of the U.S. along with white fir and spruce. Small amounts of old growth softwood timber such as Douglas fir, California redwood, and red cedar are still harvested today, but much of this wood is exported to foreign countries, particularly Japan, where it is highly valued.

Old growth cypress, a southern softwood with remarkable decay-resistant properties, was used occasionally by Milwaukee builders for siding, shingles, doors, window sash, and general interior millwork. Cypress became increasingly popular in Milwaukee and the Midwest as the white pine supply dwindled during the early twentieth century. The durability of old growth cypress is almost legendary among seasoned carpenters and builders. Cypress was used for exterior millwork and trim at least until the early 1930s, and was frequently advertised as "The Wood Eternal." Old growth cypress trees, like the old growth white pines, are nearly extinct today. Cypress has a grain much like pine, but ranges in color from a light yellowish brown to dark brownish red or chocolate. When it is cut, cypress gives off a distinctive, heavy aroma from the natural resins that make the wood, along with California redwood, the most decay resistant softwood that grows in North America. Cypress is found principally in the southern and South Atlantic states. Cypress is a premium material that rewards its owners with low maintenance and outstanding durability. Some second growth cypress is available, but it is not generally stocked in midwestern lumber yards, and is not as decay resistant as the old growth variety.

Most construction professionals agree that old growth construction lumber is inherently superior to today's construction lumber, which is cut from much younger and smaller trees. The harvesting of younger trees has resulted in lumber with more defects, such as knots, which reduce strength and serviceability. Lumber from younger, smaller diameter trees also contains a higher proportion of so-called juvenile wood which has poor stability and is subject to twisting, bowing, shrinking, and decay. Juvenile wood comprises the youngest 5 to 20 annual growth rings in a tree and has lower strength and density than the mature wood found in the outer growth rings. Thus, in the 40-year-old tree commonly harvested today, up to half the diameter of the log could be juvenile wood. Sapwood, the outermost growth rings in a log just inside the bark, is very vulnerable to decay regardless of the age or species of the tree. Within a living tree, sapwood functions to store food and transport sap. It is recognizably lighter in color than the inner part of the tree, which is called the heartwood. Sapwood and juvenile

wood, both of which are relatively undesirable as building materials, can both be present in the same piece of modern finished lumber because of the comparatively small diameter of the harvested timber. The thickness of the sapwood layer varies considerably from one wood species to another. Southern yellow pine trees, for example, widely used for construction lumber today, might have sapwood layers up to six inches thick. To combat this problem, chemical preservatives have been developed that can greatly increase the decay-resistance of the young lumber containing sapwood and juvenile wood now commonly used in construction.

Three-foot-wide white pine boards at a sawmill in Minnesota in 1912.

Minnesota Historical Society

Old growth timber, 300 to 400 years old, was an outstanding natural resource that will never be available again in significant quantities. A house made of old growth lumber has intrinsic structural value that should be considered when assessing the economic feasibility of an extensive restoration. Preserving sound, old, high quality wood might be more cost effective in the long run than replacing it with poorer quality new lumber that has less stable structural qualities and decay resistance and may require more frequent maintenance and replacement.

LUMBER SELECTION

Almost as important as the wood species, the orientation of the grain in a piece of wood is crucial to its durability, particularly if it is exposed to the weather. Lumber is classified as being either edge-grained or flat-grained, depending on the orientation of the annual growth rings on the flat surface of the board. Other commonly used terms for edge-grained lumber are quarter sawn and vertical grain.

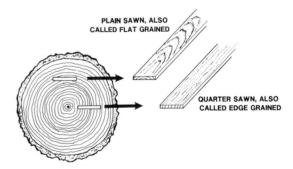

PLAIN SAWN, ALSO CALLED FLAT GRAINED

QUARTER SAWN, ALSO CALLED EDGE GRAINED

THE ORIENTATION OF THE GRAIN ON A BOARD DEPENDS ON HOW IT WAS CUT FROM THE LOG.

Edge-grained and flat-grained boards.

Flat-grained lumber is also called plain sawn. A flat-grained board has a broad, leaflike grain pattern because it is cut from a log with the annual growth rings at an angle of 45 degrees or less to the wide surface of the board. Edge-grained lumber is produced by sawing a log with annual growth rings at about a 90 degree angle to the wide surface of the board, which results in a grain pattern of closely spaced, continuous lines. Because of the large diameter of the old growth trees, they yielded a larger amount of highly desirable edge-grained lumber, which has a tendency to resist warpage, shrinkage, and decay better than flat-grained lumber. Flat-grained boards from large diameter, old-growth trees, however, are believed to be less susceptible to cupping and warping than flat-grained boards from smaller diameter, younger trees.

Edge-grained surfaces of any wood species, compared with flat-grained surfaces, shrink and swell the least and are the best for holding paint in exterior applications such as siding and trim. Ideally, flat-grained boards should be installed in areas protected from direct exposure to rain and sun.

BASIC WOOD FRAME CONSTRUCTION

Most houses in Milwaukee are made of wood frame construction, which means that a wooden skeleton provides the structural support for the walls, floors, and roof. An important function of siding and trim on the exterior of a building is to keep the frame dry so it does not deteriorate. The vertical wood framing members forming the walls are called studs; joists are the thick horizontal planks placed on edge that support floors and ceilings; and rafters are the sloping framing members that rest on top of the outside walls and support the roof. One important difference between modern houses and those built before about 1940 is the framing system of the exterior walls.

Well into the 1930s, most houses were built with the balloon frame method, which means that the exterior side wall studs in a two-story building are continuous from the foundation to the rafters. After about 1940 most builders switched to the platform or western style of framing in which the wall studs are no more than one-story in height and a subfloor or platform is built on top of the first floor to provide a base for building the second floor.

① Clapboard Siding
② Building Paper
③ Sheathing
④ Joist
⑤ Stud
⑥ Foundation

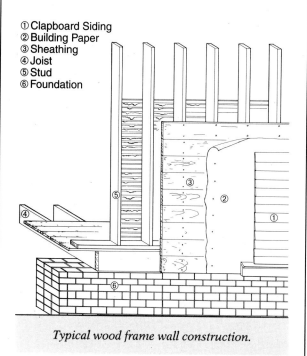

Typical wood frame wall construction.

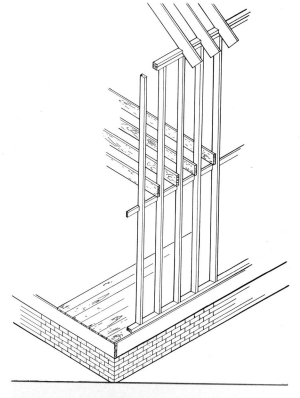

Balloon framing.

Balloon framing requires extra labor to build compared with platform framing, but it produces impeccably straight, strong walls which are less likely to shrink in height as the framing lumber dries out. Wood shrinks across the width of a framing member, not the length, and the absence of any horizontal framing members in a balloon framed wall means less chance for vertical shrinkage. This is an important consideration because siding material applied over a wood frame building (such as wood siding, cement stucco, or brick veneer) could crack, buckle, or deform from vertical shrinkage of the frame.

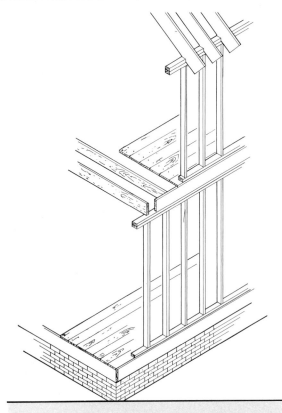

Platform or western style framing.

DECAY AND HOW TO PREVENT AND REPAIR IT

When wood is properly maintained against its two main enemies, decay-causing fungi and insects, it can provide centuries of service. Wood is most susceptible to decay when exposed to repeated cycles of wetting and drying. Those conditions foster the growth of microscopic, threadlike plants called fungi that destroy wood by feeding on it. Wood deteriorates more rapidly in warm, humid areas that promote the growth of fungi than in cool or dry areas. Wood that is moist, and consequently soft, can attract insects such as carpenter ants that destroy wood by nesting in it. In general, wood will not decay if it is kept constantly dry or if it is kept continuously wet.

Dry rot is a common type of decay found in wood in Wisconsin. Broadly speaking, dry rot refers to an advanced state of decay in which wood loses its strength and can easily be crushed into a dry powder. A roof leak over a beam that subsequently dries out to a brown, crumbly condition would be a common example of what most people call dry rot. The term dry rot is misleading because wood must be damp in order to decay. Originally, dry rot got its name because it appeared to be decay that mysteriously occurred while the wood was in a completely protected, dry environment, but it was actually caused by an unseen source of moisture. Dry rot can also form inside walls due to condensation from bathrooms and kitchens.

Chemical preservatives can greatly extend the service life of virtually any wood, even if it has a poor natural resistance to decay. Common preservatives available at hardware stores can be liberally brushed-on or the bare wood can be immersed in a preservative solution for a few minutes. When the preservative has thoroughly dried, the wood should be painted. Preservatives applied at the job site can be very helpful in preventing decay and insect damage in both new and old wood.

Pressure-treated lumber is a popular building material today for many outdoor projects. The lumber is commercially prepared in a high pressure chamber that drives the preservative deep into the wood, if not completely through it. The wood is usually warranted by the manufacturer for periods ranging from a decade up to the "life" of the purchaser.

Pressure-treated lumber is nothing new. The first known American commercial operation for injecting preservatives into wood under pressure began in 1838 on the East Coast. The modern era of pressure treating lumber in the U.S. began during the 1870s. Treated construction lumber was used extensively in Milwaukee as early as 1875 when pressure-treated wood prepared by the O. Thilmany Wood Preserving Company was used to build several large ice storage houses for local breweries. Some years before that, the Thilmany Company had started in business by treating wooden blocks for use in paving city streets.

Various wood preservatives have been injected or soaked into wood over the years. Today the most prevalent chemical used for pressure treating is chromated copper arsenate (CCA). The inorganic arsenic contained in this solution, which helps prevent rot and insect damage, is toxic to humans if ingested. There is no evidence that treated wood by itself presents an immediate health hazard, but the Environmental Protection Agency recommends wearing gloves when handling the wood, wearing a face mask in the presence of treated wood dust, and, after working with the material, to wash one's hands before eating. Wood products treated with CCA should not come into contact with food.

Treated wood is an excellent choice for use in inherently damp locations such as the structural framing of a porch, deck, or for fence posts. Because the preservative does not always completely saturate each piece of lumber, whenever treated wood is cut or drilled, the hole or cut end should be treated with a brushed-on wood preservative. Most 2-inch-thick lumber gets thoroughly treated, but on larger dimension lumber such as posts, there may be only a 1-inch penetration on the faces and a 12-inch penetration from the end grain. Most pressure-treated wood is southern yellow pine, which readily soaks up the preservative.

Architectural details such as these can often be restored at less cost than removing them and installing vinyl or aluminum trim and siding.

There are some drawbacks to using treated lumber. Treated lumber as it comes from the lumber yard is heavy because it often has a moisture content of 70 percent or more of the actual weight of the wood. Most common, non-treated construction lumber, in contrast, has a 19 percent moisture content. As a result, in addition to weighing more, pressure treated lumber will shrink considerably as the moisture evaporates. This can mean that treated wood used for trim boards installed with close-fitting joints is likely to develop unsightly gaps as the wood dries and shrinks. Treated lumber is usually allowed to dry for at least six months after it is installed before painting because evaporating moisture in the wood is likely to cause the paint to fail if it is painted any sooner. As treated wood is allowed to dry, it can develop surface cracks, called checking, in the direction of the grain. After finish painting, checking can allow moisture to seep back into the wood behind the paint layer, which will, in turn, cause the paint to peel as the moisture works its way to the surface of the wood. Treated lumber also has a tendency to twist, cup, and warp as it dries, which can create an unsightly appearance depending on the application and lead to gaps at joints that will allow water penetration and insect infestation within walls.

Using a clear (knot free) grade of wood that has a good natural resistance to decay is always preferable for exterior applications such as trim and millwork where appearance and durability are important considerations. Construction woods classified as resistant or very resistant to decay are old growth cypress, cedars, and redwood. Expect to pay a premium price for a good grade of these woods, if they are available at all, since cypress is dif-

ficult to obtain at any price. Western red cedar has excellent decay-resistance properties and is still readily available today. Red cedar is widely used for siding, trim, and shingling and can range in color from a deep, reddish brown that is sometimes difficult to distinguish from California redwood to a light tan color. Top-grade cedar lumber, usually called "D-select" in building trade terminology, is virtually knot and defect free, and is the best choice in the long run for most exterior finishing applications on older houses. Lesser grades with numerous knots, such as "number 3 and better" are more difficult to keep painted and have a "rustic" appearance that is out of place on an older house. Regardless of the wood's natural decay resistance, it is a good practice to apply a quality wood preservative to all sides of any wood before installation, either by a short soak or a liberal brushing. Classified as moderately resistant to decay are second growth or young growth cypress, Douglas fir, eastern white pine (the species that grows in Wisconsin), and two species of pine that grow in the southern states: long leaf and slash. Woods with only slight or no resistance to decay are hemlock, western and eastern fir, yellow poplar, southern yellow pine, and most of the other species of pine not already mentioned. When choosing any wood species, it is important to remember that juvenile wood near the center of the tree and the outer rings of sapwood invariably have poor natural resistance to decay.

Some types of softwood construction lumber hold paint better than others. Southern yellow pine, which comprises much of today's construction lumber, is considered difficult to keep painted. White pine is considered to be much more receptive to paint as are certain of the premium softwoods in use today such as cedar, cypress, and redwood.

NAILS

Knowing something about the history of nails can be of help when trying to distinguish between original construction and later alterations in a building. For example, finding that wire nails were used to attach some pieces of exterior trim might be indicative of a post-1900 alteration or repair if most of the other trim work was installed with square cut nails. It is also important to know what type of nail to use for what purpose.

The most common nail used in the nineteenth century is the old-fashioned square nail, which is most correctly called a cut nail because it was cut from a sheet of flat iron or steel with a special machine. The round, steel wire nails that are commonly used in construction today were introduced around 1890. Cut nails were hand-made by blacksmiths for centuries until the first nail-making machines were invented in the late 1700s. The relative merit of using cut nails versus wire nails was a topic of hot debate among carpenters during the 1890s, but by about 1910 the switch to less costly wire nails was virtually complete in the building trades.

Although cut steel nails are still made today, it is not necessary to use them in rehabilitation work, even if that was what was originally used. Cut nails do have some interesting and useful attributes, however. For one, the tip was blunted rather than sharply pointed like today's wire nails. Cut nails possess impressive holding power because, as the nail is driven in, the blunt tip pushes downward on wood fibers that in turn wedge against the side of the nail to hold it tightly in place. Sharp-pointed, common wire nails on the other hand, tend to split the wood fibers as they are driven into a board and have inherently less holding power. The blunt tip of a small cut nail can also reduce the chance that a driven nail will split the wood. Even today, it is a practice among some carpenters to cut off the sharp tip of a modern wire nail before driving it into wood that is vulnerable to splitting, such as near the edge of a board.

In order to enhance the holding power of smooth common wire nails, the "cement coated" nail was introduced during the early twentieth century and is still popular today. The nail has a thin coating of a special resin, not really cement, that greatly improves the nail's holding power. Cement coated nails are often used today to assemble the basic framing members and attach sheathing to a house. Annular wire nails are made with small rings forged into the shank in order to increase holding power. These nails are often used for installing wood siding.

To prevent either a cut or wire nail from rusting when it is exposed to the weather, the nail must be galvanized, which means that it has been given a thin, factory coating of rust-resistant zinc. Restorers often find that old non-galvanized cut or wire nails used for exterior work have rusted extensively. Although galvanized nails were introduced at least by the 1880s, they apparently were not widely used in construction until the early twentieth century. Non-galvanized roofing nails that rusted away quickly were cited as a major cause of premature failure of wooden shingle roofs during the late nineteenth century. Always use galvanized nails in an exterior application when the nail head could possibly be exposed to moisture, especially when installing finish trim or siding. Non-galvanized nails, even if covered with a thin layer of exterior paint or stain, will quickly rust and cause unsightly staining on exterior surfaces. There are two general types of galvanized nails: hot dipped and electroplated. Hot-dipped galvanized nails are usually preferred because they have a much thicker coat of rust-resisting zinc than electroplated nails.

EPOXY REPAIRS

Modern epoxy resins are perhaps the most innovative and promising materials for restoring damaged, decayed, and broken wood. Many basic epoxy repairs require no special

Original wood trim should be saved whenever possible. The simplified modern trim on the left pales in comparison with the original, highly detailed brackets and moldings.

skills other than patience and common sense. Properly used epoxies can result in a finished product that will instill a sense of satisfaction that historic material has been preserved, often at a cost far less than replacement. There are many types of epoxies on the market today, but rotted and damaged wood can be successfully repaired only with the few wood epoxies that are specifically formulated for that purpose. Quality epoxy materials are expensive, but they are permanent and remarkably strong.

Wood epoxy repair is usually a two-step process. First, decayed, dry, porous wood is soaked with a liquid epoxy material called a consolidant that solidifies and restores strength to the decayed material. Holes are often drilled in the decayed area so that the liquid can completely penetrate the decayed wood. Soaking the interior of the wood is important since merely treating the surface of a decayed piece of wood can lead to additional deterioration later. Second, large gaps, cracks and holes are filled with a thick epoxy paste that, after hardening, can be sanded, sawed, nailed, and carved. After finishing and painting, the repair work should be imperceptible. When patching surface holes or imperfections in dry, structurally sound wood, it is a good idea to "prime" the repair area with liquid epoxy immediately before applying the paste filler. Wood epoxies should not be confused with auto body paste fillers, which are not recommended for wood repair. Wood epoxies, unlike auto body fillers, have the special characteristic of being able to expand and contract with the natural movement of the wood. Because epoxies work by a chemical process, the setting time depends upon the amount of catalyst added and the surrounding air temperature.

Photos courtesy of Abatron Inc.

Rotted wooden sill in need of restoration.

Structural epoxy being applied to a rotted corner.

WOOD REPAIR USING STRUCTURAL EPOXY COMPOUNDS

The damaged corner after shaping and finishing.

After painting, the repair is invisible.

It is important to follow the manufacturer's directions carefully and to protect your skin and eyes from direct contact with epoxies. Mix epoxy in small batches because the working time is usually short. Since the epoxy material itself is costly, it is best to take your time and carefully follow directions to avoid mistakes and waste.

The decision to use epoxies should be based on the historic importance and replacement value, including labor, of the damaged wood. Epoxies are an excellent choice to fill in gouged and marred, but otherwise sound, wood features such as old wood doors, porch posts, brackets or ornamental features. Epoxies can also be used to repair rotted structural members, such as beams or rafters, but that type of application requires construction professionals and is usually beyond the ability of the average homeowner.

WOOD SIDING

"Clapboard" is the commonly used name for plain, beveled wood siding. This is the most prevalent siding type found in Milwaukee. The origin of the word clapboard remains uncertain. The Middle Dutch word "clapholt," meaning to crack or split wood, has been cited as a possible source because the earliest clapboards were made by hand-splitting boards from logs. The word has also been attributed to the English, who hand-split boards for barrel staves and called them cloveboards. Over time, the word reportedly evolved into "cloboards," "claboards," and finally clapboards.

DROP SIDING

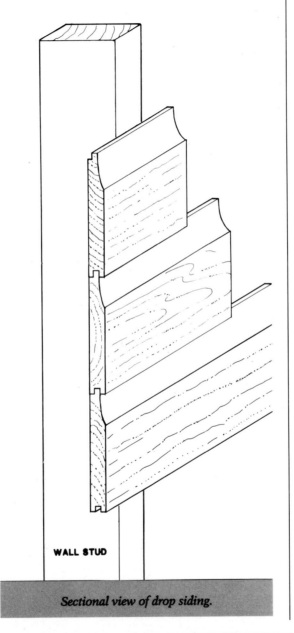

WALL STUD

Sectional view of drop siding.

Drop siding, the other major type of horizontal wood cladding, is boards that are installed directly on the wall framing without sheathing. In Milwaukee, it was used principally on barns and outbuildings rather than on houses. Drop siding is made in a variety of standard shapes. The boards are joined horizontally by a tongue and groove, or by an overlapping joint called a ship lap. Drop siding is, in fact, sometimes called ship lap. Finding exact replacement material for old drop siding may be difficult, because of subtle changes over the years in profiles and standard lumber sizes.

Clapboards or bevel siding are most commonly made today of western red cedar. White pine, redwood, and occasionally cypress are available by special order from the areas of the U.S. where these woods grow. Old growth white pine siding, the type most commonly used in Milwaukee in the past, has survived in good condition after 200 years of service on many New England buildings. Bevel siding is made in nominal widths of 4, 6, 8, 10, and 12 inches. These sizes are termed nominal because they are what the width of the board is before final finishing at the mill. The actual width of these sidings is one-half inch less than the named size. Wood siding milled today will occasionally not exactly match old wood siding in size or thickness. This is an important consideration when replacing a few isolated boards. In rare cases, exact size replacement siding may have to be custom milled.

The amount that each piece of siding overlaps the next varies according to the type of siding and the desired visual effect. Much of the wood siding used on older Milwaukee houses is nominally 4 inches wide (between 3-1/2 and 3-3/4 inches actual measurement) with about a 1/2 to nearly 1-inch overlap, leaving an exposure between 2 1/2 to 3 inches. The wider sidings are typically overlapped a minimum of 1 inch.

Clapboards being produced by radially-sawing white pine logs on vintage machinery, as was common before 1875. Clapboards cut from a log in this manner are edge grained and hold paint better and last much longer than flat-grained wood.

Donnell's Clapboard Mill

Several grades of wood siding are available, but most old houses require the use of clear (knot-free) material. Siding is usually sold in bundles with a random mix of flat-grain and edge-grained board. This is acceptable for siding replacement on older houses. For a premium price, some lumber yards sell bundles of clear, all edge-grained siding (also called vertical grained). Compared with lesser quality material, siding that is knot-free and vertical grained will initially cost more, but it will hold paint or stain better and last longer.

Western red cedar is the most common bevel wood siding material used today. It is softer, lighter, and more flexible than the old white pine siding used on most of the city's older houses. When installing red cedar siding, it is usually a good idea to drill pilot holes in the siding before nailing to prevent splitting. Use a drill bit that is smaller than the actual diameter of the nail.

Siding made of eastern white pine, still considered the best siding material by some experts, is again being manufactured at a few small mills in the eastern U.S. At least one mill uses sturdy, turn-of-the century woodworking machinery to make high-quality, all edge-grain, radially-sawn clapboards from 150-year-old trees. The owners claim that their number one premium clear pine clapboards, made like those a century ago, should last for more than 200 years when properly installed and maintained. Their claim is based on similar white pine clapboards more than 200 years old that have been documented on colonial era buildings in the eastern U.S. The clapboards are a maximum of eight feet in length and probably would be similar to the type of clapboards made in Milwaukee before about 1875. Radially sawn clapboards are better than the clapboards made later, which were mass produced in longer lengths with newer types of machinery. Radial sawing was replaced in the late nineteenth century with plain sawing, which was, by comparison, were more economical in that it made fuller use of a saw log, but produced clapboards that mostly had a flat grain which will not last as long or hold paint as well as the harder-to-produce edge-grain clapboards. If you are looking for an exceptional quality wood siding material, consider edge-grain, radially-sawn white pine clapboards.

Some homeowners may wish to consider installing new, factory painted, real wood siding that is typically guaranteed for up to ten years against peeling and cracking. This siding should not be confused with pre-finished hardboard or Masonite® siding, which are made of a composition material. Some construction professionals believe that factory painted wood siding and trim will become increasingly popular in the coming years. Because the siding is painted by machine under closely monitored factory conditions, and the bare wood is never exposed to the deteriorating effects of the weather before the painting process, the finish is considered to be particularly durable. Most of the factory painted wood siding is made of cedar, but it is also available in the eastern white pine species that was originally used to build many of the older houses in Milwaukee. Although factory painted wood siding has only recently been introduced, it appears to have promise as a "low maintenance" alternative to non-historic substitute sidings made of metal and vinyl.

Wood siding is usually milled today with a smooth, planed surface on one side and a rough-sawn surface on the flip side. Although technically either side can be used as a face, a rough-sawn appearance is not appropriate for the city's older houses, which were invariably sided with smooth, clear material for a finely finished appearance. Lesser grade, rustic-looking siding that contains large, conspicuous knots should not be used on older houses.

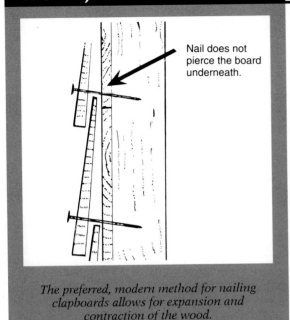

The preferred, modern method for nailing clapboards allows for expansion and contraction of the wood.

HOW TO NAIL CLAPBOARDS

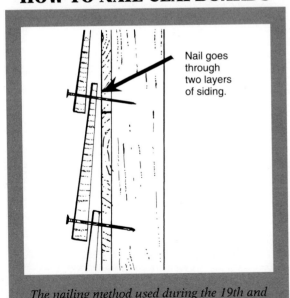

The nailing method used during the 19th and early 20th centuries is not recommended with today's clapboards because it may split the wood.

Paint or stain can peel prematurely, however, when applied to a wood surface that is too smooth. Unlike old siding, most modern bevel siding is extremely smooth because it is finished with high speed planing machines that tend to compress the wood fibers, thereby closing the surface pores in the wood and restricting the proper adhesion of paint. "Mill glaze" is a common term used to describe this machined finish. A quick, light sanding with an 80 grit sandpaper will slightly abrade the surface and make it more receptive to paint or stain. Before painting, some builders purposely leave newly installed wood siding exposed to the weather for a week or two in order to remove the mill glaze, although this is not a recommended practice. Research has shown that exposing new, unfinished wood siding to the weather for even a brief period before painting will remove some of the natural resins in the wood and contribute to a decrease in the longevity of the painted finish. If new, unfinished wood siding has been exposed to the weather for an extended period of time, it should probably be coated with a quality, paintable wood preservative before priming and painting in order to restore some of the resinous qualities of the wood.

Exterior siding and millwork should be installed with corrosion-resistant nails. Aluminum or hot-dipped galvanized nails, or even the more costly stainless steel nails, should be used for this purpose. Common steel nails, including those usually used with air-powered nail guns, will corrode easily and cause staining of the wood and paint. Nails should be long enough to penetrate into the studs and sheathing at least one inch. Avoid using nails that will penetrate the stud more than about 1-1/4" because the nail could

pierce an electric cable that might run through a hole in the middle of the stud. Five- or six-penny ring shank (also called annular) nails are usually sufficient. All vertical joints between clapboards should occur over a stud with each end nailed to that stud. Bevel siding is usually nailed far enough above the bottom, or butt, of the board so that the nail does not penetrate the course it overlaps. This method, in theory, allows the clapboard to expand and contract without splitting, but is not practical if the overlap is great. Most of the old siding in Milwaukee is nailed through two courses simultaneously at the bottom of each clapboard. With today's siding, this type of nailing might cause splitting and cracks in the siding, unlike the clapboards in use before World War I, which were made of very stable, old growth wood which is subject to minimal expansion and contraction and thus less likely to split.

Complete residing with matching wood is a practice that is acceptable when preservation of the original siding is no longer feasible because of its advanced state of decay. Siding can be replaced one wall at a time, as the homeowner's budget allows. Often only one side of a house will actually warrant complete replacement, while the others may be in repairable condition. Walls facing west and south are naturally prone to more deterioration than north and east facing walls because of greater exposure to sun and driving rain.

Before an entire wall of wood siding is replaced with new material, the course lines of the old siding should be marked on a long board or stick called a story pole. The story pole will record the layout work of the original carpenter, who probably combined some

A house in the process of being resided with new cedar clapboards to match the original siding.

Use a backsaw to cut out the damaged section of clapboard.

With a sharp chisel, carefully split and chip out the damaged clapboard section.

SPOT REPLACING A CLAPBOARD

Using a hacksaw blade with one end wrapped in tape for a hand grip, cut off any protruding nails that would be in the way of sliding in the new clapboard. Drive a small wooden wedge under the edge of the clapboard above to aid in inserting the new board.

Use a small block of wood to tap the new clapboard into place and then nail.

mathematical calculations with perhaps a little "eyeballing" to make the bottom edges of the clapboards line up evenly with the tops of window and door casings and the bottoms of frieze boards. The course line for the new clapboards can then be marked on the building with the story pole. A frieze board or some other horizontal trim board above the area to be sided is usually a reference point from which the layout marks are made. In addition to the clapboard course lines, the story pole shows the heights of door and window casings. The story pole can then be used for layout on gable end walls as well by aligning it with the tops of window casings. The course marks on the story pole indicate the location of the bottoms, or butt ends, of the clapboards. It is an excellent idea to prime the back sides of all new trim and wood siding before installation to prevent cupping and moisture penetration which can cause peeling of the finish paint.

As an underlayment for new siding, staple or nail 15-pound builder's felt over the old sheathing. As an alternative, consider using one of the new synthetic wind barriers that stop air infiltration but still allow water vapor generated inside the house to pass through. The new wind barriers are very popular in new construction and, when properly installed, should serve well to increase the energy efficiency of older houses as well. Do not install plastic sheeting as an underlayment because it could cause condensation inside the walls which can lead to the decay of the structural framing.

The outside corners of a clapboard sided building are finished either by butting the clapboards against vertical corner boards, or by mitering the clapboard corners. A miter is a joint made with the ends or edges of two pieces of lumber cut at a 45 degree angle and fitted together to form a clean, sharp corner. Mitered corners are labor intensive and were installed to create special design effects usually in more expensive buildings. Mitered corners are an impressive architectural detail, but they tend to open up, allowing moisture to get behind the siding. When replacing a mitered clapboard, it is essential to prime the cut end to seal out water that would cause the joint to open. If a building was designed with mitered corner siding, it should be retained as a design feature.

Corner boards are always installed before the siding which is then butted up to them. A homemade wooden siding gauge to hold one end of the clapboard while the other end is fitted and nailed is invaluable for a one-person installation. Make at least two of these gauges because the other will double as a marking

An 1870s cottage as it looked in 1977 when it still retained much of its original character.

NEW WOOD SIDING SHOULD MATCH THE APPEARANCE OF THE ORIGINAL SIDING

This 1990 photo of the same house shows that the new front windows and the new, rustic, board-and-batten siding have completely changed the architectural character of the house.

gauge when fitting a clapboard to a corner board. Metal gauges with built-in scribing wheels to mark siding so that it could be cut to fit tight to a corner board were a common tool of the past and might still be found in usable condition at antiques stores.

For reasons of economy, particularly in buildings constructed in the 1860s and 1870s, bevel wood siding was sometimes applied directly to the studs without sheathing. In this application, the siding often deteriorated or does not hold paint well and many restorers choose to completely replace it. If the siding is in relatively good condition, it can be spot-repaired like any other clapboard-sided wall. If the siding is completely removed, it is recommended that the exposed wall cavity be insulated with fiberglass batt insulation that has a vapor barrier on the side of the insulation that faces the interior of the building. New sheathing such as plywood, oriented strand board (a composition board made of glued-up wafers of wood) or traditional, nominal one-inch-thick plank lumber should be installed over the wall studs. Filler strips of wood the thickness of the new wall sheathing should be carefully cut to size and installed around the old window and door casings after the trim is removed for a proper appearance when the trim is replaced. After the corner boards, window and door casings, and fascia boards have been built out to the proper thickness, and the trim reinstalled, the building can then be resided.

SIDEWALL SHINGLING

Decorative wooden shingles were installed on sidewalls in an almost endless combination of patterns beginning in the 1880s to give individuality to even very small and otherwise simple houses. Sidewall shingles are similar in appearance to wooden roof shingles, although some sidewall shingles were thinner and of a lesser grade of wood than typical roof shingles because their application did not demand as great a resistance to weather. Because they are installed on a vertical surface which will shed water, they have a much longer service life, if kept painted or stained, than roofing shingles. Many examples of sidewall shingling are still in excellent condition after 100 years. Sidewall shingles, like roof shingles, are finished with a slightly rough surface after being milled so that they will hold paint or stain better. Frequently, shingles were dipped in stain before installation, sealing them on both sides and thus contributing greatly to their longevity. This is still an excellent practice.

Sidewall shingles of a uniform width are known as dimension shingles, and they are still manufactured today in a wide variety of ornamental butt patterns virtually identical to those manufactured 100 years ago. Square butt wooden shingles of random width, however, are probably the most common, and they adorn the upper floors and gable areas of hundreds of houses in Milwaukee. Shingles on sidewalls are sometimes installed in a method called double coursing. This is done by using a lower grade shingle under the shingle exposed to the weather. The exposed shingle's butt extends about one-half inch below the butt of the under course. Most old sidewall shingles in Milwaukee are made of white pine or cedar. Today, practically all wooden shingles are made of western red cedar, although redwood, a more expensive material, is also available.

Replacing damaged or missing wood sidewall shingles is relatively simple. Often the most difficult part of the job is reaching the area to be repaired, which is usually on the second story or in the gable area. Use wood wedges to raise the butt of the shingle directly above the defective or missing one. A damaged shingle can be removed by carefully splitting it in pieces along the grain with a wood chisel and hammer. Do not damage the adjacent or underlying shingles which are not

A house with wooden sidewall shingling.

to be removed. At least two courses of nails will hold each shingle in place. Old iron nails tend to be corroded and weak, and by using a chiseling action with a hammer and flat pry bar, the old nails may break off flush with the surface, making it easier to slip in the new shingle. A better tool to use, designed specifically for this purpose, is a shingle ripper. It is not a common homeowner's tool, but if you are doing extensive replacement of any type of shingles, it is invaluable and well worth the investment.

Push the replacement shingle, cut to proper size, up as far as it will go under the upper course. Then drive two four-penny box nails into the shingle at an angle at a point as high up on the shingle as possible. Use a nail set when it becomes difficult to strike the nail without damaging the shingle above it. Finally, drive the butt of the replacement shingle up flush with the rest of the course by striking a wood block held against the bottom of the shingle with a hammer. Do not strike the shingle directly with the hammer. Remove the wooden wedges so that the upper course of shingles lays flat over the top of the new shingle, and the repair is complete.

If an entire wall of shingles is to be replaced, carefully record the exposure of each shingle on a story pole, as you would if you were replacing old clapboards. Note that the bottoms of the old shingles will invariably line up with the tops of window and door casings. By using a story pole, you will be able to duplicate the spacing of the old shingles without having the laborious task of calculating the spacing of each course as the original carpenter had to do. Make an effort to duplicate the size and design of the old shingles. Unless otherwise specified, shingles ordered today will be delivered in bundles of random width pieces ranging between three and ten inches wide. Old shingles were never less than about five inches in width, and installing a three-inch-wide shingle is not recommended today under any circumstances except, perhaps, in undercoursing. Some decorative wood shingles with shaped butts used in the nineteenth century might not be commercially available today, but they should be easy to duplicate using square butt shingle stock. A bandsaw is probably the best tool for cutting decorative patterns, but a good, hand-held jig saw with a narrow, sharp, fine-toothed blade will also work. A table saw can be used to cut the shingles to the proper width. Decorative shingles must be cut individually, instead of stacked because the wedge shape of the shingle will produce undesirable variations in the pattern.

Installing a completely new wall of shingles is labor intensive since each small shingle is attached with two nails. This requires much more nailing and fitting than installing beveled wood siding and takes longer. This is an important consideration since most shingling is located high upon the building, and you will be working from a ladder or scaffolding. Therefore, it is desirable to utilize as many labor-saving devices as possible, such as the story pole described earlier. Snap a chalk line between the bottom story pole marks and lightly tack a good straightedge, such as a 1 x 4, to the line. Butt the shingles to the straightedge and nail them. Continue this procedure up the wall. Outside corners, if they are part of the installation, are alternately lapped in a procedure called lacing. Allow one outer course to protrude slightly past the corner, butting the shingle on the adjoining wall

plane to it. Trim the protruding corner with a box plane and a small utility knife.

TRIM

Exterior wooden trim and moldings are essential to defining and accentuating the architectural style of a house and giving it a sense of scale. White pine was the most commonly used material for trim, but mahogany, a highly decay resistant and expensive imported wood, was used occasionally for turned exterior decorative features such as small decorative columns and porch spindles. Every effort should be made to preserve original exterior wooden trim, particularly carved or complexly machined pieces which would be difficult and expensive to duplicate today. High quality wood epoxy fillers and consolidants can be used to permanently repair even severely decayed or damaged decorative wood features. Badly damaged decorative trim will probably have to be removed from the building in order to properly restore it.

Exact size replacement lumber for old houses is not stocked in lumber yards today, because, along with decreases in lumber quality over the years, there have been slight, but steady, decreases in standard lumber sizes. These differences need to be considered when purchasing replacement lumber. Most older trim boards measure a full one-inch-thick or more. Today, the thickness of a board stocked as a nominal one-inch-thick is actually only three-quarters of an inch thick. In many cases a slight difference in thickness or width between a piece of replacement wood and the old material is not objectionable. Often replacement wood can be unobtrusively shimmed or blocked from behind to make fin-

ished surfaces flush. However, for some applications, replacement lumber may have to be custom planed to match the thickness of an existing board. Not to be overlooked as a good source of trim material is old, used, framing lumber sold by demolition contractors that can be remilled to new specifications. The wood has to be completely free from any nails or metal objects before being milled, however, so a common metal detector, used by many

An 1880s Victorian house with elaborate wood trim.

A typical worker's cottage of the 1880s or 1890s that has been stripped of its original detailing.

How such a cottage might look with its architectural detailing restored.

hobbyists, is an excellent tool for locating hard-to-see or imbedded nails before sending reclaimed old growth wood to be remilled. Some local lumber yards and millwork shops offer custom thickness planing services for the homeowner. These businesses may, however, be reluctant to plane old, salvaged lumber because of fear that hidden nails may damage their machinery. Some carpenters have small, portable, thickness planners and are capable of milling exact-size replacement lumber at the job site for a reasonable fee. They may be willing to use salvaged lumber.

Restorers will also encounter problems with finding basic replacement moldings. New, off-the-shelf moldings, although they may superficially appear to match old molding profiles, usually do not. Some short runs of molding might have originally been made by carpenters using hand-operated molding planes, although power woodworking equipment was used extensively as early as the mid-nineteenth century to mass produce most of the millwork used in a house. Virtually any old, machined molding or spindle can be duplicated today by local woodworking shops and restoration carpenters. However, the cost

for such custom services can be very high depending on the amount of millwork needed and the complexity of the profile. Repair of damaged or decayed sections of existing wood moldings with wood epoxies is often the most economical and practical solution.

Bargeboards and elaborate wooden gable ornaments were other common and very prominent decorative features of many houses. Although most houses retain their bargeboards, relatively few gable ornaments have survived. After reaching their peak in popularity during the 1870s and 1880s, many were removed over the years to facilitate the installation of substitute siding, to reduce maintenance or to make the buildings look more modern. Gable ornaments and barge-boards are purely decorative elements and do not perform any structural function. The simplest types could be assembled on the job site by carpenters with only a few shop-made pieces of wood. Fancy, turned gable ornaments that were mass-produced to adjust to any roof pitch were relatively inexpensive and trimmed the gable peaks of even very modest cottages. For very expensive residences, gable ornaments were custom designed by architects and made to order in millwork shops.

The decision to reproduce a missing gable ornament for a house should be carefully researched. First, look beneath the gable peak for evidence that would indicate the presence of a gable ornament, such as old nail holes where the missing ornament was attached or old paint marks. When reproducing a totally missing ornament, research old pattern books, historic photos, and catalogs to find a proper design. It is often helpful to search for a simi-

Raking Crown Molding

Mitered Corner

Level Crown Molding
on a Vertical
Fascia Board.

In order to produce a proper mitered corner on this dormer, the raking crown molding must be shaped to a profile different than the level crown molding.

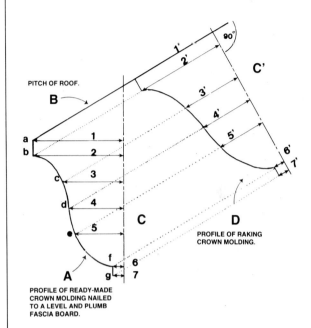

PITCH OF ROOF.

B

C'

a
b

c

d

C

D

PROFILE OF RAKING
CROWN MOLDING.

A

f
g

PROFILE OF READY-MADE
CROWN MOLDING NAILED
TO A LEVEL AND PLUMB
FASCIA BOARD.

① DRAW PROFILE OF READY-MADE CROWN MOLDING (A) AND ESTABLISH PROPER ROOF PITCH LINE (B).

② ESTABLISH REFERENCE POINTS a THROUGH g ON THE GIVEN MOLDING PROFILE AND FROM THESE POINTS DRAW LINES PARALLEL TO THE ROOF PITCH LINE.

③ DRAW CONSTRUCTION LINES C AND C' AS INDICATED.

④ TRANSFER THE MEASURING LINES 1 THROUGH 7 TO CONSTRUCTION LINE C' AS INDICATED. 1 equals 1', 2 equals 2', etc.

⑤ THE MEASURED DISTANCES FROM C' WILL DETERMINE NEW REFERENCE POINTS TO DRAW THE PROFILE OF THE RAKE MOLDING THAT WILL CORRECTLY MITER WITH THE GIVEN LEVEL MOLDING.

NOTE: ONLY SEVEN MEASURING LINES ARE SHOWN HERE BUT MORE CAN BE ESTABLISHED TO INCREASE THE ACCURACY OF THE PROFILE.

How to determine the profile of a raking molding that will correctly miter with a level molding.

lar house with its original ornament intact and use that as a model for the reproduction.

Another type of trim that is very typical of old houses is the crown molding that was used to trim the cornice. Because of its exposure to the weather, this piece frequently needs replacement or repair, particularly the pieces that trim the raking cornice of a gable. When considering replacing or installing crown moldings or trim on a raking cornice, it should be kept in mind that fitting two pieces of molding together at a mitered corner, such as where the trim on a horizontal eave meets the trim on the raking angle of the gable, can be far more complicated that it appears. In many old buildings, crown molding is typi-

cally used to form a continuous band of trim along the edge of the horizontal eave and up the sloping edge of the gable. Replacement of this ornament presents special problems because the horizontal eave crown molding and the sloping gable crown molding, called a rake, are actually two different molding profiles specially designed to form a perfectly mitered corner. Horizontal crown molding similar in appearance to nineteenth century crown molding is still stocked in several different sizes by most lumber yards, but the exact profile of the raking crown, which is flatter and longer in profile than horizontal crown molding, depends on the roof pitch. Years ago lumber yards probably stocked raking crown molding for a few different roof

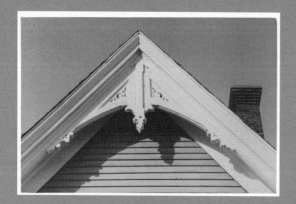

Timbered Victorian Gothic Gable Ornament c. 1872.

Pierced Victorian Gothic Gable Ornament c. 1875.

Scroll-sawn Victorian Gothic Gable Ornament c. 1880.

VICTORIAN GOTHIC AND QUEEN ANNE GABLE ORNAMENTS

Queen Anne Fan Gable Ornament c. 1885.

Queen Anne Spindlework Gable Ornament c. 1890.

Queen Anne Sunburst Panel Gable Ornament c. 1890.

Victorian Gothic Bargeboard, 1874.

Victorian Gothic Bargeboard, 1876.

Queen Anne Bargeboard, c. 1890.

BARGEBOARDS

Elizabethan Revival Bargeboard, c. 1900.

Tudor Revival Bargeboard, 1908.

Craftsman Bargeboard, c. 1913.

pitches, but carpenters often had to have the raking molding custom-made at a millwork company or made at the job site with hand-operated molding planes. In either case, a carpenter had to know how to precisely determine the profiles of compatible level and raking crown moldings. Today, raking molding is strictly a custom-made item, and the illustrations in this chapter show how to determine its correct profile. Trying to use a standard crown molding for both the eave and rake will result in a clumsy-looking joint where the two meet, since the profiles will never exactly match. If at all possible, it is advisable to preserve an original raking crown molding with epoxy consolidants and wood preservatives or else use it as a pattern to cut a new reproduction raking crown molding.

SUBSTITUTE SIDING

For some homeowners the dream of an elegantly painted, old, wood-sided house is diminished when confronted with the reality of peeling paint and decayed trim. Other restorationists become frustrated when a new paint job on an old house begins to fail within just a few years. One of the most frequent solutions to these problems, installing substitute siding made of aluminum or vinyl, is not a good alternative if the historic architectural character of the building is to be preserved.

Substitute sidings have their place in the construction of modern buildings, but they are often a poor choice for installation on the fine old houses in Milwaukee that were built during an era of unsurpassed craftsmanship in wood. Substitute sidings are appealing at first glance because they promise relief from

the expense and drudgery of painting, but there are numerous hidden drawbacks.

Consider these facts about substitute siding:

* Maintenance is not actually eliminated, as is sometimes advertised, but is merely deferred, since substitute sidings such as aluminum, steel, and vinyl eventually require repainting to restore a factory-fresh look. The fact that paint manufacturers now formulate paints that are specifically advertised to cover aluminum, steel and vinyl siding indicates that substitute sidings have to be recoated eventually. At least one major paint maker also states that vinyl siding should never be repainted with a color darker than the original factory color in order to prevent warping of the siding.

* Vinyl siding is plastic and its ability to withstand the harmful effects of ultraviolet light from the sun has not been proven over time.

* Vinyl can crack, especially in cold weather.

* The factory-applied colors of substitute siding are limited, and do not lend themselves to the accurate recreation of multi-color historic paint schemes.

* Covering an older house with substitute siding can actually decrease its resale value among the increasing number of buyers who prefer original, traditional siding materials.

* Substitute sidings have a tendency to look dated very quickly. Asphalt, asbestos tile and wide steel or aluminum siding were all

popular in their day, but are now considered to be old fashioned and are being removed from many houses today. Wood siding is timeless and will never go out of fashion.

* Substitute siding systems cannot replicate the trim work and detailing that make older houses works of art and give them their architectural character.

With few exceptions, the application of substitute siding hides historic details that are important to the architectural character of a house. Trim around windows and doors, under eaves, and at the corners of a building are often removed or completely obscured to accommodate substitute sidings. Existing trim can be left uncovered in most installations, but this costs more and often results in awkward detailing where the siding meets the trim. Inevitably all siding materials become damaged over time. Wood siding is much easier to replace and repair than synthetic sidings which, over time, become difficult to match with exact replacement material. One of the worst problems with synthetic siding is that it tends to hide the physical deterioration of the building rather than to stop or prevent such problems. Some sidings act as exterior vapor barriers, trapping excess water vapor which condenses within the wall cavity and damages wood framing and sheathing. Substitute sidings that are installed to conceal severely deteriorated wood surfaces might buckle and come loose from the building as the underlying wood it is anchored to continues to decay. Wood siding, on the other hand, allows internal moisture to harmlessly escape, in effect, to let the building breathe.

Shown in the 1930s this Queen Anne style house still retained its original character.

By the 1980s, asbestos siding installed in the 1940s covered the exterior, and the porches had been enclosed.

By 1991, vinyl siding had been installed to cover the dated-looking asphalt siding applied 50 years earlier. The house has lost all of its original architectural character.

Milwaukee County Historical Society

SUBSTITUTE SIDINGS CAN DESTROY ARCHITECTURAL CHARACTER

Over time, virtually all substitute siding seems to acquire an undesirable, dated look. The early, simulated brick and stone asphalt and cement tile sidings so fashionable fifty years ago are now themselves being covered over with the vinyl or metal substitute sidings popular today. Steel siding succumbed in popularity to aluminum which has recently been eclipsed by vinyl. A decade ago aluminum was one of the most popular siding materials, but today, because of cost, vandalism, and maintenance problems, it is already one of the least-used sidings in America. The home improvement division of a major U.S. retailer, which once actively promoted its use, included the following criticisms of aluminum siding in a recent advertisement for the firm's vinyl siding: "Aluminum siding dents easily, shows scratches easily, and has problems caused by corrosion, too. And aluminum is not a good insulator...it conducts heat, which can be bad for your pocketbook." Vinyl, the current rage in the substitute siding industry, will no doubt be replaced by yet another "miracle" product in the future.

Wood siding, by contrast, has never gone out of style. It is a traditional material that has been in continuous use throughout the history of building in the U.S. and still has the distinction today of being considered a quality, even luxury, cladding material.

If after carefully considering all of its drawbacks, you ultimately decide to install substitute siding over your wood cladding, keep the following guidelines in mind if you wish to preserve the historic character of your old house:

* The width of new siding must match the old clapboards.

* Do not select wood grain-look sidings because original clapboards never looked like this; they were smooth.

* All original trim around windows and doors should be left uncovered.

* Do not cover decorative brackets, cornice moldings, eaves, or soffits.

* Do not cover sidewall shingles because this material is remarkably durable and low in maintenance and there are no substitute materials made that can accurately reproduce the look of many patterns of wood shingles.

This historic house has been sided with aluminum, but great care was taken to preserve nearly all of the original exterior wooden trim so that the building largely retains its historic appearance when viewed from a distance.

A dramatic transformation occurred when the asphalt siding was removed from this late 1860s cottage exposing the original wood siding and trim.

REMOVING SUBSTITUTE SIDING

Removing substitute siding to expose the original underlying wood clapboards and trim can be an experience similar to opening a time capsule. The actual demolition is often a relatively quick process, and the results of uncovering long-hidden historic siding and decorative features can be dramatic and rewarding. The work is simple and straight-forward, but a few precautions should be taken because some of the most common older siding materials contain asbestos fibers which pose a health threat if inhaled.

In general, if a substitute siding is not made of aluminum, vinyl or steel, it probably contains some asbestos. The earliest types of substitute sidings, installed during the 1930s, 1940s, and early 1950s, were made in two basic types: hard, slate-like, tile siding made of cement asbestos; and soft, simulated brick and stone siding with a consistency similar to that of roofing shingles made of asphalt and an asbestos-bearing fiber. Cement asbestos tile siding was frequently installed over a rock lath underlayment, which is a gypsum board material that smoothed the installation surface and functioned as an insulator, but it was just as often installed directly over the old wood siding without the rock lath underlayment. The soft asphalt siding materials typically were manufactured to a thickness of five-eighths of an inch including a core of asbestos-bearing insulation and were usually installed in sheets directly over the old wood siding on lathing strips.

Asbestos is a natural mineral that separates into very strong, fine fibers, some as small as the particles in cigarette smoke. Breathing airborne asbestos fibers has been associated with the disease asbestosis, a non-cancerous respiratory ailment that scars lung tissue. Symptoms of the disease often do not appear until many years after exposure. Asbestos has also been linked with cancers of the lung and the lining of the abdominal cavity. The potential of an asbestos-containing material to release fibers is dependent upon its degree of friability. Friable means that it can crumble under hand pressure and emit virtually invisible asbestos fibers to float in the air. Asbestos siding materials are generally considered non-friable and unlikely to emit airborne fibers unless they are broken or subjected to sawing operations. Asbestos came into use because it is a good insulator, fireproof, lightweight, and almost indestructible. It was in use at least as early as the fifth century B.C. in textile production. In modern times, asbestos has been an essential ingredient of many building materials including roofing, siding, pipe and wire insulation, and floor tile. In recent years government mandates have curtailed the use of asbestos, but it is still used in the manufacture of some building products. Government regulations call for an end to the use of asbestos in new products by 1996.

There are currently no government regulations regarding the removal of exterior asbestos siding, but the material must be sealed in plastic bags and taken to a landfill that is approved for the disposal of asbestos products. It is advisable to wear a half-face respirator with a high efficiency particulate (HEPA) filter when removing asbestos siding. The respirators are relatively inexpensive and are an invaluable addition to a rehabber's tool box because they have many other uses, such as filtering out paint vapors as well as other potentially harmful dusts and airborne chemicals encountered in the course of building construction and restoration. The respirator should also be used during siding removal as a precaution against breathing any lead-bearing dust that might be trapped behind the substitute siding from old, deteriorated, lead-based paint. Do not wear a common facemask because it will not filter the tiny asbestos fibers. Work clothes should be washed separately from other laundry, or else disposable plastic clothes called "moon suits" can be purchased at a reasonable cost from asbestos removal supply companies. Tools used to remove the siding should be washed thoroughly after use.

The fastest way to remove most tile-type siding is with a flat pry bar and a hammer. However, this method increases the risk of breaking the siding tiles releasing asbestos fibers into the air. A more cautious approach is to use a metal punch and hammer to drive the nails holding the asbestos siding tiles into

This house was an ugly duckling, before the asphalt siding was removed.

Removing the asphalt siding revealed the long hidden beauty of the house.

the wood behind it. The tile siding can then be removed in one piece. Nails holding the soft asphalt type of simulated brick and stone sidings in place are usually located in the fake mortar joints. Work down from the top of the house since that is how the siding is lapped.

When the substitute siding is removed, the paint on the old clapboards is often completely deteriorated, leaving the siding sooty and dark. What little paint remains can usually be scraped away easily. Look for the scars or outlines of moldings or decorative features over doors and windows that might have been removed to install the substitute siding. Make tracings or patterns of the scars so they can be used later to design and fabricate new trim pieces. Often a projecting belt course or drip course made of molding and canted siding or shingling was removed between the first and second stories to allow the substitute sidings

to be installed flat. Another frequently removed feature was the angled board at the bottom of the clapboard wall, called a water table, which was designed to direct water away from the foundation of the building.

Some of the old clapboards may need replacement, particularly if water leaked between the substitute siding and the original wooden siding, but most people find the original wood siding in good to excellent condition. The numerous holes left by the nails used to attach the substitute siding must be patched. Although a good grade of wood filler or putty will do the job, it is worthwhile to consider using one of the new, high quality wood epoxy patching and consolidating materials that can be sanded smooth when dry resulting in a permanent, almost invisible repair. Although epoxies are expensive, a little material in this application goes a long way. Epoxies have the virtue of not shrinking, cracking or falling out over time like some of the more common patching materials.

When wood siding is found in a bare, very dry condition, it is essential to restore some of the wood's original, supple surface qualities to allow the proper adhesion of new paint or stain. Primer and paint will often peel prematurely when applied to wood that is extremely dry. Wood can be rejuvenated with either a quality, commercially-prepared, paintable wood preservative or a very acceptable homemade solution consisting of: three cups of varnish, one ounce of paraffin wax, and enough mineral spirits (or paint thinner or turpen-

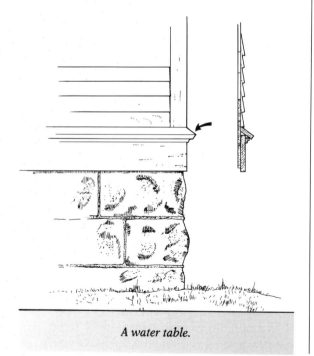

A water table.

tine) to make one gallon. Paraffin wax, used for canning, is available at most food stores. In government tests this mixture proved to be as effective as some commercially-made water repellent preservatives. After applying the solution, let it dry for about two or three days, and then prime the wood with a high quality oil base primer followed by your choice of finish paint. Weathered wood often has extensive small cracks called checking that must be filled, preferably with epoxy, before painting to keep water out. Paint alone, no matter how thickly applied, will not sufficiently bridge and seal these cracks.

If the base wood is dirty, it should be cleaned by brushing, scraping, and if absolutely necessary, scrubbing with clear water. Avoid detergents or similar common cleaners on bare wood because they may soak in and later cause problems with paint adhesion. To remove very fine, deep-seated dirt, consider using one of the new products formulated to remove dirt from natural wood decks. These solutions also act as wood rejuvenators.

PAINT REMOVAL AND REPAINTING

The key to a good and lasting paint job is a stable base. Excessive paint buildup and moisture are the two most common causes of paint failure. Excessive moisture can enter the building through faulty roof and chimney flashings, leaky or overflowing gutters, defective roof shingles, and missing or deteriorated trim. Escaping interior moisture can also cause exterior paint to peel. Modern living conditions that include more showers, baths,

and cooking than was common many years ago can create large amounts of interior moisture. In a large home, excessive interior moisture may manifest itself in the form of peeling exterior paint in only a few areas. Two common solutions are to use a dehumidifier or to install an exhaust fan in the kitchen, bathroom or other areas of high humidity. Homes heated with steam or hot water have inherently higher humidity levels than homes heated with forced air furnaces.

Excessive paint buildup causes the paint to fail when the thickness of the paint prevents it from expanding and contracting at the same rate as the wood siding. This causes the paint to crack, often down to the bare wood, allowing moisture to get behind the paint. The moisture then dissolves the bond between the paint and the wood siding causing the paint to flake off. The only solution to excessive paint buildup is to remove the paint down to the bare wood. Other than causing peeling, excessive paint buildup obscures the crisp edges of the architectural details on older houses and detracts from the intended appearance of the building.

Once any moisture problems have been corrected, the remedy for extensive peeling paint is complete removal of all the remaining loose paint to bare wood. Usually this does not mean that the entire house needs to be stripped, just problem areas. Treat any area where paint has peeled to bare wood with a quality, paintable wood preservative before priming and repainting. Wood siding that is checked or severely weathered will probably not hold paint for long and should be replaced or the cracks filled with epoxy fillers. A good paint job can last up to seven years.

Stripping paint is an unpleasant task, and there are few advisable shortcuts. Some safety precautions should be taken during the process because old paint may contain lead which is a potential health hazard. Any house built before 1978, the year in which the sale of lead-bearing paint was banned, may contain some lead-based paint. This does not necessarily present a health hazard unless the paint is removed or peels off. Lead was used because it made the paint more durable, but even a century ago, the potential health hazards of leaded paint, primarily to house painters, were recognized.

The Painter, Gilder and Varnisher's Companion, which was a reference book published in 1860, identified lead poisoning, then called the "painter's colic," as "the most common and the most dangerous to which painters are liable. [This illness] arises with painters from breathing in the fumes and handling the different preparations of white lead." The book also noted that "the business of a painter and varnisher is generally, and not without reason, considered an unhealthy one. Many of the substances which he is necessarily in the habit of employing are of a nature to do injury to the [body]."[1]

Although lead-based paint was usually the material of choice for exterior painting before World War II, other types of paints were also used during that period. In fact, an older wooden house usually has many layers of several different types of paint. The commercial production of zinc-based paints as a less-toxic alternative to lead-based paint, begun in France in the late 1700s by a man named LeClair, who was a master painter and paint manufacturer. LeClair's zinc-based paint became very popular in France, and it was eventually specified for all painting work done for the French government.[2] Imported French, zinc-based paint could have been used in America any time after about 1800.[3] However, the widespread use of zinc-based paint was probably not common until after 1850 when domestic zinc-refineries were in operation. It is possible that zinc-based paints were introduced to the Milwaukee area at least by the 1860s when one of the first large zinc refineries began operating relatively close by in the city in Mineral Point, Wisconsin. Pure zinc-based exterior paint produced a smoother, more uniform texture than leaded paint, and is currently not known to present a health hazard. However, small amounts of pigments, some of which did contain lead, were often used to tint the white zinc base. Titanium-based paint, introduced about 1918, also became very popular. Currently, it is not known to present a health hazard. Casein paint, which has a milk base, was also used before 1900. It should be kept in mind that all paint, no matter when it was made, contains chemicals that are potentially toxic to humans if ingested.

The safest method to remove lead-based paint from flat surfaces is with a heat plate that softens the old paint so it can be easily scraped away. Heat guns are useful for removing paint from trim and wooden details where heat plates will not work. The use of heat guns to remove paint from siding is potentially dangerous, however, and not recommended because hot air from the guns can sometimes pass through cracks in the siding and sheathing to ignite objects or debris inside the wall, such as birds' nests, building paper, and old sawdust. Open-flame torches are not recommended because the intense heat can start a fire or vaporize any lead in the paint. Lead vapors are dangerous because, if inhaled, they are quickly assimilated into the blood stream. Low levels of lead in the blood can cause high blood pressure, irritability, or depression, while high levels can cause severe medical problems including mental retardation or death. Sanding and scraping lead-based paint can create lead dust that can easily be inhaled.

Failing paint caused by excessive moisture penetration due to leaking gutters.

Always wear a half-face respirator with a high-efficiency particulate (HEPA) filter, which is designed to filter lead particles. An ordinary dust mask will not filter lead dust or vapors. Paint chips containing lead should be carefully swept up or collected in a dropcloth and disposed of in a place where children cannot get at them. Leaded paint chips are known to have a sweet taste when ingested, making them a dangerous attraction to small children who are prone to put things in their mouths.

Chemical paint strippers can be used with excellent results, but should be applied with care because many contain toxic chemicals such as methylene chloride. Paint strippers that work quickly and efficiently are usually expensive. Working with inexpensive products can yield poor results and make the process more labor intensive than it needs to be. When stripping vertical surfaces, it is advisable to select a stripper with a thick consistency that will not quickly run off. Keep in mind that chemical strippers work faster in warm weather and the faster that a chemical stripper can dissolve the paint, the less damage will be caused to the wood. It is generally advisable to wait for temperatures above 65 degrees, because if a chemical stripper has to remain on the wood for long periods of time, it can often severely raise the grain of the wood. "Raised grain" is a braille-like effect of the wood grain that may occur during any stripping process because the wood surface slightly expands as it absorbs water and other chemicals. Before repainting, some hand sanding may be necessary to level the surface of newly stripped wood.

Architectural trim that can be removed such as shutters, brackets, balusters, and small, solid, wood columns can be sent to a commercial wood stripper. Some firms dip the wood in a vat of chemical solution that eats the paint away, while others use a hand stripping process. The dip-strip method has been known to deteriorate wood glue, which can cause ornamental features made up of small pieces of wood glued together, such as cornice brackets, to come apart.

Some accelerated methods of removing paint from wood such as high pressure power washing and sand blasting are not recommended. High pressure power washing, also called water blasting, removes paint by bombarding it with a pressurized water jet that exerts a force of several hundred pounds per square inch. In some cases the water can actually penetrate the exterior sheathing of a building and damage interior finishes. While this method does remove some paint, it also tends to force water deep into bare trim and siding. Because the wood is usually painted before most of the moisture can escape from the wood, the new paint often peels prematurely as the wood dries.

Some practitioners of power washing mix a fine grit sand with the water to act as an abrasive that speeds the paint removal process. This method is more harmful than water blasting alone because the cutting action of the sand scars and pits wood detail and raises the grain of wood siding.

Sandblasting, which utilizes a stream of fine, dry grit sand propelled by compressed air, is completely inappropriate for the removal of paint from exterior wood surfaces. Wood detail can be scarred beyond recognition by sandblasting; flat areas of wood such as siding and trim are often left with pronounced, unnatural looking raised grain that is objectionable for historic buildings and produces a poor surface for paint adhesion. Beware of any contractor who claims that sandblasting can be controlled so that the paint is removed without damage to the historic woodwork since the quality of a sandblasting job is determined entirely by the skill and sensitivity of the operator and there is a lot of margin for human error. Sandblasting also poses the danger of lead contamination, since old paint, which usually contains lead, is pulverized by sandblasting into a wind-borne dust which can contaminate nearby soil as well as the residual blasting sand. In some cases, people have gathered the spent blasting sand for use in children's sandboxes, unaware of its potential lead contamination. Lead, if ingested or inhaled even in small amounts, is toxic to small children.

PAINTING

Choosing the proper paint scheme for your house is crucial to the success of any exterior renovation. Homeowners are rediscovering the value of a tastefully-designed multi-color paint scheme that can subtly call attention to wooden siding, trim, and architectural detail. The use of multi-color paint schemes in house painting was very common until the 1920s, but declined rapidly after that. Designing a historic, multi-color paint scheme, either by conjecture or scientific analysis, takes time and patience even for professionals. If the original paint colors on a house are uncovered, they might not suit the tastes of today's owners who may choose instead to create a new color design based on historic paint schemes.

Although today many modern paint manufacturers offer a wide range of paints and color charts tailored specifically for painting older houses, into the 1930s, many painters mixed their own paint colors starting with a base of white lead ground in oil to which small amounts of color, drier and turpentine were added. Needless to say, some painters were more skilled than others in producing pleasing, consistent hues of color. Ready-mixed paints like those used today were commonly available at least by the early 1880s. In 1867, the Averill Chemical Paint Co. patented the first ready-mixed paint, but it was relatively unpopular because painters could still mix a better quality product. Henry A. Sherwin's 1876 invention of a new paint grinding mill paved the way for the high-quality ready-mixed paint in use today.

Lead-based paints, which are no longer available, are generally thought to have been more durable than today's lead-free paints, and to some extent this is probably true. Paints sold today are made either with an oil base, which requires mineral spirits for clean-up, or latex base, which requires water for clean-up. Both types of paints have their merits, and deciding which is best for your house is usually a matter of personal preference and experience. Many painters still prefer oil base paint for exterior work because of its superior workability and a perception that it is more durable. Older paints also often contained a small amount of mercury which curtailed the formation of mildew. Mercury, too, has been removed from paints in recent years and replaced with modern fungicide additives that many painters do not feel are as effective.

An illustration from a 1917 paint catalog.

If wood is new or has been completely stripped, some restorers are choosing to finish it with a so-called solid color or opaque stain which is available in a wide variety of custom colors and produces a flat (meaning no gloss) finish like paint, but is much thinner in consistency. The advantage of solid color stain, according to proponents, is a reduction in peeling over the years. Using solid color stains over new or stripped wood does seem to cut down on preparation work when painting time comes around again, but recoating may have to be done more frequently. Opaque stains are made in both latex and oil base, although many painters seem to prefer the oil base variety.

To summarize, here are a few basic tips on painting an older house:

* Scrape all loose paint thoroughly and sand the edges to avoid an "alligatored" look.

* Use a dropcloth around the foundation to catch paint chips which are almost certain to contain lead and could contaminate the soil next to the house if they are not cleaned up.

* Treat any bare wood with a paintable wood preservative, let it dry, and then prime the spots before applying a finish coat of paint. Using a wood preservative can lengthen the service life of the paint.

* Avoid painting in direct sunlight or on very hot days.

* Oil base paint may be applied when the temperature does not fall below 40°F., but a minimum temperature of 50°F. is usually required for latex based paints to dry properly.

* Heavy dew can streak latex and oil base paints that have not dried, so it is advisable to avoid painting near sunset.

* When using solid color stain products over bare wood, a primer is not required, but two finish coats are generally recommended to produce a better-looking, more even, longer-lasting finish.

* Do not use semi-transparent wood stains on old buildings.

PAINT COLORS

A house built between the late 1870s and about 1895 was typically painted with up to five different colors, usually chosen from a palette of deep, rich hues of red, brown, green, gray, olive, and yellow. Before 1900, moveable window sash were typically "picked out" in a color that was darker than the trim and body of the house, usually black, dark green or reddish brown. Visually, this technique creates the impression that the windows recede into the facade rather than project, as painting them a light color does. Major trim pieces such as the water table (located between the bottom course of siding and the foundation), the corner boards, and cornice moldings (located at the tops of windows and along the eaves and gables) were typically painted with a trim color that "outlined" the house. The major vertical and horizontal elements of the porch were outlined in a similar fashion. Some painters, architects and homeowners preferred dark colors for the body of the house and lighter colors for the trim, but the reverse is also appropriate. When recreating a Victorian paint scheme, beware of excessive detailing, such as picking out small or minor trim members with accent colors. If authenticity is your goal, you should also resist the temptation to imitate the "painted lady" pastel color schemes which were first popularized in San Francisco about 20 years ago. Although they are attractive and eye-catching, these color schemes are not actually historic, even for San Francisco, and both the colors and placement of the paint generally do not follow the intention of nineteenth century designers.

Around 1895, architectural tastes began to favor lighter, pastel colors for the body, although window sash and some other architectural trim elements were still often picked out in darker, contrasting colors. Partly in reaction to the somber, fussy, multi-hued paint schemes of the late nineteenth century, many Victorian-era houses were repainted stark white or in light pastel colors in the early 1900s and have remained that way down to the present.

House painting from the early 1900s through the 1930s was typically simple, incorporating as few as two, but more typically three colors. Wood clapboard siding was usually a light color; trim, an intermediate color; and window sash and wood shingling a relatively dark, contrasting color. If the house had different cladding materials on the first and second floors, generally the first story would be light and the second story darker.

There are now a number of books available on the correct colors to paint older houses. Looking at these would be an excellent way to familiarize yourself with historic paint schemes. If you are seeking to determine the true original colors of your older house, however, you may wish to have paint on protected areas of the house analyzed by a professional color consultant. Currently the methods of historic paint color analysis are either microscopic examination of a paint chip or the "cratering" or "discing" technique. Microscopic analysis is considered the most accurate when done by a professional, but it is more time consuming and consequently more expensive. Cratering/discing means using fine sandpaper to make a small circular depression completely through a painted surface in order to reveal concentric layers of paint that can then be examined with a magnifying glass.

With either method, an historic color is determined by using optical magnification to match the oldest paint stratum to modern color cards or paint samples. The accuracy of paint analysis ultimately depends upon the skill and expertise of the technician. In order to do a proper paint analysis, many paint samples have to be taken from various places on the exterior of a painted building. Cratering is usually done at the job site, while microscopic analysis is typically done with small samples that are taken to a laboratory. Microscopic paint analysis can also be helpful in determining the approximate age of an addition or alteration.

Often a multi-layered paint chip will peel off cleanly to bare wood with a visible color on the back side, but that is typically the color of the priming coat used by painters years ago rather than the color of the original finish coat. If you uncover a layer of paint that you wish to have duplicated, you may take the chip to one of the many local paint dealers that have a computer color analysis and mixing system and have them determine a formula and mix a matching paint. Once you have determined a possible paint scheme, it is advisable to purchase the smallest quantities of the paint available (usually quart sizes) and apply them to a test patch area. Carefully study the colors at different times of the day before making a final decision. ∎

FOOTNOTES

[1] **The Painter, Gilder and Varnisher's Companion,** Philadelphia: Henry Carey Baird, 1860, pp. 177-178.

[2] Dalton B. Faloon, **Zinc Oxide.** New York: O. Van Nostrand Co., 1925, p. 6.

[3] **Glass, Paints, Varnishes and Brushes.** Pittsburgh: Pittsburgh Plate Glass Co., 1923, p. 10, paint section.

BRICK, MORTAR,
STONE AND STUCCO

**BRICK, MORTAR,
STONE AND STUCCO**

BRICK, MORTAR,
STONE AND STUCCO

BRICK, MORTAR,
STONE AND STUCCO

BRICK, MORTAR,
STONE AND STUCCO

When Milwaukee's first permanent settlers arrived in the 1830s, they had no idea that the brownish clay under their feet would produce the golden-cream colored bricks that would earn the community its "Cream City" nickname. An abundant supply of local limestone complemented the city's unique brick as a building material. Limestone was widely used for building masonry foundations, but it was also pulverized and burned in a kiln to produce lime that was then mixed with sand and water to make mortar. Limestone and cream brick were the principal masonry materials used in construction in Milwaukee until about 1900 when red brick began to be imported in quantity and stucco came into use. Practically all of the houses built in the city prior to 1900 had cream brick or limestone basement walls and chimneys. Repairing deteriorated mortar joints and cleaning years of grime and paint from Milwaukee's celebrated cream brick, if done properly, can restore the warm glow of the city's native building material.

As the manufacture of cream brick in Milwaukee declined during the first decade of the twentieth century, Milwaukee builders imported brick from other parts of the country. The new bricks were usually harder than Milwaukee's local brick, came in many different colors and surface textures, and were laid in hard mortar made with Portland cement rather than the soft lime and sand mortar that had previously been used. During the 'teens and 'twenties, locally-made concrete blocks began to replace brick and limestone as the preferred material for basement walls. Stucco also became a popular exterior cladding material during the early twentieth century.

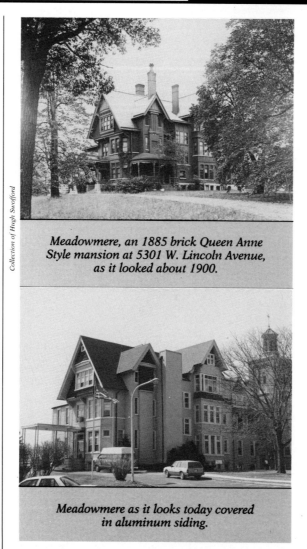

Collection of Hugh Swofford

Meadowmere, an 1885 brick Queen Anne Style mansion at 5301 W. Lincoln Avenue, as it looked about 1900.

Meadowmere as it looks today covered in aluminum siding.

Masonry products traditionally rank among the most enduring of building materials, but their restoration should be thoughtfully undertaken because mistakes are often as permanent as the material itself. Historic brick buildings should never be covered with vinyl or aluminum siding. Proponents of putting siding over brick claim that it can be cheaper to install siding than to restore the brick. To the contrary, a good masonry restoration job will far outlast any synthetic siding product, making the cost of masonry restoration, when calculated over the life of the building, much less expensive. Furthermore, if the brick and mortar have deteriorated to the point where they are beyond feasible restoration, which is seldom the case, they would make a poor and potentially unstable base to which to attach aluminum or vinyl siding. Siding would hide the problems that caused the brick to fail without solving them, and the building could continue to deteriorate behind the siding to the point where it could become unsafe. Furthermore, siding over brick destroys the original character of a building and, in the long run, decreases its resale value because a brick structure typically commands a higher price than a sided house.

BRICKMAKING IN MILWAUKEE

Milwaukee is famous for its locally made cream-colored brick. Before working with cream brick, it might be helpful to know something about its history. The earliest brickmaking in Milwaukee began in 1835 or 1836, according to differing historical accounts. The manufacturing process was crude and required considerable hand work. Horses turned a large wheel in a circular pit to mix and temper a combination of clay and sand. Then the pliable clay mixture was formed into brick shapes by packing it into wooden molds. The bricks were then briefly air-dried before being fired in kilns for a period of a week or more.

Previous Page: Victorian ornamental brickwork.

This 1870s engraving of the brick-making process shows clay being excavated from a hillside and loaded into a horse-drawn wagon. Clay, water and some other minor ingredients were then shoveled into the brick making machine which mixed and formed the clay into brick shapes. Before being fired in a brick kiln, the so-called "green" brick were allowed to air dry in the sun in long rows. Workers are shown building a kiln to fire the air-dried brick.

The first brickmakers in Milwaukee expected red brick to result from firing the red-brown Milwaukee clay, but an unusually high content of calcium and magnesium in the clay gave the brick a unique, soft, golden-yellow color instead. Cream brick, as it was soon known, grew in popularity in Milwaukee and in other cities. Milwaukee's brickmakers were justly proud of their unique product. In May of 1859, the schooner M. S. Scott sailed from Milwaukee to Hamburg, Germany carry-

ing, among other things, samples of Milwaukee's cream brick to the mayor of Hamburg. The Germans were impressed with the Milwaukee brick and imported a quantity of it for use in ornamenting new buildings. It is not known if there are any buildings surviving in Germany today that feature Milwaukee cream brick. The popularity of Milwaukee cream brick was reflected by the fact that as late as the 1920s a large paint manufacturer headquartered in the eastern U.S. sold a ready-mixed house paint in a cream color called "Milwaukee brick."[1]

Much of Milwaukee's cream brick was made at the Burnham brothers' brickyard, which was located on the south bank of the Menomonee River Valley between South 13th and South 21st Streets. The Burnham brothers, George and Jonathan, together with an employee, Stoddard Martin, revolutionized the brickmaking process by inventing one of the first practical brickmaking machines in the United States. The machine, which was patented, allowed the Burnhams to make their product faster and cheaper than their competitors and enabled a greater number of people to purchase a product that previously had been affordable only by the affluent.

Milwaukee's cream brick was made in two types — common and pressed. The pressed brick were the most expensive, selling for about twelve dollars per thousand in 1853 from the Burnham yards, while the common brick sold for half that amount. The pressed brick were molded under pressure, and, after firing, they were uniform in size and color and had very smooth faces and sharp, square corners. Today, pressed cream brick is rela-

tively rare, and finding salvaged brick to match original pressed brick can be difficult.

Common bricks, on the other hand, were not subject to great pressure when packed into the molds before firing, and they were very porous, had blunt corners, and their sizes and colors tended to vary. The finished size of the common bricks made in the same batch could vary significantly, with the result that one can expect to find size differences in the brick used in the same wall. Cream brick sizes also tended to vary from manufacturer to manufacturer in the years before the establishment of uniform sizes. For example, the oldest known cream brick house still standing in Milwaukee was built by Alanson Sweet in 1845 at 1216 South First Street of odd sized, long, thin brick that are believed to have been handmade in a small, nearby brickyard that was located at the corner of South First and West Washington Streets. Pressed brick was used where appearance was vitally important, such as on the front of a building, but it was generally too expensive for utilitarian purposes such as constructing the side and rear walls of commercial buildings and basements, which were built with the less expensive common cream brick. Most of the cream brick buildings still standing in the city today are faced with the better grades of common brick. Cream bricks have a distinct top and bottom side. In most older brick, the top can be distinguished from the bottom because it is much rougher. The top is also slightly wider than the bottom, which means the brick is actually slightly wedge-shaped. Modern brick does not have this distinction. Cream brick was generally laid with the so-called top side facing up. Bricklayers could quickly distin-

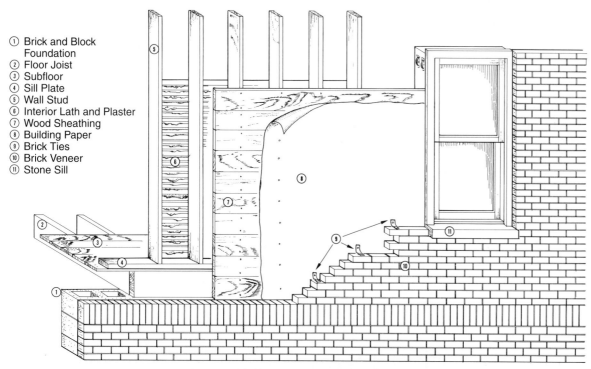

① Brick and Block
   Foundation
② Floor Joist
③ Subfloor
④ Sill Plate
⑤ Wall Stud
⑥ Interior Lath and Plaster
⑦ Wood Sheathing
⑧ Building Paper
⑨ Brick Ties
⑩ Brick Veneer
⑪ Stone Sill

TYPICAL BRICK VENEER CONSTRUCTION.

A single wythe of brick covers the wood framing of the house. Brick ties, nailed to the wooden sheathing and embedded into the mortar joints, hold the brick in place.

guish the top from the bottom by the feel of the brick as they took it from the pile.

The majority of brick houses in Milwaukee are brick-veneered, which means that the brick is an outside facing used to cover a wall built of wood frame construction. Most brick-veneered houses are built basically the same as wood frame houses except that a skin of brick is substituted for the outer layer of wood siding. Some houses, primarily those built between 1910 and 1930, are built with con-crete block or clay tile walls which are faced with brick veneer.

Houses built with solid load-bearing brick walls are now very rare in Milwaukee because this was an old method of construction used for houses only during the early years of set-tlement. Most of these houses were located in the center of the city and have mostly been demolished. The thickness of a brick wall is described as "single wythe" for a one-unit-thick brick wall, "double wythe" or "two wythes" for a two-unit-thick wall, and so forth. Most of the solid brick houses in Milwaukee have walls of three or more wythes in thickness.

Milwaukee cream brick has not been manu-factured since the 1920s. Salvaged antique cream brick is a popular building material for restoration projects and new construction in the Milwaukee area as well as in many other areas of the country where the brick is still valued for its unique qualities.

HISTORIC BRICK CONSTRUCTION METHODS AND PROBLEMS

Here are a few key terms commonly used in discussions about the repair of historic brick and masonry.

Repointing (tuckpointing): The process of replacing deteriorated mortar in brick or stone masonry. Usually this involves removing deteriorated layers of mortar to a depth of about 3/4 of an inch and then repacking the joints with matching fresh mortar.

Spalling: Splitting or chipping of the brick surface. Usually caused by water trapped within the brick that expands when it freezes, shearing off thin shards from the face of the brick.

Efflorescence: A white powder or stain on the surface of brick or mortar caused by nat-ural salts in the mortar or brick that are dis-solved by moisture passing through the brick that then crystallize on the surface of the

Applying the mortar and spreading it evenly over the brick with the edge of a trowel.

Laying the brick.

Leveling the brick with a string line.

BASIC BRICKLAYING

Cutting off excess mortar from the brick.

Tooling horizontal joints with a sled runner jointing tool.

Tooling vertical joints with a smaller jointer.

masonry as the water is drawn to the surface and evaporated by the sun.

Repointing or tuckpointing an old brick wall is a very common remedy for sealing small cracks and replacing modest amounts of eroded mortar. However, in some cases, it may be necessary to actually rebuild a portion of a brick wall in order to restore its structural integrity. No amount of tuckpointing, for example, would restore a bulging or bowed brick wall that is delaminating from a building. Loose brick, too, usually must be removed from a building, cleaned off, and then reset in fresh mortar. Noticeable movement of a brick wall along large, step-like cracks may also call for relaying some brick rather than simply tuckpointing to seal the gaps.

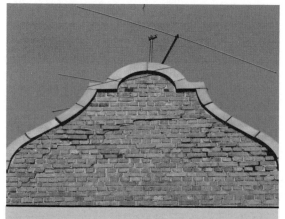

Large, step-like cracks and loose bricks often connot be repaired by tuckpointing, and, instead, a portion of the wall may have to be completely taken down and rebuilt using the old brick and new mortar.

Correctly diagnosing the problems of an old brick wall requires skill and experience that many homeowners may not have. You should consult a qualified masonry contractor or construction professional who is experienced with the restoration of old masonry. Remember that some contractors may be unnecessarily discouraging about the feasibility of restoring an old brick wall if they are not familiar with historic buildings.

The deterioration of historic masonry can usually be attributed to the effects of time and weather, although some problems with old masonry work may be the result of defects in the original materials or workmanship. Understanding some of the problems builders faced a century ago can help with the planning of a restoration project and lead to an understanding of why some old masonry walls are more durable than others.

Quality control in the manufacture of handmade and early machine-made brick was difficult, and in almost every brickmaker's kiln there were some underburned, second quality brick which the brickmaker sold as such at a discount. In general, brick that are hardburned have good weatherability and were ordinarily put on the exterior of a wall, while the softer or underburned brick were used for courses called "backing up" which were not directly exposed to the weather. It is important to realize that when salvaging brick from walls that are two or more wythes in thickness that the interior brick might not be well-suited for direct exposure to the weather. Underfired brick also have reduced load-bearing capacity. Even if attempts were made to originally use better or first quality common brick on the exterior of a building, some underfired brick might have been mistakenly mixed in, and this might partially account for an isolated spalled brick in a wall. Milwaukee builders and architects, however, were generally very conscious of brick quality. A standard part of the architectural specifications for residences designed by Milwaukee architects Rau and Kirsch during the 1890s, like those of many other architects, required that "all brick used in the walls to be good, hard, and well-burned."

Brick quality is generally not a major factor in deterioration problems with old brick. A brick wall that has stood for 50 or 100 years undoubtedly is made with quality products. However, understanding how brick were made and their differing grades may help to explain, for example, why an occasional isolated brick in a wall has spalled when other factors such as excessive water penetration have been ruled out. Too often contractors have pointed out a few isolated spalled brick as justification for coating an entire wall with a masonry sealer to prevent additional spalling that probably would never have actually occurred.

BRICK CLEANING

Milwaukee's masonry buildings have been subject to years of pollution from the bustling urban environment surrounding them. The surface of porous cream brick acts like a magnet for soot, smoke and other airborne dirt and over the years much of the original golden luster has been hidden under a layer of black grime. Milwaukee pressed brick, smoother and less porous than the common brick variety, is less likely to hold dirt and is easier to clean. To cover the stains of pollution and age, cream brick and other brick masonry were often later painted. Today, most homeowners seek to remove the layers of paint and dirt from cream brick to recapture part of the original architectural elegance of the "Cream City." Don't overlook the fact that much of the city's remaining cream brick is in the foundation walls of thousands of wood-frame houses. Cleaning the visible courses of a brick basement, particularly a tall, raised brick basement, could have a substantial impact on the appearance of the building.

Most masonry buildings are cleaned for cosmetic purposes rather than to preserve a structure. Dirt and soot on Milwaukee cream brick, for example, rarely endanger a building, and the dirt may, in fact, even act as a protective skin that provides continuing protection from airborne pollutants. Some restorers prefer to repair defective mortar joints and leave the "patina" of age on their buildings instead of cleaning the brick, although this approach is more typical of buildings like churches than houses.

The techniques for safely removing paint and dirt from any type of brick masonry are basically the same. It is always preferable to use the gentlest means possible to clean brick. In rural environments, where airborne dirt and soot have been minimal over the years, old masonry can sometimes be cleaned by a low-pressure wash with clear water and some hand scrubbing. This is seldom the case, however, for masonry buildings in urban environments, which will almost invariably require a more aggressive cleaning method. The most frequently used method today to safely clean historic masonry is a combination of chemical cleaners, strippers, and a gentle, non-abrasive power wash used with clear water.

It is important to understand that cleaning brick is a somewhat risky venture because the aesthetic results cannot be guaranteed, and even the gentlest cleaning methods can sometimes cause damage to the masonry. Cleaning, for example, might loosen or erode mortar, which means that additional money would have to be spent on repointing. Cleaning brick may not return the building to the like-new condition hoped for by many restorers, particularly if extensive weathering or other discoloration of the brick appears as unsightly blotches even after a thorough cleaning. This is more likely to occur on a commercial building or a factory than a house, however. Stripping the paint from a masonry wall might also reveal the scars of imperfect alterations or bad repairs made in the past. Brick buildings were often painted to hide flawed brick surfaces or to unify walls patched or altered with brick that did not match the original brick.

Badly sandblasted brick.

Before beginning any masonry cleaning project, examine the type of paint and/or dirt covering the surface. Often there is a layer of dirt, modern paint, historic paint and coal soot on the masonry, not all of which can be removed with the same cleaner. If this is the case, both the cost of the job and the time to do it will increase.

Cleaning brick is a fairly complicated procedure requiring a combination of the correct chemicals, patience, and know-how. Unfortunately, some well-intentioned restorers mistakenly resort to abrasive blasting methods to clean masonry because the results are dramatic and quick. One of the principal villains in the effort to preserve historic masonry is sandblasting and other abrasive cleaning techniques. A building that has been sandblasted is not eligible for listing in the National Register of Historic Places because the structure is considered by the Federal government to have been irreparably damaged. Developed during the nineteenth century to clean rusted iron and steel, sandblasting is simply the process of bombarding the brick with a fine, abrasive sand propelled at high velocity by compressed air. It is not actually a method of cleaning the surface of masonry, but rather it removes the outer surface containing the dirt and stains to expose clean inside layers of the stone or brick.

When used on brick, sandblasting has a particularly disastrous effect because the thin, hard-fired, outer weathering surface of the brick is often completely destroyed, exposing the soft, inner, baked clay layer of the brick, which is highly vulnerable to rapid deterioration from wind and water. Sandblasted brick has a cratered, unnatural appearance, and the eroded surface will actually stain and attract dirt more rapidly than before the so-called cleaning. Unlike a chemically-cleaned building, once a building has been sandblasted it will have to be sandblasted again and again with increasing frequency to retain its clean appearance.

The use of sandblasting to remove the weathered surface from stone buildings began about the turn of the century, in some areas of the country, although it does not seem to have been commonly used on brick structures until after World War II. When used on stone, sandblasting will dull the detail of carved work, and flat, hand-dressed building stone will lose forever some of the subtle, light-reflective surface qualities left by the chisel marks of skilled stonecutters from a bygone era.

Beware of sandblast practitioners who claim their method is safe for masonry when done by a skilled operator. Sandblasting invariably destroys a layer of masonry and creates conditions that can lead to accelerated deterioration in the future. Despite years of educating the public about the dangers of sandblasting masonry, it is still widely practiced. A newer, but equally unacceptable, variation on sandblasting that appears to be gaining in popularity is the water-sand blast, which, instead of compressed air, typically uses a high pressure water jet mixed with fine abrasive sand. Practitioners of the water-sand blast method claim that the water reduces the abrasive action of the sand to a gentle cleaning, but in reality the surface of the masonry is still eroded, though perhaps not as dramatically. Air-blasting masonry with glass beads, walnut shells or other abrasives should be avoided for the same reasons as sandblasting and water-sandblasting.

Pressurized water blasting, also called power washing, is acceptable for cleaning masonry when used without any added abrasive agent and provided that the water pressure does not exceed 500 pounds per square inch (p.s.i.). Water blasting at higher than 500 p.s.i. can damage masonry, force water deep into the interior of the building and pit the surface of the brick as well. The success of any pressurized water blasting project depends on the type of nozzle being used, along with the skill of the operator. It is possible, even with low-pressure water, to blast snake-like patterns in brick if a narrow-dispersion nozzle is used and the water wand is held too close to the building. Lower pressure power washing today is typically used in combination with chemical cleaners that are brushed or sprayed on the building to loosen dirt, grime, and paint and then subsequently washed off. Be sure that any water blasting work is carried out before Fall, or at least in time for any water that is pushed into the brickwork to evaporate before the weather dips below freezing.

There are many chemical brick cleaners on the market today. Most of those that are effective on porous, historic brick, such as Milwaukee cream brick, contain hydrofluoric acid. Do not confuse this with the hydrochloric' (muriatic) acid commonly used for cleaning mortar stains from brick. Muriatic acid will dissolve mortar, but it won't clean brick.

As well as other firms, there are two Milwaukee-area companies, American Building Restoration and Diedrich's Chemicals that make chemical brick cleaners that have proven effective in cleaning Milwaukee cream brick as well as other types of historic brick

masonry. Brick cleaning chemicals are potentially dangerous, and the large-scale use of chemical cleaners is a job for professional contractors who are familiar with the chemicals and the type of brick being cleaned. When both paint and dirt have to be removed from brick, at least two types of cleaners have to be used. Also, when lead-based paint is removed from brick, it must be carefully collected because lead is a health hazard and can contaminate the soil around the building. When stripping paint from brick, one chemical manufacturer recommends laying plastic sheeting around the building over a bed of hay. To contain water runoff during rinsing operations, a plastic gutter should be placed against the side of the building. The lead-based paint residue collected in the gutter must be disposed of in an approved manner.

Before cleaning any large area of brick, small test cleaning patches should be made to determine both the effectiveness of the cleaner and whether the chemicals will harm the bricks or mortar. If the chemical seems too harsh on the test patch, it should be diluted and retested.

Because historic bricks and mortar vary widely in chemical composition, it is impossible to determine beforehand whether a proposed chemical will cause any particular brickwork to dissolve or deteriorate. The cleaner should not roughen the surface of the brick or create small holes by dissolving impurities on the brick surface left over from the manufacturing process. Compare the hardness of the mortar in a test area with a nearby uncleaned section by scraping with a knife. Chemicals that are too aggressive can cause deterioration of the mortar and thus lead to expensive repointing work. If you are contracting for masonry cleaning, you should specify in a written contract that the contractor must apply chemicals to a test patch which will be evaluated and approved before full-scale cleaning can begin. Because chemicals react differently during colder temperatures, you should make sure that the test panel and the full cleaning project are done in similar weather.

Cleaners that contain hydrofluoric acid may be harmful to certain types of stone, particularly marble and granite, so precautions might have to be taken to protect these materials. Brick cleaning chemicals can also etch the surface of window glass. There are products available that can be brushed on like paint over a window to protect it during the cleaning process and then peeled off later like a plastic sheet. Check with the chemical manufacturer to determine any potential side effects chemical cleaners may have on other building materials. After cleaning a building, it is common for efflorescence to appear on the brick. Consider using one of the commercially-prepared efflorescence removers if the problem is extensive.

SEALERS

The two general types of masonry sealers, water-repellant and waterproof, are generally not recommended for use on historic buildings except for masonry that is permanently buried or backfilled with earth. Masonry sealers are nothing new and various formulations have been in use for at least 120 years. An 1877 recipe for a waterproof coating consisted of preparing a two-part solution as follows: "Dissolve Castile soap in water, three-fourths of a pound to the gallon. Make another solution by dissolving one-half pound of alum in four gallons of water. Both should be completely dissolved before using. First lay on the soap boiling hot, taking care not to form a froth on the brickwork. Let this remain 24 hours to become dry and hard; then apply the alum-wash which may be at a temperature of 60 or 70 degrees and allow it to remain 24 hours before repeating the soap wash. Repeat the washes until the wall is impervious to water."[2]

Although today's sealers are sophisticated blends of modern chemicals, the basic concept of blocking the flow of water through the surface of the masonry has not changed since the formulation of the primitive soap-wash technique. Waterproof coatings, in general, make a masonry surface completely impermeable to water. Water-repellent coatings, on the other hand, condition the masonry surface to resist and repel water but not to be impervious to it. The danger of waterproof coatings is that they completely block the normal flow of vapor through the masonry. In an above-ground wall, moisture trapped within masonry can freeze in a harsh northern climate and cause the surface of the brick or stone to spall or pop off. Sealers should be considered only as a last-resort to water penetration problems in above-ground masonry. The correction of defects in flashings, gutters or roof overhangs is often the proper remedy for directing water away from masonry walls. Sealers can be considered in cases where brick has been damaged by sandblasting or severe spalling and no other means can prevent the brick from absorbing damaging amounts of excess moisture.

Contractors often recommend the application of water-repellent masonry sealers after brick has been cleaned to maintain a clean appearance, but water-repellent sealers last only a few years before recoating is necessary and do not seem to be cost effective. Keep in mind that the pollutants that originally stained the brick, such as coal dust and smoke from wood-burning stoves and furnaces, are no longer present in the air, and any cleaning job today should last for many decades before another cleaning is required, if ever. A water-repellent sealer will also slightly change the tone and color of the masonry, which in some cases is objectionable from an aesthetic point of view.

PAINTING BRICK

There are relatively few known buildings where the cream brick was painted as part of the original design of a house. More often the brick was painted years after the house was built primarily to hide accumulated soot and grime or to disguise mismatched masonry alterations. If the cream brick was painted very early in the history of the house, as was sometimes done to simulate more expensive red brick, a painted brick finish might actually be part of the historic character of the building. In this case, some thought should be given to retaining the paint.

Unlike the glossy or semi-gloss modern paints typically used on brick today, the paint historically used on brick was flat, meaning it had no gloss or sheen. Red was perhaps the most common color for painted brick, and the mortar joints were sometimes picked out separately in black or white. Years ago, three to four coats of paint were recommended to make a good painted brick finish. One painting authority in 1907 wrote that the first coat should be made up of pure white lead and dark Venetian red in oil, a small quantity of brown japan, and a little turpentine. After the first coat dried thoroughly, a second coat of the same material was applied but thinned down a little more with two parts of raw linseed oil, one part turpentine, and some paint drier. Next, all minor imperfections in the brick were filled with putty made of whiting (which is calcium carbonate or chalk) and linseed oil stained with Venetian red to match the color of the second coat. The third coat was made up of dark Venetian red and yellow ocher in oil, thinned with equal parts of boiled linseed oil and turpentine, and a small amount of paint drier. The finish coat, which had to be perfectly "flat" showing no gloss or reflection in imitation of natural brick, was made in the following proportions to make one gallon: five pounds of French yellow ocher ground in japan, four pounds of Venetian red (also ground in japan), three pounds of the finest Cliffstone whiting, and 1/2 pint of boiled linseed oil. This mixture was then thinned with 1/2 gallon of pure turpentine and then, finally, strained in a fine paint sieve or cheese cloth to make it ready for use. Because the oil in the paint could produce a slight sheen, some painters preferred an alternative finish coat of brick dust, Venetian red, yellow ochre, varnish, and turpentine. This mixture, which used no oil, reportedly produced a finish on the brick with no perceptible sheen or gloss. Only one finish coat was applied. After it was dry, the mortar joints were painted white with a mixture of pure white lead in oil, thinned with turpentine and a little paint drier. Paint for black mortar joints, which were popular in the nineteenth

century, was a mixture of lampblack ground in japan, a small amount of boiled linseed oil, and turpentine. The mortar joints were painted with the aid of a straightedge that was used to guide the painter's hand rather than the tip of the brush. The horizontal joints were usually painted first and then the vertical joints were filled in. It was considered a good

The "red" brick in this ca. 1900 photo of 1843 N. Palmer Street is actually Milwaukee cream brick that is believed to have been painted red as part of the architect's original design for this 1881 house.

practice for the paint to be drawn in a smooth, even line that extended just beneath the joint and onto the brick to give a straighter, more uniform appearance. Merely painting the actual mortar joints alone sometimes produced a ragged-looking joint that many painters of the era found objectionable.

The painting method and materials described above undoubtedly produced a paint finish that was markedly different from today's paints. Of course, when brick is painted today, the mortar joints are never painted separately in a different color. The complexity of a multi-layered early paint job on brick might explain why it can be very difficult today to remove all of the historic paint from a brick wall that was painted in the nineteenth or early twentieth centuries.

Before repainting, the brick surface must be scraped to remove any loose or peeling paint, and any defective mortar joints should be repointed. The old formulas for brick paint contain lead-based materials that are no longer available today. If you choose to repaint a historic brick wall, select a modern paint that produces a "flat" finish and is recommended for exterior use on masonry surfaces. Latex-based paints are recommended. Test the color on a small patch on the building and study the color during different times of the day before making any final decisions. If you choose to paint-in the mortar joints in a different color, as was sometimes historically done, make test patches to develop a technique that will produce professional-looking results.

MORTAR

Mortar quality has always been a major concern of builders and architects. Mortar holds brick, stone and concrete block together and also serves as the filler that compensates for small differences in the size of the masonry units to create an even, uniform wall. The quality and type of mortar used affects both the finished appearance and the strength of any masonry wall. Mortar joints comprise as much as one-quarter of the surface area of a typical brick wall. Before restoring or rebuilding any historic masonry wall, it is important to recognize and understand the differences between modern mortars made with large amounts of Portland cement, and historic lime mortars that contain little or no cement. The correct blend of lime mortar is vital to the success of rebuilding or repointing a wall made of historic brick.

Lime mortar, a traditional material used for centuries, is simply a mix of lime paste and sand. There was little or no Portland cement in most of the mortar used during the nineteenth century for residential buildings. Lime is an ancient building material, and the process for making it is quite simple. Common limestone rock, which is made up mostly of calcium carbonate, is quarried and then crushed, screened, selected, washed, and graded. The selected stone is then placed in kilns where it is heated up to 2500 degrees Fahrenheit. This process evaporates the moisture from the rock and also removes certain gases such as carbon dioxide. The product that results from heating the limestone is called quicklime, and it is a very caustic material. When it comes in contact with water, a violent reaction occurs that is hot enough to

Drawing of a lime mill in 1885. On the third floor crushed limestone was loaded into the top of the oil-fired kiln and then "burned" at an extremely high temperature to convert it to a powdery substance called quicklime used for making mortar. The quicklime was removed at the bottom level and then packed into barrels or loaded in bulk into railroad cars. The water tank provided a supply of water to cool the exterior of the hot kiln.

cause the water to boil. In years past, masons would purchase dry quicklime and then add water to it, a process called hydrating or "slaking" the lime. However, before the lime could be mixed with sand to make mortar, it had to soak for a week or more before it was ready for use. Masons then mixed the lime paste with sand to make a mortar. Lime and sand mortar hardens very slowly and becomes stronger with age. Decades after a wall is built, some lime mortar in it might still be uncured.

The care and handling of lime was also important to early builders. According to one late 1890s writer, "Lime should never be stored in a cellar, or in any place where it is damp, as it will lose half its virtue in a very short time in such a place, and the mortar made with it will never give satisfaction. To ensure good and lasting work, the mortar should not be used until it has been made at least ten days. It will be better to stand fourteen days if conditions will permit."[3]

Lime as it is used today is purchased in a dry, factory-hydrated form which eliminates both the need for soaking it prior to use and the danger of the chemical reaction of quicklime and water. To test old mortar for a high lime content, remove some from deep within the joint and mix it with vinegar. If the mortar has a high lime content, it will react with the acidic vinegar and form bubbles.

Lime mortar is relatively soft and slightly water soluble, and, therefore, an excellent companion for use with the relatively soft, hand-made or early machine-made, cream brick of the late nineteenth and early twentieth centuries. One of the significant attributes of lime-rich mortar is that small cracks in it are self-healing. As water and air flow into a crack in lime mortar, a reaction occurs with the uncured lime which then slowly dissolves to fill in the void and restore the integrity of the joint. The common proportions of lime to sand were about three to five measures of sand to one measure of lime. Three parts of sand to one part of lime formed a good mortar that was perhaps the most popular mix used by builders during the late nineteenth century. Too much lime in the mix caused the mortar to shrink and crack as it set, while too little lime made a weak mortar. It was reportedly common for architects of years ago to visit the job site to inspect a small batch of mortar mixed in the proportion of about one part lime to two parts sand to serve as a standard. By making himself familiar with the appearance of this standard mortar, the architect was then able to determine the quality of the mortar being used on a job at a glance.

Lime mortar can lose its binding properties when exposed to the continuous dampness that a foundation wall or basement might be subjected to. Many early masonry basements in the city were built with pure lime mortar, the strongest of lime mortars, to compensate. Recognizing the inherent weakness of lime mortar in damp locations, builders in the 1890s began using a harder, less porous mortar made with Portland cement, lime, and sand much like the mortar in use today. Portland cement was invented in 1824 by Joseph Aspdin, a mason in Leeds, England. He burned limestone and clay together in a kitchen stove creating a gray powder that came to be called Portland cement because of its resemblance to the stone quarried on the British Island of Portland. The use of Portland cement was slow to catch on at first, and there were numerous quality-control problems as well as a mistrust of the material because it was new. In 1890, only 335,000 barrels of Portland cement were produced in the U.S. By 1905 that figure had increased to more than 35 million barrels. These production figures indicate that before the early 1890s Portland cement mortar was probably relatively uncommon in America, although the first known American Portland cement factory was built in 1878 by David O. Saylor at Coplay, Pennsylvania.

Although Portland cement made a much stronger, harder mortar, it is important to remember that harder mortar is not necessarily better in terms of its durability. Despite the strength and hardness of the mortar itself, a slight shifting or settling of the wall can easily break the bond between the brick and mortar. Unlike the lime-rich mortars of years ago, Portland-cement-rich mortar is not self-healing, which means that cracks, unless repointed with new mortar, will continually allow moisture to penetrate the wall. Even small cracks in Portland cement mortars are a major concern because they are permanent and create an easy path for water to enter the building and cause further deterioration.

The drying process of mortar can have a significant impact on the strength of a wall. Old Milwaukee cream brick, as well as other early brick, is inherently porous. Therefore, it is important to wet the brick first before laying them in mortar in order to keep the brick from rapidly absorbing the moisture in the mortar. This is particularly important if the bricks are laid during dry, hot weather. A poor bond can result if the mortar drys too rapidly. Keep this fact in mind if you are relaying old cream brick in new mortar.

In summary, it is important to try to match the strength of the original lime mortar when repointing the joints in an old masonry wall. A historic brick wall naturally expands and contracts slightly with changes in temperature and moisture. As the bricks expand during hot or moist weather, the relatively soft, compressible, lime-rich mortar can absorb some expansion and then flex back into shape when the bricks contract during dry, cold weather. Portland cement-rich mortar, on the other hand, is rigid, non-compressible, and inflexible. Not only will cracks occur in the mortar joints that can lead to harmful moisture penetration of the wall, but damage to the brick can occur over time if Portland cement-rich mortar is used to repoint the front edge of a lime mortar joint. This happens because the soft lime mortar in the back of the joints will compress as the brick expand, but the hard, rigid, Portland cement-rich mortar at the front of the joints will not, causing the front face of the brick, which is softer than the Portland cement mortar, to crack or chip.

REPOINTING

Severely eroded mortar joints must be cleaned out and refilled with fresh, matching mortar in a process called "tuckpointing."

Because lime-rich mortar is relatively soft, it tends to wear away over time from constant exposure to wind, water, and sun. Repointing, also called tuckpointing, is the process of replacing deteriorated mortar with fresh mortar. Ideally, the best repointing jobs are those that are undetectable from the original mortar. Matching the color and blending new mortar with historic mortar takes skill, patience, and sometimes a bit of luck. The erosion of mortar joints is never uniform across the face of any brick wall, and, typically, only certain areas require work. Too often, an entire wall is repointed, resulting in needless extra expense. If you are going to clean the brick, it is advisable to wait until that work is done before beginning a repointing project.

Preparing the joints for new mortar is a relatively simple process, but it is often rushed, which can result in irreparable damage to the brick. The first step, removing deteriorated lime mortar from joints between the brick, is a straightforward job that can be best accomplished with the least danger to the brick and the worker with a special hook-like tuckpointer's rake that is pulled across the joint or lightly tapped with a hammer. A hammer and tuckpointing chisel, called a plugging chisel, are also commonly used. Unfortunately, many contractors and homeowners try to speed up the job by using an electric saw equipped with a masonry blade to cut out the old mortar, but, in the process, the saw blade often carves away part of the brick as well. When used to clean out vertical mortar joints, power saws or grinders are particularly prone to make cuts into the bricks above and below the joints. As a result, a wall repointed in this way will often have clumsy, wide mortar joints that lap over the cut edges of the brick that are completely out of character with the originally intended appearance of the brick wall. Although some operators are more skilled than others in the operation of power tools and are less likely to damage the brick, handwork methods using a rake or chisel are always preferable since there is less likelihood of damage due to human error or lack of skill than is the case with a high speed saw blade.

Removing old mortar with an electric grinder is a technique that requires great care to prevent damage to the edges of the brick. Using a hammer and chisel is usually preferable, although the removal of hard Portland cement mortar sometimes requires power tools.

By using hand tools, the worker is much more likely to remove only the loose, deteriorated mortar. The speed and fast cutting action of an electric tuckpointing saw, besides potentially damaging the brick, can result in too much mortar being removed. Probably one of the best power tools currently available for removing old mortar is an air-powered chisel often used by stone carvers. This tool is lightweight, creates less dust than a saw, and minimizes the chance of damage to historic masonry. Most homeowners are capable of removing deteriorated mortar from joints by hand-work methods, and thus might be able to assist a masonry contractor with a repointing job. A contractor might be willing to work with a homeowner by helping to decide where mortar should be removed, letting the owner rake out the defective joints, and then coming back later to actually install the new mortar.

Removing deteriorated mortar with a tuckpoint rake.

When all deteriorated mortar has been cleaned out to a depth of 3/4 to 1 inch, the joints to be filled should be washed out with clear water just prior to the application of fresh mortar. When the new mortar is applied, the joint should be damp but not dripping wet. Ideally, masonry experts recommend that a lime mortar wall should be repointed with new lime mortar mixed in the proportion of one part of lime to two parts of sand as a starting mixture. However, workability, durability, and the water resistance of the mortar can be improved if Portland cement is substituted for no more than 20 percent of the volume of lime used in the mortar. This would result in a mortar with the volumes of approximately ten parts sand, one part cement, and four parts lime.

Some restorers might choose to buy commercially prepared bags of mortar mix, which are varying blends of Portland cement and lime to which mason's sand and water must be added. The five basic mortar types available today, which vary considerably in compressive strength or hardness, are known as types M, S, N, O, and K (every other letter in the term MASON WORK). The most common and readily available mortar is type "M," which is the hardest of the commercial mortar mixes. It is often the only type of mortar mix available at most hardware stores and large homeowners' building supply stores. Because of its hardness, however, it is not recommended for tuckpointing a historic cream brick wall. Type "K" mortar has a compressive strength or hardness that most closely approximates historic lime mortar, but it is not easy to obtain. Type "O" is probably the next best acceptable substitute.

By about 1910, improvement in brickmaking technology resulted in harder bricks that were designed to be laid with hard, Portland cement mortars. Architects in some areas of the country routinely specified a mortar of one part Portland cement to two or three parts sand. In the Midwest, however, it was common during that time to use a mixture of pure cement mortar and pure lime mortar. The preferred proportions of lime, cement and sand varied among masons and architects. One relatively standard mortar was made by first mixing two parts (by volume) of sand, some water, and one part quicklime, which was allowed to "slake" or stand for a week or more. Just prior to use, one part of the lime mortar was combined with three parts of a Portland cement mortar composed of one part Portland cement and two parts of sand. Using today's factory-hydrated lime eliminates the need for a slaking process, and the mortar can be mixed in the proportion of eight parts sand, three parts Portland cement, and one part lime. Type "N" premixed mortar would probably be a good approximation of this formula.

Colored or tinted mortar was produced in two general ways: using a natural colored sand, ground granite or other stone (ground oyster shells were occasionally used), or by the use of artificial mortar colors. A sample of the old, historic mortar can be crushed and examined with a magnifying glass to determine the type, color and size of the original sand. It might be impractical, however, to obtain sand to match the original, and modern restorers often have to rely on the use of artificial mortar colors alone to produce a new batch of mortar with an acceptable hue.

Commercially prepared mortar colors made from iron oxides are recommended because they tend to resist fading and have good weatherability. Dark mortar pigments that contain "carbon black" should generally be avoided because this type of color tends to fade noticeably over time. Excessive use of pigments can substantially reduce mortar quality and, as a rule of thumb, the amount of color should not exceed ten percent of the weight of lime and Portland cement in any batch of mortar.

Matching the color of historic mortar is a trial and error process. Before actually applying new mortar, some test batches of mortar

Proper tuckpointing is not simply a matter of packing new mortar into joints as this poorly repointed wall illustrates. A good tuckpointing job should blend with the original mortar joints.

have to be made. Start by wetting some of the dry, historic mortar you want to match, and then mix a sample of new mortar. Next, add colorant until it approximates the color of the old, wetted mortar. Let the mortar sample dry and assess the result. Vary the amount of colorant in successive test batches as needed until you arrive at an acceptable color match. Apply the new mortar to a test area (preferably on a small, inconspicuous area), and allow it to dry. Then judge the results before repointing a large area.

Mortar can be applied to the joints with a grout bag (which looks like a baker's bag used

A properly tuckpointed wall.

GRAPEVINE JOINT   BEADED JOINT

THESE TWO JOINTS ARE USED MAINLY WITH STONE RATHER THAN BRICK.

V-JOINT   STRUCK JOINT

WEATHER JOINT   RAKED JOINT

CONCAVE   FLUSH JOINT
(OR HALF-ROUND) JOINT

Mortar joint styles.

for decorating cakes), or by pushing it into the joints with a knife-like tuckpointing tool, which comes in several different widths. A tool for applying mortar which looks and works much like a common caulking gun is also now available for less than $100. Regardless of the method used for applying the mortar, do it as neatly as possible, and avoid smearing mortar on the face of the brick. Apply the mortar in 1/4-inch layers, packing each layer into the corners. As soon as a layer has set up slightly, but is still damp, apply the next layer. When the final layer begins to set up slightly, it must be tooled to match the style of the historic joints. There are several different ways of finishing mortar joints. Flush or struck joints are made with a bricklayer's trowel. Most other mortar joint styles are made with simple but specialized forming tools called jointers. The V-joint, half-round, raked, and grapevine style joints are each made with different jointing tools. Contractors' supply houses typically carry a good selection of these tools, but an unusual tool, such as the grapevine jointer, would probably have to be special-ordered. The finish of the mortar joints is vitally important to the appearance of any brick wall. Some masons also use a fine bristle brush on the tooled joint to simulate the weathered appearance of the old, existing mortar.

Shortly after the completion of a tuckpointing job, it is fairly common for white stains called efflorescence to appear on the brick around the new mortar. A number of restoration chemical manufacturers market products to remove efflorescence. You also have the option of doing nothing to remove the efflorescence and eventually it might weather away. You might also try scrubbing efflorescence with a stiff natural bristle brush to remove it.

SPALLING

When a brick spalls, the hard, thin, weather-resistant outer layer of the brick shears off to expose the relatively soft and porous interior, which is then subject to rapid deterioration. Spalled brick serve as a path for water to enter the building. The only remedy for a severely spalled brick is to cut or chisel it out and replace it with a new matching brick of the same size and color. Sometimes the brick can be chiseled out in one piece and then reversed to expose the undamaged back side of the brick. Spalling of the brick on the entire face of a wall is serious and indicates a problem that needs to be addressed, but minor spalling problems generally do not warrant the removal of the brick. Minor spalling can be caused in the manufacturing process by underfiring the brick so that it does not have sufficient hardness to resist the effects of expansion and contraction due to temperature variations. However, even hard-burned bricks can spall if they are repeatedly subjected to a combination of extensive exposure to water runoff and freezing temperatures. This is a serious situation that must be addressed because it is important to divert water away from brick to the greatest extent possible to reduce the potential for spalling. Spalling can also be caused by tuckpointing soft brick with hard Portland cement mortar.

Spalling causes the face of a brick to pop off and expose the soft, sponge-like inner layers of a brick that can be seen in this photo. Compared with intact brick, spalled brick will absorb more water and dirt.

STONE

1060 E. Juneau Avenue has extensive stone trim.

For many years, limestone was considered to be one of the best materials for foundation walls and footings and was used extensively for window sills and other decorative trim on masonry buildings. Most of the limestone used in the Milwaukee area was quarried locally. For a few very costly houses, limestone veneer was used to cover entire exterior walls. Sandstone, another common building stone used in Milwaukee, is a porous, brown, red or tan-colored stone used almost exclusively for trim purposes since it is generally too soft for use in loadbearing walls such as foundations. Because it is relatively soft and easy to work with, it was a favorite material for carved stone ornament. Other building stones, such as marble and granite, were only very sparingly used in residential construction because of their cost and rarity.

Unlike sandstone, limestone is highly resistant to deterioration from water and capable of supporting very heavy loads. Locally-quarried limestone was known for its superior strength and durability when compared with limestone from other states. Many older houses rest on raised basements that are faced above the ground level with impressive and very costly-to-duplicate "rusticated" limestone, which is the name for rectangular or square building stones with a rough or rock face. New rusticated limestone building blocks can still be obtained at Wisconsin limestone quarries to replace deteriorated old blocks. A raised, rusticated, limestone clad basement is an important and highly visible architectural feature of a Victorian house, particularly since it was not common before 1910 to plant bushes, evergreens or even flowers around a foundation, as we do today. Below the grade level where appearance was not important, smaller, randomly-shaped limestone blocks referred to as "random rubble" were often used. Early masons often built the limestone basements in such a way that gravity basically held the wall together and mortar was used primarily to fill the voids between the stones. For this reason, limestone basements are remarkably durable. There are reports that some early limestone basement walls were laid up "dry," that is to say, without the use of mortar, and then the joints on each side of the wall were "pointed" or filled with mortar.

Deteriorated mortar joints in a limestone foundation may need repointing, which can be done in the same manner as repointing brick. Because limestone is very hard, it can often be repointed with mortar that is harder than the lime-rich mortar used to repoint historic brick. Using a medium strength mortar, such as Type "N," is generally recommended for limestone, especially when the joints above ground are finished with beaded or rope-like mortar joints, which require extra strength because they are more vulnerable to damage from weathering. The distinctive-looking beaded joint, which was commonly used in the nineteenth century with large, rusticated

Gustave Pabst's limestone clad house under construction at 2230 N. Terrace Avenue in 1907.

Milwaukee County Historical Society

A Milwaukee County limestone quarry about 1930.

water that includes a fungicide. Acid rain in our atmosphere has also been shown to be highly damaging to sandstone and, to a lesser extent, limestone. To stop sandstone from further erosion due to water penetration, a special chemical stone strengthener, such as Conservare® H, made by ProSoCo Inc., can be applied to consolidate the outer layers of stone without impeding the necessary passage of normal levels of vapor through the stone.

The concave jointer shown in the top photo is used to produce the protruding rope-like mortar joint shown in the bottom photo that was very popular for stone masonry during the late nineteenth and early twentieth centuries.

limestone blocks, can be replicated with a special, jointing tool which generally costs about five dollars.

Generally, the sandstone used in the Milwaukee area has not held up very well over the years, and much of the carved sandstone trim has eroded extensively. As a first step to analyzing what is causing the deterioration, examine the sandstone during a heavy rain to determine if the problem is caused by excessive water penetration that might be corrected through the repair of defective flashings or gutters. Excess moisture can also foster the growth of moss and lichen on the porous surface of sandstone and cause extensive damage. Fungal growth should be removed through scrubbing or with a power wash with

While cleaning limestone is actually seldom necessary because dirt and grime tend to naturally wash off its hard, non-porous surface, the porous surface of sandstone tends to attract and hold dirt. In general, limestone and sandstone should be cleaned with alkali-based chemical cleaners formulated for use on stone and not the acid-based cleaners used on brick, since the latter can damage stone. Although it is difficult to keep acid-based cleaners away from sandstone and limestone trim on a brick building that is being cleaned, research seems to indicate that skilled personnel can reduce the exposure of stone to the acid and minimize or even eliminate damage. In extraordinary cases, a temporary metal flashing can be installed above the stone to deflect acidic brick cleaning chemicals from washing over the stone.

STUCCO

Stucco is a plaster-like exterior wall finish usually applied over a reinforcing base, such as wood or metal lath, that is securely anchored to the building. In America, stucco originally consisted of lime, sand and water. It did not become popular as an exterior sheathing material until the turn-of-the-century when Portland cement was added to the mix, which greatly improved its weatherability. Stucco is very durable, but is susceptible to damage from water that might seep behind it through cracks or defective flashings around doors and windows. If small cracks are promptly sealed and flashings are maintained, stucco can last indefinitely, as many 80-year-old examples in Milwaukee attest.

A stucco house at 4918 West Washington Boulevard built in 1922.

If left unrepaired, cracks and other defects in stucco will lead to additional deterioration until large patches of stucco literally fall of the building. It seems that properly installed stucco jobs have an indefinite lifespan while defective installations usually begin to fail very soon after completion. If the cement stucco cladding of your old house has stood the test of time, perhaps 60 years or more, chances are you have an excellent quality stucco job that will last indefinitely if properly maintained.

It might be necessary to make repairs to sections of stucco that have been damaged or neglected for many years, but it is rare that the entire stucco finish on a house would have to be replaced. Local contractors who specialize in stucco repair are capable of making high-quality, lasting repairs that duplicate the original material as closely as possible in texture and appearance. Any homeowner contemplating

stucco repair should become familiar with basic stucco restoration techniques in order to better evaluate the work proposed by a contractor or to be able to make quality "do-it-yourself" repairs.

The word stucco, according to one source, might be derived from an old German word, "stucchi," which means "crust." Stucco is an ancient material that traditionally was applied directly over masonry and mud-adobe walls. American Portland cement stucco construction methods were pioneered in the late nineteenth century. The most common stucco application is over wood lath but there are also many examples of stucco applied directly over concrete block, hollow terra cotta structural tile, and brick.

Stucco-clad houses became popular in America after the turn of the century as architects and builders sought a new cladding material to use as an alternative to the traditional wood and brick siding long in use. Technological advancements in the manufacture of Portland cement, a key ingredient in stucco, helped pave the way for a boom in stucco construction. Stucco became closely associated with early twentieth century architecture, and many homes designed in the Arts and Crafts, Prairie, Bungalow, Mediterranean, and Tudor Revival styles were completely sheathed with stucco or at least featured large areas clad in stucco in combination with other materials such as brick or wood. Stucco was particularly appealing because it can be finished in a variety of textures and colors and offered a fresh new look and a smooth monolithic finish. Homes built today are sometimes sheathed with a synthetic stucco system called an exterior insulation and finish system or EIFS for short. EIFS typically consists of a base of rigid foam insulation, covered with a

Defective stucco is removed exposing the original wooden lath.

To create a strong bond between the old material and the new patch, the repair area is coated with a bonding agent.

New metal lath is attached to the old wooden lath and the cement stucco base coat is applied.

REPAIRING DAMAGED STUCCO

When the stucco base coat is dry, a finish coat of stucco is applied by a compressed air method to match the texture of the old stucco.

There are many different ways to texture stucco. Here, the craftsman applies a stipple finish with a brush to duplicate the texture of the original stucco.

A top coat of high quality, latex-based stucco paint was rolled on to finish the job.

① Brick and Block Foundation
② Floor Joist
③ Subfloor
④ Sill Plate
⑤ Wall Stud
⑥ Interior Lath and Plaster
⑦ Wood Sheathing
⑧ Building Paper
⑨ Furring Strip
⑩ Exterior Lath
⑪ Two-Coat Stucco

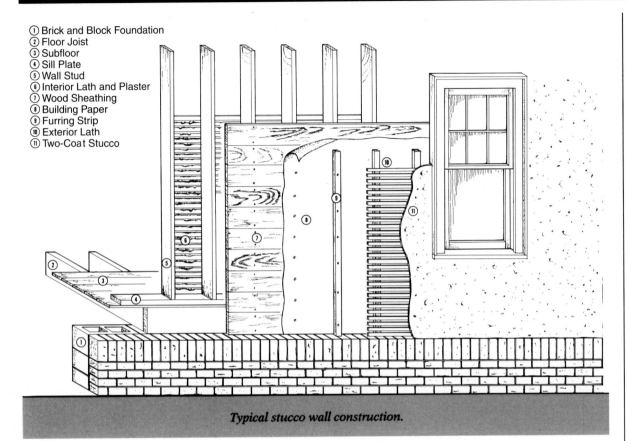

Typical stucco wall construction.

The premature structural failure of some early twentieth century stucco occurred because builders and architects experimented with various new types of lath, mortar, and flashings. Many of these failures resulted from moisture problems, usually due to using too much lime in the mortar, with the result that the steel lathing rusted out or the wood lathing rotted away. Large patches of stucco then fell off as the lath disintegrated. Some of the first metal lath used was uncoated steel, but after rust problems became evident, builders and manufacturers switched to rust-resisting galvanized or painted metal lath and reformulated the stucco recipe to have a higher proportion of Portland cement. One of the more common stucco mixes was three parts sand to one part Portland cement.[4]

This 1920s advertisement illustrates a stucco cladding system that was probably used on some Milwaukee area houses.

reinforcing mesh of fiberglass or metal, a basecoat of synthetic stucco about 1/16 to 1/4 inch thick, and a thin, simulated-stucco finish coat. The popularity of EIFS nationwide in new construction points not only to the renewed interest in stucco, but also the desirability of preserving and repairing historic Portland cement-over-lath stucco finishes on older buildings. Many of the highly sculptural, bold, traditional stucco finishes, however, cannot be convincingly or economically duplicated using synthetic stucco materials because the stucco coating is not thick enough. As a result, in most cases you should not attempt to repair historic Portland cement stucco finishes with EIFS systems.

Another popular modern stucco system uses a concrete board (much like a sheet of interior drywall) as a base over which thin finishing coats of cement stucco are applied. More durable than the EIFS foam board stucco systems, the concrete board stucco systems may be a possible alternative for the replacement of entire walls of historic stucco if applying stucco over traditional metal or wood lath is not a viable option.

Builders also quickly learned that properly installed metal flashings around windows, doors, and other junctions between stucco and wood trim were vital to prevent water from getting behind the stucco and causing premature failure. Improvements were made to wooden lath also, such as factory-treating it with a creosote preservative and beveling the edges to create a dovetail lock when the stucco was applied over it. One manufacturer of a system of treated lath and premixed stucco claimed that the life of a home sheathed with its product "cannot be reckoned by years — it is a matter of generations."

After stucco failed, it was common years ago to completely strip off all of the remaining stucco and reside the house with a new material such as cement asbestos shingles, asphalt siding, or wood clapboards. Seldom did the replacement siding replicate the architect's intended appearance. If you suspect that your early twentieth century house might have originally been stuccoed, you should consult the original building permit which might specify the original exterior wall material.

Stucco repair is a multi-step process, and the key to making a lasting repair is in the preparation work. First, all loose, crumbly and deteriorated stucco must be removed from the building. Wooden lath beneath the stucco should not be removed unless it is rotted. In order for the new stucco patch to bond properly to the old wooden lath, however, a special liquid bonding agent should be applied to the lath and the edges of the surrounding old stucco. One of the best known professional quality products for this purpose is "Eucoweld," available from masonry and plaster supply firms. Application of the bonding agent is a critical step because without it, the old, dry wooden lath and stucco will too rapidly absorb moisture from the new stucco causing cracks in the patch. It might be helpful to think of the bonding agent as a "primer"

This Frank Lloyd Wright design house located at 2722 W. Burnham Street was completely stripped of its old replacement siding (shown in the top photo) and reclad with new stucco to restore the original character of the building (bottom photo).

that helps create a good, strong connection between the old and new materials.

After the bonding agent is dry, preparation continues with the installation of new, diamond mesh, galvanized metal lath which is screwed, nailed or stapled over the old wood lath to further ensure a good bond between the new stucco and the building. A two-coat system of stucco, probably the most common in the Milwaukee area, will finish the patching process. The precise portions of Portland cement, sand, and lime in the stucco will vary from contractor to contractor. One ingredient used in the base coat by some contractors is a special latex admixture that gives the stucco, when dry, a small amount of additional flexibility to prevent cracking. The base coat, which is usually about 1/2 inch thick and applied with a trowel, may also be reinforced with short, thin strands of fiberglass. Traditionally, many stucco mortars were reinforced with the long, winter hair from goats or cattle years ago.

The method of applying the finish coat will vary widely depending upon the desired finish. Some stucco finish coats were sprayed on by a compressed air method, others were trowelled, and still others were splashed or slapped on with a mortar-laden brush. Small, light-reflective quartzite pebbles were also sometimes used in the finishing coat to create a special pebble dash effect.

The final phase in stucco repair is usually painting. There has been some debate over whether it was ever appropriate to paint stucco. Although most stucco houses have been painted over the years, particularly to cover weather stains and minor repairs, it was a common practice years ago to tint the wet stucco itself during the mixing process to eliminate the need for painting. Some of the popular standard colors offered by one stucco materials manufacturer during the early 1920s were Alba White, Shell Pink, Sienna Buff, Ivoril Cream, Granistone Gray, and French Gray, in addition to other colors made to order. The original stock colors of tinted stucco account for most of the colors used on stucco today.

The central problem with paint on stucco seems to be the paint itself. Historically, oil base paints were used. These act as a vapor barrier and subsequently peel as moisture from inside the house tries to escape through the porous stucco. Latex paints are recommended for stucco by experts today because these paints can breathe, so to speak, and allow moisture to pass through them to some degree without peeling. Only those latex base paints specifically formulated for use on stucco should be applied and these may require some searching for. Do not expect to find a good quality stucco paint at every hardware store.

Frequent repainting of stucco, particularly when poor quality or inappropriate paints were used, can make a mess of the finish. To remove peeling layers of paint from stucco, a low pressure power washer, using not more than 500 pounds per square inch of pressure, can be used. Stucco can vary in hardness from building to building, which means some stucco will safely withstand more water pressure than others. Water pressure should be adjusted after experimenting on a small test area. New latex base stucco paint can then be applied with a high nap roller. If the paint is properly applied to a well prepared base, stucco should not require frequent painting. If you have original unpainted stucco in good condition, you should avoid painting it if at all possible.

TWO COMMON MASONRY PROBLEM AREAS

Foundations

A typical brick foundation under an older Milwaukee wood frame house is an impressive piece of masonry work being about 14 inches thick and containing more than 18,000 bricks for an average sized 24 by 44-foot house. Older houses in the city derive part of their distinct architectural character from the fact that they were built on raised basements that project two feet or more above the ground. Unusually tall raised brick basements are a key architectural element of Milwaukee's well-known "Polish flats." Structurally, the foundation has the vital job of supporting the rest of the house above it. Homeowners are most frequently confronted with repairing foundation damage and defects caused by water or poor soil conditions. Among the most common symptoms of foundation ills are water in the basement, bulging or cracked

Constructing a basement for a new building on West Lincoln Avenue about 1910. Building a brick basement wall today would be prohibitively expensive.

Kwasniewski Collection Univ. WI at Milwaukee Golda Meir Library foundation walls, and settlement, which causes the building to sag or tilt out of plumb. Foundation repair is not a particularly rewarding job because much of the work is hidden from view below ground, it can be very expensive, and it may result in little or no improvement in the appearance or resale value of the building.

Keep in mind that if you discover extensive foundation damage, it probably took decades to develop. Usually there will be plenty of time to carefully assess the situation and arrive at a sensible course of action, so do not panic and rush into a contract for costly and possibly ineffective repairs. With a basic knowledge of foundation construction and common problems, the homeowner should be able to make informed decisions about how to make proper repairs. Most foundation systems are built like an inverted "T" with a brick, stone or concrete block wall resting on a much wider base called a footing which distributes the weight of the wall over a larger area of soil to provide a broader base of support. A footing is essentially a little pad made of thick stone slabs or poured concrete about 2 feet wide and 10 to 12 inches thick. The typical 14-inch-thick brick basement wall resting on a footing is usually made of three rows of 4-inch-wide bricks plus a small air space between the inner row and the two outer rows. The air space was designed to insulate the wall and stop moisture from the surrounding subsoil from seeping into the basement. Brick foundation walls made this way were common for residential construction in Milwaukee into the 1920s, although concrete block was introduced around 1900 and had become the preferred material for basement walls by the mid-1920s. From the mid-nineteenth century through the 1890s the foundations of substantial houses were often built of limestone blocks or were made of brick veneered with limestone.

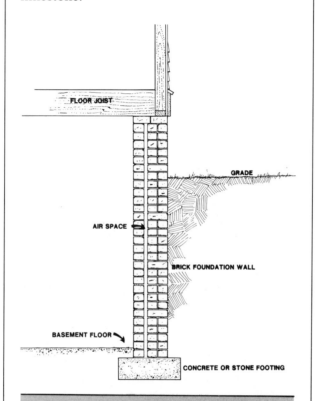

Typical brick basement wall construction.

By the early 1920s, the technique of building foundations with poured concrete had been perfected and it has remained one of the most common ways of constructing foundations. Foundations today are typically built with drain pipes (called drain tiles) that are buried along the inside and outside perimeters of the footing to collect ground water and drain it to a catch basin in the basement where it can be pumped out to the city sewers. Although drain tile has been used for a long time, many old houses do not have any foundation drainage systems or, at best, have some drain tiles buried under the basement floor along the inside perimeter of the footing. Historically, the exterior of a brick or stone basement wall below the soil level was protected from moisture penetration with a plaster-like water-resistant coat of mortar called parging. Over the years, this parging tends to disintegrate, which consequently exposes the brick and mortar joints below ground to potentially damaging amounts of moisture.

The roof drainage system, including gutters, flashings, downspouts, and sewer pipes they drain into, is often responsible for many of the moisture problems in older basements. Extensive foundation damage, which can go undetected for many years, has been caused by defects in the piping system that drains runoff water from the roof to a sanitary sewer pipe beneath the basement floor. It was a common building practice before 1940 to connect downspouts to the sanitary sewer system rather than to have the roof runoff water spilling over yards, driveways, and sidewalks. Typically, a metal downspout is connected near the ground level to a clay or cast iron sewer pipe that extends to the bottom of the foundation before turning back under the basement floor to meet the main sewer pipe. The vertical section of sewer pipe buried against the foundation is subject to rupturing and deterioration that can consequently cause the runoff water to pool against the foundation below the grade level. If this happens, the slow deterioration of the bricks and mortar in the foundation can continue, mostly unseen, for years. In the vicinity of the cracked or damaged pipe, bricks in the two outer courses of the foundation will loosen as mortar between them breaks down and washes away. Wet spots will appear inside the basement, and some spot settling and cracking may occur as soil is eroded from under the footing. Any below-ground cracks or holes in the foundation are also potential locations for mice and other small rodents to enter the house. To detect this type of problem, after a rain, look for telltale moisture in the basement in those places where a downspout receiver sewer pipe is located on the outside of the foundation wall.

The clay pipe that meets the metal downspout can rupture or break below ground which will send damaging amounts of water cascading against the foundation, unseen, for years.

One solution for a cracked or deteriorated downspout receiver pipe is to excavate, replace the pipe, and repoint, relay or replace loose bricks. Because the pipe usually extends no lower than about five feet below the level of the surrounding landscaping, it is possible for a homeowner to do the excavation with a pick and shovel. New clay pipe is still available to replace the deteriorated section, although you may want to opt for using PVC plastic plumbing pipe of the same diameter instead, since it is not subject to deterioration. Clay pipe sections are usually mortared together, and mortar is also placed around the joint where the metal downspout enters the sewer pipe. If you do install a PVC sewer pipe, it is advisable to include a "clean-out" fitting which has a screw-like plug in the side of the pipe that can be removed to facilitate cleaning.

Some homeowners may choose the option of abandoning a defective downspout sewer pipe and installing a standard downspout and splash block to direct water away from the foundation. Excavation and foundation repair may still have to be done, however. This option may not be practical on many small city lots, which have little room for proper surface drainage.

Much of the soil in the Milwaukee area has a high clay content, which can cause problems for foundations built on it. Clay tends to retain more water than other types of soil and then swells considerably when it freezes. The top layers of clay soil next to a foundation can freeze as deep as three feet, and the expanding soil can crack the mortar joints of a brick, stone or block basement wall. This problem can often be alleviated by improving drainage around the foundation. Some situations call for adding dirt fill which is clay-free or low in clay content around the foundation and to fill in depressions which could be holding runoff water. Where space permits, a ribbon of gently mounded earth can be integrated into the landscape to keep surface runoff water away from a nearby foundation. Trees growing near the foundation that have extensive shallow root systems that retain water, such as the weeping willow, should be removed. Gutters and downspouts should also be checked for proper functioning.

Waterproofing paints applied to the inside of the basement wall to solve excess moisture problems do not stop the penetration of moisture into the masonry and therefore are not considered effective. Waterproofing basement paints are, however, a good choice to reduce normal dampness, although not water penetration, and to create a vapor barrier in preparation for the construction of basement living or recreation areas.

To control water infiltration problems in an old foundation, some contractors recommend the installation of plastic or concrete drain tiles buried around the perimeter of the footing or a few feet below the ground level to catch excess water and drain it away. This is an extreme measure that should be approached with caution because the large-scale excavation of dirt around an old foundation invariably disturbs the balance between the brick or stone, the mortar, the footing, and the surrounding earth. Before installing drain tiles, a civil or structural engineer should be consulted, and all other methods of eliminating the water problem should be considered first. If you decide on a solution that requires the excavation of the foundation, the exterior of the foundation wall should be carefully examined when it is exposed. Mortar joints should be repointed where necessary, and the wall below the grade level should be treated with a parging composed of a new coat of cement/lime/sand plaster and then topped with a brush or spray coat of bituminous waterproofing, which is a black, tar-like material made for such purposes.

A settling foundation built on poor soil or fill that continues to settle over the years is a major problem that usually requires inspection by a structural or civil engineer. It was common for developers years ago to fill swampy or low-lying areas in order to create buildable lots. Dirt fill can continue to settle for decades taking along with it any foundation built on top of it. Some minor settling in a foundation is common, but noticeable, uncomfortable pitching of interior floors and severe, step-like cracks in basement walls are

A crack meter will record movement in a cracking wall.

indications that serious settling problems are present. A simple device called a crack meter that is attached to a crack in a masonry wall will record over a period of months any movement in the crevice.

When major settling problems are present and no other readily identifiable cause can be found, samples of the soil beneath the foundation should be taken in order to analyze the soil type and load-bearing capacity. New, wider footings spread over a greater ground area may have to be installed. In extreme cases, the soil directly beneath the footing may be too unstable to bear the weight of the building, and concrete, column-like footings called caissons will need to be poured into holes drilled beneath the foundation that extend to hard, load-bearing soil or bedrock. These measures, which are very costly, would be very rarely required for a residential building, but might be justifiable to preserve a particularly valuable older house.

CHIMNEYS

A chimney is simply a hollow shaft, usually built of brick in an older house, that carries off smoke and fumes from heating equipment such as a furnace, fireplace, water heater, or woodburning stove. To prevent hot embers or hazardous fumes from leaking back into the building through gaps between the bricks, the interior of a brick chimney, called the flue, is often lined with either a thick coat of cement plaster or a separate clay pipe. A leak-free lining is important to the safety of a chimney. It is equally important that the chimney be built to the proper height above the roofline in order to create an air flow, called a "draw," that will exhaust the smoke and fumes.

Rebuilding the rooftop portion of the chimney and repairing the lining are the most common chimney restoration projects.

If there is no fireplace and the functional need for a chimney has ceased as a result of the installation of a high-efficiency furnace and hot water heater that vent through the wall, it is possible to abandon a masonry chimney. However, even if the chimney is functionally obsolete, it might still be an important architectural feature of the house and should, therefore, be preserved. A chimney can be "mothballed" by capping the opening in the top with a sheet metal cover or a stone cap. This is considerably cheaper and easier than demolishing it.

Most pre-1930 houses, even modest cottages, were originally topped with ornamental brick chimneys. Maintaining or restoring an ornamental chimney top can add greatly to the period appearance of a house. Although the tops of chimneys tend to deteriorate because of constant exposure to the weather and high temperatures, there are still many fine examples of sturdy, original, ornamental brick chimney tops existing in the city, that can serve as models for rebuilding the top of a chimney that has been removed or has been badly altered in a subsequent rebuilding.

Many chimneys need only minor brick repointing work, which should be done according to the specifications listed in the repointing section of this chapter. Sometimes, however, the chimney has deteriorated so drastically that it has to be rebuilt from the roofline up. Masonry joints in a rebuilt chimney that come in direct contact with hot gases should be made with special "refractory" mortar. Regular mortars made with Portland cement and lime are not suited to withstand prolonged contact with high temperatures inside a chimney flue. The sections of a clay flue lining, for example, should be joined with refractory mortar, but the outer brick casing around it could be built with regular mortar. It was not uncommon for late nineteenth century architects to specify that the top four brick courses of the chimney should be laid with a hard, Portland cement-rich mortar to fuse the top into a rigid mass that could better resist the effects of weather and the hot gases in the flue.

The height of the chimney above the roof is critical in order for it to properly draw out the smoke and fumes generated by the fireplace or furnace. According to the state uniform dwelling code, all chimneys that depend on gravity for removal of the products of combustion must extend at least two feet higher than any ridge peak, wall or other roof within ten feet (measured horizontally) of the chimney. It is important to keep the height in mind when inspecting an old chimney because an earlier rebuilding might have removed some brick courses and left the chimney too short to draw properly. Older chimney tops are frequently trimmed with ornamental brickwork called corbeling, which is a technique of laying the brick in a stepped-out fashion to widen the wall or shaft. Corbeling is used, for example, to give the top courses of a chimney the appearance of a bulging cap. There are an endless variety of chimney designs that can be made by corbeling brick. Although corbeled brick chimneys are most frequently associated with nineteenth century architecture, they were common features on many early twentieth century houses as well, particularly those

A small corbeled brick chimney design suitable for use on most pre-1900 houses.

A Victorian corbeled cottage chimney.

built in the English-influenced styles. Corbeled brick chimneys fell out of favor after World War I, but in recent years they have again become a fashionable feature on expensive new homes of traditional design. Most experienced bricklayers should have no trouble in building a corbeled brick chimney cap, but it is advisable to supply the contractor with a design.

When a chimney top has been dismantled or when salvaged brick to match the original has been brought to the site to rebuild a chimney, it is a good idea to chemically clean the brick before they are relaid. It is difficult and often impractical to clean the exterior of a chimney top when it is in place on the roof because the chemicals can streak and discolor the roofing materials. Cleaning the individual brick when they are at ground level is a job that the homeowner can do to save the labor cost of a brick cleaning contractor or mason.

Maintaining the lining inside a chimney flue is very important. There are two types of flue liners found in older houses. Some brick chimneys were built around a clay flue lining, which looks much like a sectional, square pipe. Clay, more properly called terra cotta, is highly resistant to deterioration from the hot gases passing through it. The terra cotta industry in America was not well developed before the late 1880s, however, and therefore most pre-1900 chimneys were built as freestanding brick boxes which may or may not have been smoothly plastered on the inside to reduce the accumulation of soot and facilitate the passage of smoke and fumes without allowing them to seep back into the house. According to a recommendation published in 1878, "The chimney should be smoothly plas-

*A Victorian Gothic chimney
(1870-1883).*

*A Victorian Gothic chimney
(1870-1883).*

*A corbeled Victorian
chimney
(1870-1885).*

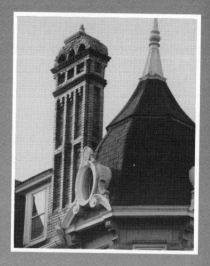

*A paneled Victorian chimney
(1885-1900).*

HISTORIC CHIMNEY STYLES

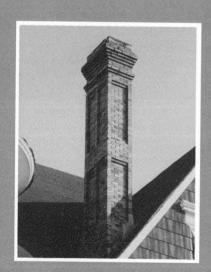

*A paneled Victorian chimney
(1885-1905).*

*A corbeled Victorian chimney
(1890-1910).*

*A Queen Anne style chimney
(1885-1895).*

*A battered, Queen Anne
style chimney
(c. 1882-1895).*

An ornate Victorian chimney with clay chimney tops (1885-1895).

An arcaded chimney (1895-1910).

A corbeled Colonial Revival chimney (1895-1910).

An Arts and Crafts style chimney with clay chimney tops (1905-1925).

HISTORIC CHIMNEY STYLES

A stone trimmed chimney (1905-1920).

A Mediterranean style chimney (1910-1930).

A Tudor Revival chimney (1900-1930).

A Cotswold Tudor style chimney (1915-1935).

tered with a mortar composed of one part fresh cow dung and three parts ordinary mortar. A chimney so plastered will soon present a hard surface nearly as smooth as glass [and] soot will not accumulate on the sides of the flue."[5] This mortar mixture is not recommended for use today, but it indicates that a plastered flue was considered a very desirable feature that contributed to the proper and safe functioning of the chimney. When the smooth plaster lining fails or deteriorates, flammable soots are more likely to accumulate in the flue, and it is also possible that some gases might seep through cracks in the mortar joints. As a safety measure, the walls of a brick chimney (whether or not the flue was plastered) were often at least two masonry units thick and separated by a small air space. However, when a chimney was built with a brick wall, only one unit thick, it increased the likelihood that a hot ember from a fireplace might pass through a small hole and ignite wood framing near the chimney stack. Old chimneys usually do not have to be completely rebuilt in order to make them safe and functional because there are now a number of different patented flue lining systems available to choose from. Relining a chimney is a job for experts and there are quite a few firms that specialize in this type of work.

It is also important to keep in mind that modern, high-efficiency heating equipment must never be vented to a conventional masonry chimney. Unlike older, less-efficient heating equipment, the principal waste product of a high-efficiency heating unit is a large volume of water vapor that can ruin a conventional masonry chimney and cause related moisture problems with interior walls located near the chimney stack. These types of heat-

ing units are designed to be vented directly to the outside through the basement walls instead of through a chimney.

A chimney with clay chimney tops.

It is advisable to have a chimney flue cleaned periodically, particularly if there is a woodburning furnace, fireplace or woodburning stove attached to it. A by-product of burning wood, particularly softwoods, is a flammable substance called creosote that can cling to the inside of a chimney flue and possibly ignite from a burning ember. Chimneys with clay flue linings are well-suited to contain a chimney fire and protect the rest of the structure against damage. However, after a chimney fire, there may be extensive cracking and damage to the flue that might require the relining of the chimney in order to make it safe to use. Cleaning a chimney flue is definitely a job for an experienced chimney

sweep. Homeowners can cut down the buildup of creosote by limiting the amount of softwood burned in a fireplace or woodburning stove.

A feature found on some old houses, particularly those built between 1910 and 1930, is a molded chimney top made of fired terra cotta. Clay chimney tops, which are seldom seen on homes of pre-1900 vintage, range in design from simple, box-like or round structures that crown the chimney to highly ornamental units that can be the focal point of a roofline. Clay chimney tops reached the zenith of their popularity during the 1920s and are particularly associated with the Tudor and Mediterranean Revival architectural styles. A good selection of new clay chimney tops is available today to replace broken originals. ∎

FOOTNOTES

[1] **Glass, Paints, Varnishes and Brushes.** Pittsburgh: Pittsburgh Plate Glass Co., 1923, p. 26.

[2] **American Architect and Building News.** January 20, 1877, p. 21.

[3] **Carpentry and Building**, September, 1896, p. 218.

[4] **Building Age**, June, 1911, p. 319.

[5] **American Architect and Building News.** November 23, 1878, p. 173.

ROOFING SYSTEMS

ROOFING SYSTEMS

ROOFING SYSTEMS

ROOFING SYSTEMS

ROOFING SYSTEMS

ROOFING SYSTEMS

ROOFING SYSTEMS

ROOFING SYSTEMS

ROOFING SYSTEMS

ROOFING SYSTEMS

Dramatic rooflines are a hallmark of many old houses in Milwaukee. Stand back and take a good look at an average house, and as much as one-half of what you see will be the roof. Although historically the primary purpose of a roof has been to shed water away from a building, a roof is also a major design element that, if properly finished, can greatly enhance the architectural character of a house.

A roof restoration ideally begins with research of old construction documents and the examination of the physical evidence to establish a history of the roof. If research reveals an early failure of the original roofing material, a restoration of a later roof material might be more appropriate. Often, a physical inspection will reveal that the original wooden shingles or slates are still on a house beneath modern asphalt roofing. Telltale screw holes in the sheathing at the ridge of the roof may indicate that iron roof cresting was once present. For houses built in 1888 and later, an original building permit that lists the original roofing material may be on file at the city building inspector's office. Other permits may also be on file indicating when a building was re-roofed or otherwise altered. Lacking sufficient physical evidence and an original building permit, the next step would be to research the Milwaukee fire insurance maps published in 1876, 1888, 1894, and 1910. These highly detailed maps, available at the Milwaukee Central Library, show the location of many city buildings, their basic foundation shapes, roofing material, and other descriptive information. The 1876 map is particularly helpful when researching buildings constructed before the advent of city building permits. The maps show that well into the early twentieth century, the majority of houses in the city were roofed with wood shingles.

There are valid reasons for replacing a roof with a material other than the original, including prohibitive cost or lack of skilled labor to do the work. Any decision to use an alternative material, however, should be weighed carefully against the primary concern to preserve or restore the historic character of the building. Of course, in the case of a flat roof that is not visible from the ground, appearance is much less of a concern and it would, for example, be acceptable to install a modern rubber membrane roof material instead of a traditional flat metal roof or built-up roof, which might be considerably more expensive.

The two most important factors in any successful roof repair are watertight construction and the selection of appropriate materials. The major components of a residential roof system are the roof covering, flashings, gutters, and downspouts. Most pitched roofs in Milwaukee today are covered with asphalt shingles, but metal, slate, clay tiles, wood shingles, and cement mineral fiber shingles are also in evidence. Metal roofing is most commonly used on flat roof decks and bay window projections. Each of these materials has its own character, adding color, texture, and pattern to the roof surface that it covers. Flashing, usually made of sheet metal, is used to seal out water in areas where the roof comes into contact with projecting features such as dormers, chimneys, skylights, plumbing vent pipes, and in the valley created where two different roof planes meet. Faulty flashings are the most common cause of roof failure. Gutters and downspouts are essential to conduct water away from a building. A house that is not fitted with properly functioning gutters and downspouts is likely to experience serious water damage to its foundation and sidewalls. It is equally important that downspouts direct water to locations where it will drain away from the foundation. A house with properly functioning gutters and downspouts may still experience foundation damage if the grade slopes toward the foundation rather than away, thus carrying water into the basement.

The shape of a roof is one factor in choosing roofing materials. Shingles, slate, or clay tile can only be used on roofs with sufficient pitch, while a flat or slightly inclined roof must be covered with a blanket of metal or synthetic rubber roofing to properly seal out water. There are four basic roof shapes commonly seen in most of Milwaukee's older residential neighborhoods: gable, hip, gambrel, and flat. Often a house may feature combinations of two or more of these roof types as well as the addition of dormers and towers which increase both the visual interest of the building and the complexity of the roofing job.

The gable roof is by far the most familiar roof shape in Milwaukee. It consists of two inclined planes that meet at a ridge over the center of the house and slope down to the sidewalls. At the ends of the house, the inclined planes form a triangular shaped wall called a gable or gable end. A hip roof is pitched on all four sides, eliminating the gable end, but increasing the amount of roofing material required compared with a gable roof covering the same area. The gambrel roof, a hallmark of Dutch Colonial Revival style houses, features a break or change in the roof slope that creates four inclined planes, two on each side of the peak. The upper plane on each side has a relatively low pitch, while the lower plane is very steep. This roof shape allows more headroom and about 50 percent more usable space in the attic compared with a gable of the same height.

The flat roof, which is structurally the simplest, presents special roofing problems because it does not shed snow and water as quickly as a sloped roof. While there are relatively few flat-roofed houses in Milwaukee, many Milwaukee houses have flat-roofed front and rear porches. A flat-roofed area atop a hip roof is a feature of many larger houses.

A hip roof.

A gable roof.

A gambrel roof.

Choosing the proper material for a roofing system depends on how long it needs to last

before replacement, the appearance desired, and budget constraints. Generally, the more costly the material, the longer it lasts. It is particularly prudent to pay special attention to the quality of the flashings and gutters because those are often the components of a roofing system that develop water leakage problems first, rather than the roof covering itself. In general, you should install roofing materials that are commensurate with the quality of your home.

ARCHITECTURAL SHEET METAL

Sheet metal is a versatile, traditional building material that can be used for any part or all of a roofing system including flashings, gutters, and the roof covering itself. The most common metals used are galvanized steel, copper, lead, lead-coated copper, terne, and aluminum.

Copper has long been considered to be the superior material for any part of a roofing system. It is expensive, but lasts indefinitely, requires little maintenance, and does not need painting. If it is damaged, it can be successfully spot-repaired. Lead, which ranks with copper in terms of cost and longevity, is easily shaped, but because of its inherent softness, it punctures and tears easily. Lead-coated copper was developed after the turn-of the century to combine the pleasing aesthetic qualities of lead — a soft, gray, mottled appearance — with the superior wearing and working qualities of copper. Runoff water from lead-coated copper will not stain brick and stone as uncoated copper will.

Terne metal is an alloy of lead and tin coated on mild steel. It was first imported to America from Wales during the early nineteenth century. Terne was apparently the most frequently used metal in residential roofing construction in Milwaukee during the late nineteenth and early twentieth centuries. The word terne means dull, which describes the material's natural finish. The steel base lends high strength while the terne plating offers resistance to rust. Like galvanized steel, terne metal must be painted or else the plating will wear off, exposing the underlying metal to rust. Rusting is not a problem with the terne-coated stainless steel now being manufactured, which is a permanent material, in the same class as copper. Old terne metal is difficult to distinguish from galvanized steel. Although terne roofs are often patched and restored, the material is not generally used for completely new roofing installations today.

Galvanized (zinc plated) steel has been the primary material used for gutters and flashings for most of the twentieth century. Because of its thin plating, the material is rust resistant, but it still requires painting. Becoming increasingly popular today is factory-painted galvanized steel that is an excellent choice for some types of metal roofs as well as flashings and gutters. The material is typically guaranteed for a period of ten years or more against peeling or fading. Of special interest for restoration projects is a new type of galvanized steel with a copper-like coating that weathers from a new penny brightness to a dark patina. Since it is difficult to make lasting watertight repairs to old, galvanized metal, it is generally better to replace it rather than attempt to repair it.

Aluminum as a building metal did not come into common use until after World War II. Today, aluminum has become one of the most popular metals for gutters, flashings, and roofing. It is the only metal many roofing contractors use today because it is lightweight, easy to work with, does not rust, and installs quickly. Aluminum cannot be soldered, and because it expands and contracts more than other roofing metals, aluminum roofs and built-in gutter systems must be designed to accommodate this movement. Pure aluminum is soft and weak, so it is strengthened by alloying it with other metals such as manganese. In spite of this, the aluminum manufactured today for use in gutters and flashings is very thin and dents easily. This is one of the principal drawbacks to using aluminum gutters.

Metal deteriorates by either chemical or electrochemical corrosion. It is important to understand these processes in order to properly design and maintain any metal roofing system. Chemical corrosion is the result of metals reacting with oxygen, water, and pollutants in the air and forming oxides at the surface. The brown and green patina associated with weathered copper is actually a thin layer of surface corrosion which acts as a skin that protects the metal from further decay. Rust on steel is another product of oxidation. Although surface rust actually slows the decay of steel, the corrosion still continues at such a rapid rate that the metal eventually disintegrates. Aluminum decays with white oxides forming on the surface during the corrosion process. High levels of air pollution can greatly accelerate the corrosion of aluminum.

Electrochemical, or galvanic corrosion, results when two different types of metal contact each other. In the presence of moisture, reaction between adjacent, dissimilar metals will produce a small electrical current which dissolves the more reactive of the two metals. The following list of the more common building metals is arranged according to what is known as the electrochemical series: (1) aluminum, (2) zinc, (3) steel (galvanized), (4) iron, (5) nickel, (6) tin, (7) lead, and (8) copper. Metals from opposite ends of this list should never be combined. For example, if copper and steel are in contact, or if rain water drains from a copper roof or flashing into a galvanized steel gutter, the steel will corrode. Electrochemical corrosion is faster than ordinary chemical corrosion because protective oxides never get a chance to form at the surface. Aluminum, which is a popular metal for flashings and gutters, is particularly subject to galvanic corrosion and should not come into contact with other metals or be subject to run off water that has passed over a different metal. For example, pressure-treated lumber, a popular building material today, often contains preservatives made with copper, and runoff water that has passed over this wood can potentially corrode aluminum through galvanic action. The galvanic action between a pair of metals close to each other in this list, such as copper and lead, is negligible, and so it is safe to combine them.

FLASHINGS

Flashings are formed from sheet metal, rubberlike membranes, asphalt roofing, or a combination of these materials. Some of these materials may not be appropriate for older houses where appearance is important.

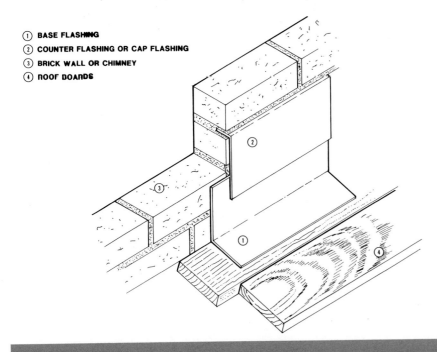

① BASE FLASHING
② COUNTER FLASHING OR CAP FLASHING
③ BRICK WALL OR CHIMNEY
④ ROOF BOARDS

Typical two-piece flashing.

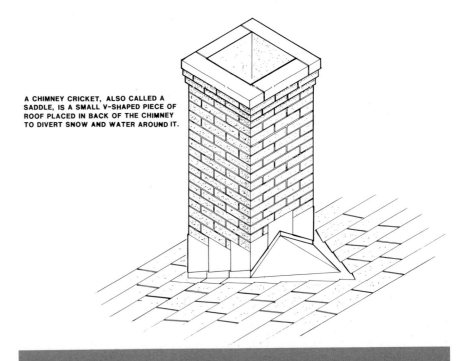

A CHIMNEY CRICKET, ALSO CALLED A
SADDLE, IS A SMALL V-SHAPED PIECE OF
ROOF PLACED IN BACK OF THE CHIMNEY
TO DIVERT SNOW AND WATER AROUND IT.

A chimney cricket.

Because replacement costs can far exceed the initial installed costs, it makes good sense to select as permanent a flashing material as you can afford for an original or a replacement installation. Patching defective flashings with sealants or cements, commonly referred to by many rehabbers as "black goop," is never more than a temporary solution.

Metal flashings around a chimney or between the roof surface and an intersecting wall, such as the sides of a dormer, are typically constructed in two pieces, the base flashing and the counter flashing, to allow for the independent movement of both the roof and wall without breaking the flashing's protective seal.

When a chimney exits the roof below the ridge, special flashing called a chimney cricket or saddle must be used at the back of the chimney. The chimney cricket is a small inverted V-shaped piece of roof, like a miniature gable roof covered with metal, that is placed between the back of the chimney and the main roof to divert water around the chimney. Many older houses in the city have developed serious leaks around their chimneys because the chimney crickets were removed or the original builders omitted them.

For most shingle roofs, a good metal for valley flashings is 26-gauge galvanized steel, which was the standard material for many years, rather than the aluminum or rolled roofing that many contractors use today. The cost difference is negligible in the long run, and galvanized steel is stronger, more appropriate historically, and should last considerably longer than rolled roofing. Chimneys and sidewalls are often flashed today with a rubberlike membrane material that is nailed and cemented into place. Little is known about the longevity of this material, and it tends to look inappropriate when viewed from the ground, but it does install quickly, thus saving labor costs. Two-piece metal flashings, although more expensive, are probably preferable. Another desirable metal roof feature is the metal drip edge that is installed at the edge of a shingle roof to prevent water from running or being blown under the shingles and, to a lesser extent, to reduce heat loss by cutting off infiltrating air under the shingles.

Copper is the best choice for flashings and gutters, especially when long lasting, expensive roofing materials such as slate or clay tile are used. The thickness of sheet copper is defined by its weight in ounces per square foot. Copper weighing 16 ounces per square foot is the minimum recommended for exposed flashings and gutters. However, on roofs of heavy slate or clay tiles, flashings made of 20-ounce copper are recommended. In cases where runoff water from copper flashings could stain stone, brick or roofing materials, the use of lead-coated copper is recommended. It is advisable to ask the contractor installing copper materials if there is any potential for staining from the metal, since that is one of the principal drawbacks of using copper.

GUTTERS

Gutter design and installation on older houses can be far more complicated than most homeowners realize. Factory-made and seamless gutters, which can work fine on new, modern design homes, are not always the answer for older houses with much steeper roof pitches and complicated roof designs. Often, the old gutters that are removed from a house were actually custom-made for that building and may be larger and shaped differently than modern seamless or factory-made gutters. Some homeowners report that new

gutters installed on their older houses do not function properly. Run-off in a heavy rain that overshoots the gutters and overflowing are common problems. This is not so much due to the fault of the installer as it is to the limitations of the gutters. New gutters typically have a smaller capacity than older gutters of the same nominal size and style as those that were made by local sheet metal shops years ago. The 5-inch size gutter is the standard size for most residential installations, but on some large older houses a 6-inch gutter may be necessary to properly drain at least certain sections of a roof. It is important to find contractors who are sensitive to the problems of building a proper gutter system for an older house.

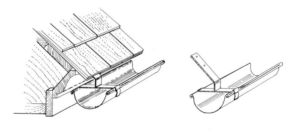

A half round gutter, also called an eaves trough, is used where the fascia is trimmed with decorative moldings. The gutter hanger is nailed to the roof beneath the shingles.

There are three general types of preformed metal gutters available: rectangular, (usually used in commercial installations), half-round, and ogee. Half round and ogee gutters (also called K-style) are the most frequently used for residential installations and come in different sizes. Half-round gutters, sold in 4-, 5-

and 6-inch sizes, are also called eaves troughs, and are the best choice if the eaves are trimmed with a crown molding or some other decorative woodwork. The 4-inch eaves trough is used only to drain small roof areas, such as a porch roof. Eaves troughs are attached to the roof with metal hangers or straps which are typically spaced about three feet apart. Straps should be nailed beneath the shingles, and never on top of them, to prevent leaks through the nail holes.

Aluminum is the most popular material for gutters and downspouts today. Aluminum gutters are usually made only in the ogee style, although a half round aluminum gutter can sometimes be found. Usually a contractor can make the gutters on the site to any length with a special forming machine. Although aluminum gutters are frequently advertised as "seamless," the gutters still have seams at inside or outside corners. These joints are riveted and caulked together or connected with a slip joint which requires periodic caulking to keep it watertight. Aluminum gutters, which are lighter in weight than gutters made of galvanized steel or copper, can be bent out of shape by winter snow and ice sliding off the roof and by ladders leaning against them. Frequently, aluminum gutters are replaced not because the metal has corroded but because they have been distorted and no longer function properly.

There is a considerable difference in quality between a modern aluminum gutter system and a traditional galvanized steel or copper gutter system with soldered joints. The latter is still one of the best overall choices for most houses. The soldered joints ensure a strong, long-lasting, watertight system, and the steel is inherently rigid enough to resist damage from sliding snow and ice. The downspout joints are also often soldered in a galvanized steel system, and the hangers for attaching them are stronger than those used for aluminum gutters. Galvanized gutters are formed in 10-foot lengths from one piece of sheet metal, and often include a flange that extends a few inches under the first row of shingles and is securely nailed to the roof sheathing. Gutters with this flange are usually called "high-back." Next to the half-round eaves trough, the high-back gutter was probably the most common type used in older construction in Milwaukee. The flange built into the gutter can prevent, to some extent, a backup of water from penetrating the roof and soaking the fascia. In contrast, aluminum gutters are sometimes made in two pieces with the flange being a separate piece, but, more typically, aluminum gutters do not have a flange at all. As a result, water backup under the shingles and rotted fascia boards are much more common with aluminum systems. The major disadvantage of galvanized steel gutters, other than their higher cost, is that they require periodic painting to keep them from rusting.

Painting new galvanized gutters requires special care because galvanized sheet metal has a film of oil over its surface used in the manufacturing process which must be completely removed in order for paint to adhere properly. A plain galvanized gutter system can be allowed to weather without paint for a year, which will naturally remove the oil, or a vigorous rubbing with a fine steel wool and turpentine will speed the process. Properly installed and maintained, however, steel gutters can last for fifty years or more. Galvanized gutters should be installed with a

slight pitch to drain water because standing water can cause these gutters to prematurely deteriorate. Through the 1930s, most sheet metal shops made their own gutters to order. In this way, the correct pitch to drain water to the downspout could be built into the gutter

One of the shortcomings of aluminum is that it cannot be soldered, making the joints susceptible to leakage. This downspout joint, although it was once tight, has opened up so that water can spill against the side of the house and penetrate the foundation causing decay.

An aluminum gutter installed with a hanger strap.

An aluminum gutter installed with the spike and ferrule system.

SHOP-MADE HIGH BACK GUTTERS CAN BE MADE IN MANY DESIGNS

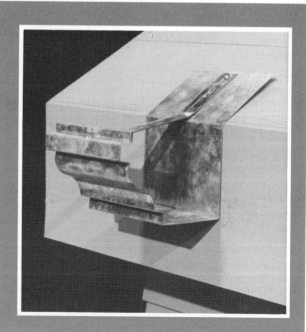

as the job required. Downspouts were often factory-made. The Milwaukee Corrugating Company (later called the Milcor Company) was a major national manufacturer of architectural sheet metal products including galvanized downspouts and gutters. After World War II, factory-made galvanized gutters and downspouts came to dominate the market, but still were installed with field soldered joints. In the 1960s, aluminum gutters and downspouts installed with pop-riveted and caulked joints became the most common gutter system. Only a few sheet metal shops still make their own gutters today. Factory-made galvanized steel and copper gutters are still commonly used today, but it is more difficult for the installer to properly pitch a factory-made, high-back gutter.

Gaining in popularity today are factory painted galvanized steel gutters which are a compromise between the low maintenance feature of aluminum and the strength of steel. Factory painted steel gutters cannot be soldered, however, because of the finish, and the sections must be pop-riveted and caulked together. As a result, there is a greater probability of leaking at the joints over time. They can, however, be made in the one-piece high-back style, like the unpainted galvanized type, which tends to prevent water damage to the fascia.

Many Milwaukee houses built during the nineteenth century were originally fitted with standing roof gutters which were also known as flush or Yankee gutters. This gutter was a simple, L-shaped piece of metal backed with a bracketed board that stood on the roof surface a foot or more above the eaves. These gutters allowed the eaves to be exposed to full view, which, as a result, were often ornamented with a crown molding, shaped rafter tails, or other decorative woodwork. This type of guttering system was always troublesome. It often quickly deteriorated allowing water to leak into the building, necessitating frequent repair or early replacement with metal gutters hung from the eaves. Because of the inherent practical difficulties with them, the restoration or retention of existing standing or Yankee gutters is not encouraged.

The built-in gutter was another gutter type that was commonly used on more expensive houses until after World War II. Like flush gutters, they are prone to deterioration, causing water to leak directly into the building. The major advantage to built-in gutters is appearance. The gutter is completely invisible from the ground since it is enclosed in a boxed cornice that can be ornamented with moldings, dentils, or brackets creating a handsome ornamental feature at the eaves line. When repairing or replacing built-in gutters, the new sheet metal material used to line the gutter should be corrosion resistant, and all joints and patches must be soldered. This precludes the use of aluminum which cannot be soldered. Galvanized steel or copper are the preferred materials. The built-in gutter should be supported by a wood box frame that has been restored to a sound condition by replacing rotted pieces and shimming it to drain properly. Carefully designed expansion joints must also be built into the gutter system. Since the wooden framing of old box gutters has usually sagged or deflected over time, rebuilding and relining old built-in gutters to properly slope toward the drains is a tricky business requiring considerable patience and expertise. As a result, it is also fairly expensive

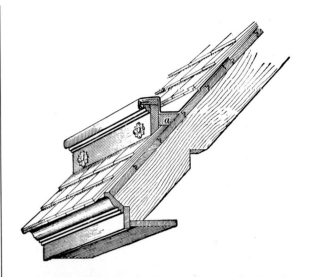

A standing gutter.

A built-in gutter.

and there are no guarantees that the completed job will drain properly. Because of the way some houses were designed, it may be impossible or aesthetically undesirable to convert to hanging gutters, in which case the built-in gutters must be retained. Although it may be expensive, repairing built-in gutters is probably the best solution in the long run if your house was designed to have them.

ROOF CRESTING

Iron roof cresting at 1535 N. Marshall Street, a house built in 1875.

Many of the city's older homes were originally topped with roof crestings and finials made of stamped sheet metal, wood, or cast iron. Many of these details failed to survive subsequent reroofings, changing tastes, and scrap iron drives during the two world wars. Old cast iron roof crestings are sometimes available from architectural salvage dealers, and several manufacturers are again manufacturing reproductions. The stamped sheet metal types are the least expensive and can be used with virtually any type of shingle roof. Ornate, lacy, cast iron crestings reached the zenith of their popularity in the 1870s but not all houses had them. It would probably be a mistake to use them on any house built after 1890. Less elaborate stamped sheet metal rolled ridge caps were used on many homes built from the 1880s into the late 1920s.

Milwaukee Public Library

The Mrs. J. H. Rogers House, formerly at the corner of N. 13th Street and W. Wisconsin Avenue, showing the wooden roof cresting about 1875.

The poor-man's roof cresting of the nineteenth century was made of wood and could

Rolled metal ridge caps.

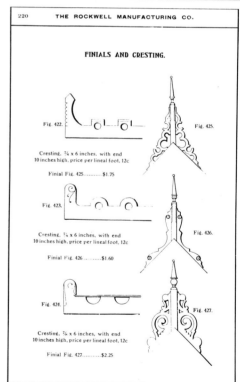

Pattern book plans for wooden roof cresting.

assume a wide variety of shapes. Because of rot, few original examples survive today. While wood has a much shorter service life than metal and requires frequent painting, decorative wooden crestings are relatively easy to duplicate and are appropriate for enhancing even relatively modest wooden cottages. They were commonly used from the 1850s into the 1890s.

ASPHALT SHINGLES

Most sloped roofs in Milwaukee are covered with asphalt shingles or their successor, fiberglass shingles. Both are made from a base mat over which asphalt and mineral granules are applied. They are generally fairly inexpensive, easy to apply, and even the least costly type can be expected to last about 15 to 25 years. Asphalt shingles have a base mat made of asphalt-saturated felt, while fiberglass shingles, as their name implies, feature a fiberglass base. Both are virtually identical in finished appearance, but some fiberglass shingles are lighter in weight. Fiberglass shingles have increased in popularity since their introduction about 20 years ago because research has shown that they provide superior moisture resistance which prevents curling, buckling, and blistering of the shingle. It is advisable to choose a shingle that has an Underwriter's Laboratory Class A fire rating.

Asphalt shingles, which were introduced during the 1890s, are being manufactured today in a wide variety of styles, textures and shapes. The three-tab asphalt shingle is the most widely used today because it installs quickly. Each of the tabs looks like an individual shingle after installation. Another type of shingle, T-lock shingles, give the roof a basketweave appearance and are often used to cover an old, rough roof that might otherwise have to be torn off.

The thick butts of Winthrops lie snug against the roof, doubling its wearing thickness where exposed to weather and casting the attractive shadow lines of the old wooden shingle.

The colors—tile red, sea green, blue black and golden buff—are permanent. The surface is crushed slate firmly embedded in everlasting asphalt.

A 1925 advertisement for asphalt shingles.

Perhaps the largest variety of asphalt shingles was available during the 1920s when architects and designers focussed particular attention on the appearance of a roof. Some of the 1920s shingles, like some of today's asphalt shingles, were aimed at duplicating the look of wooden shingles and slate. Some of the old asphalt shingles were actually wedge-shaped and installed like individual wooden shingles. Other asphalt shingles of the 1920s were shaped like thick, rectangular, individual roofing slates and came in colors such as red, blue-black, green and sunset to approximate the common colors of slate. The slate and wood look-a-likes were popular with the English, Mediterranean and French styles of period revival architecture. Still to be found on some older houses, the Dutch lap shingle is a large rectangular shingle that is no longer made. The hexagonal shingle is another early twentieth century shingle that may still be seen on some older roofs, but it, too, is no longer available.

A recent development is asphalt shingles that are styled to look somewhat like wood shingles or slate. It is debatable whether these products actually do resemble wood or slate once installed. Often called dimensional, heavyweight, or architectural shingles, they are designed to show deep shadow lines and are considerably thicker in appearance than conventional asphalt shingles. The lower half of each shingle is actually two shingle thicknesses laminated together. Because of their extra weight, these shingles typically feature a manufacturer's warranty of 30 years or more. Expect to pay a premium price for dimensional asphalt shingles and, before buying, compare the costs and longevity with other roofing materials that may yield better aesthetic results.

A new shingle roof can be installed directly over one or two layers of old roofing material and still be in compliance with the Milwaukee building code. If there are three layers of old roofing, however, all of the old roofing material must be removed before re-roofing. Many old houses in the city retain their original wood shingle roofs beneath a layer or two of asphalt shingles.

Although the building code allows up to three layers of roofing, it is good practice never to exceed two layers of shingles on a roof, particularly when one layer is wooden shingles. Old layers are often badly deteriorated, making a poor base for applying the new shingles. Waves and sags can develop in new shingles that are installed over old shingles, contributing to the early deterioration of the new roof as well as resulting in an unsightly appearance.

Removing all of the old roofing material allows a thorough inspection to be made of the roof sheathing boards for rot and damage. Defective roof boards are usually replaced by the roofing contractor on a time and material basis. Expect considerable debris around the house during a tear off. Some contractors may reduce the problem by using protective tarps over bushes and plantings around the house. Vibrations caused by workers on the roof can shake loose interior light fixtures, pictures and mirrors, so appropriate precautions should be taken.

Asphalt shingles should be hand-nailed when installed over the narrow roof sheathing boards which were typically used in the construction of older houses. Many roofing contractors today use air-powered nail or staple guns to attach asphalt shingles, but the guns

T-Lock asphalt shingles give a roof a basketweave appearance.

Kwasniewski Collection Univ. WI at Milwaukee
Golda Meir Library

Hexagonal roofing shingles are no longer made.

FOUR TYPES OF ASPHALT SHINGLES

Heavyweight or architectural shingles are designed to add distinctive shadow lines to a roof.

Standard 3-tab shingles are today's most common roofing material.

make it impossible for the roofer to tell if a fastener has been driven into the roof board or into a small space or joint between two roof boards. Hand nailing virtually assures that every nail will be driven into solid wood, providing a sound and lasting means for attaching the shingles. Standard galvanized roofing nails are also considered by many contractors to be more durable and rust-resistant than the nails or staples that are specially manufactured to be used in air-powered equipment.

Many of the city's old houses have what is called skipped sheathing where the roof boards were installed with wide spaces between them. This allowed air to circulate around the backs of the original wooden shingles so they wouldn't rot so quickly. When all the old roofing material is removed from a skip-sheathed roof, a new layer of plywood or other continuous sheathing must be installed over the old sheathing to provide a proper base for the new asphalt shingles. This, of course, increases the cost of the job.

A good roofer will install asphalt shingles in straight courses that lay flat on the roof, and the shingles will be trimmed in impeccably straight lines at the valleys and gable ends. When roofing over an existing asphalt shingle roof, there should be no perceptible waves or cupping of the new shingles even after several years of wear.

WOOD SHINGLES

Wood shingles, the most common roofing material used on Milwaukee houses until well into the twentieth century, are enjoying a resurgence in popularity for rehabilitation projects. Wood shingles have a unique character all their own, and no visually convincing substitute for them has yet been developed. The thick end of the shingle which is exposed to the weather on the roof is called the butt, and it can be rectangular in shape or decoratively sawn, adding distinctive pattern, texture, and deep shadow lines to a roof. It was a common practice during the nineteenth century to paint or stain wood shingle roofs in traditional Victorian colors, adding to the architectural character of a house as well as extending the life of the roof.

It is important to note the difference between wood shingles and wood shakes, both of which are made today. Wood shakes are thick, rustic-looking slabs that are split from a log, sometimes by hand, while wood shingles are uniformly sawn by machine into smooth, thin wedges. Wood shakes are not appropriate for use on older houses in Milwaukee because

A Victorian style patterned wood shingle roof with color stained shingles.

this material was not in use in the city at the time the existing housing stock was built.

Wood shingles are commonly sold in bundles of random widths ranging between 3 inches and 6 inches or more. Shingles cut to a uniform width are called dimension shingles and include those that are decoratively sawn. Factors that affect the service life of wood shingles are the pitch of the roof, wood species, preservative treatment, and the type of nails or fasteners used.

The sawn wood shingle on the left is appropriate for installation on late nineteenth and twentieth century homes. The thick, split "shake" on the right has a rustic appearance that would look out of place on the older houses found in the Milwaukee area.

Wood shingles were made from cedar, cypress, redwood, white and yellow pine, spruce, and even oak. It has always been known that some woods are more durable for roofing purposes than others. For example, the **Cyclopedia of Architecture, Carpentry and Building,** published in 1917, stated that, "Cypress shingles have been known to last more than a hundred years, redwood shingles from twenty-five to fifty years, and cedar shingles from twelve to twenty years." Cypress wood, known for its superior resistance to decay, but now in very short supply, is one of the best woods for shingling purposes. Intact cypress roofs that are 100 to 200 years old have been documented in the eastern U.S.

A distinctive English cottage "thatch" roof made of steam-bent wooden shingles wrapped around specially built eaves to simulate the appearance of a genuine thatch roof.

For many years, white pine was the preferred material for wood shingle roofs in Milwaukee and other northern cities because of its abundance, low cost and durability. During the 24-year period before 1912, one source estimated that 85 billion white pine shingles were produced by the timber industry in Wisconsin, Michigan and Minnesota.[1]

White pine shingles are no longer being mass produced because good quality white pine timber is now in short supply.

Most wood shingles available today are made from western red cedar, a decay-resistant softwood. Experience has shown, however, that today's cedar shingle roofs are not as long-lasting as the ones installed before 1930. This is partly due to a general decline in the quality of the wood available today, since the supply of old-growth timber available for use in construction has nearly disappeared. Most lumber today comes from relatively young, fast-growing trees and does not have the innate durability of the much older, virgin timber used by nineteenth and early twentieth century builders. Installation practices have also

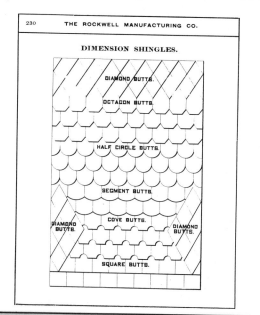

Shapes of wood shingles used in the 19th century.

changed over the years. Traditionally, it was a common, though not universal, practice to install wood shingles over spaced roof sheathing boards. Although this type of construction created a drafty attic, it did allow air to circulate under the shingles, drying them quickly when they became wet and thus extending their life. One turn-of-the-century building manual unequivocally stated that wood shingles will rot when installed over non-spaced wood roof sheathing. Current research tends to substantiate that wood shingles are more prone to decay when installed over the continuous wood sheathing used today. Unfortunately, in most cases, the use of skipped sheathing is not possible today because of energy conservation requirements and the trend to convert attic space to living areas.

The decline in the quality of the wood available has made a new wood shingle roof less resistant to its two main enemies — water and ultraviolet light from the sun. The sun draws out the wood's natural protective oils, allowing water to more easily penetrate the wood and create a cycle of wetting and drying that leads to decay.

Maintenance is one of the key factors to preserving a new wood shingle roof. Most wood shingle roofs installed today are left unstained so that they will weather to a natural dark gray or brown. Staining the shingles will repel water and extend the life of the roof and is highly recommended. It was a common practice to apply stain or preservative to wood shingles during the late nineteenth and early twentieth centuries. Many roofs, however, were allowed to simply weather without a preservative not so much for aesthetic reasons, but because a wood shingle roof was inexpensive and easily replaced, and the first growth shingles used had an inherently long life anyway. Today, however, installing a new, wood shingle roof is a costly undertaking and it makes particularly good sense to apply some type of stain or preservative to extend the life of the shingles. Paint should never be applied to a wood shingle roof because it is much thicker than a stain and can cause conditions that trap damaging amounts of moisture inside the shingles. Years ago, carpenters, rather than roofers, usually installed wood shingle roofs. They recommended dipping the shingles in stain or preservative before installation and then topping the roof with a brush-coat of stain after the job was done. In 1922, a carpenter, who described himself as an "old timer," wrote in a building trade publication that, "Wood shingles are not permanent. But when properly treated with stains, they become much more so than when left in their natural state, and besides that, the appearance is considerably enhanced."[2] This type of treatment is still an excellent practice. Historically, shingle stains were usually dark brown, dark red, dark green, and medium green. Research has revealed that some nineteenth century builders finished wood shingles with a mixture of red brick dust and linseed oil and that wood roofs were oiled periodically to extend their life. Most of the stains, however, were creosote-based, which is a product that is no longer available because of its health hazards. There are, however, many excellent shingle stains and preservatives on the market today that are available at lumber yards and paint dealers. With periodic re-staining or coating, it is possible that a modern wood shingle roof could be made to last the 50-year life span that most nineteenth century roofs had.

Trade Mark Registered in U. S. Patent Office.

A Shingle Stain That Preserves
A Combined Wood Preserver and Shingle Stain.

Shingles treated with this Creosote Stain will neither warp nor rot, as the stain penetrates into the wood and remains there. This stain will not wash off and discolor the rainwater. The preserving liquid, by penetrating into the wood, remains to protect it from the weather and does not evaporate. One gallon of this Creosote Stain will cover 100 square feet of shingles, two coats. When dipped, 2½ to 3 gallons will cover 1,000 of the regulation 4x16-inch shingles. Two-thirds of the length of the shingle only need be dipped. A lighter colored stain than the shade really desired should be applied to old shingles and, in order to obtain the best results, two or even three coats should be applied. The most important feature of our shingle stain is the preserving quality of the liquid. The coloring we use is high in quality and will give to your shingles a desirable, dull stained effect. Shingles should never be painted, because the paint leaves a ridge at the butt end of the shingles which holds moisture under the lap, causing the shingles to rot. Our Improved Creosote Shingle Stain penetrates the shingles and follows the pores and grain of the wood up under the lap and absolutely prevents rot and decay. The cost of this stain is a little more, but in buying it you know you are getting the best.

Order According to Catalog Number and Color.
See Opposite Page.

| 1-Gal. Can. Shpg. wt., 15 lbs. Per Gallon... | 70c | 25-Gal. ½ Bbl. Shpg. wt., 250 lbs. Per Gallon... | 60c |
| 5-Gal. Can. Shpg. wt., 50 lbs. Per Gallon... | 65c | 50-Gal. Bbl. Shpg. wt., 500 lbs. Per Gallon... | 55c |

For Color Samples See Opposite Page.

A 1917 Sears advertisement for shingle stain.

In terms of choosing a shingle material, strong consideration should be given to installing shingles made from white oak, a hardwood which is believed to be much more durable than other wood species for shingling purposes. Historically, white oak shingles were not commonly used in the Milwaukee area because of the ready availability of white pine shingles. Builders in the south, however, have used white oak shingles for generations because of the material's superior durability and exceptional resistance to decay. Builders in England have long preferred shingles made of white oak to other wood species. Even the Roman historian Pliny wrote in 77 A.D. that, "The most suitable roof shingles are got from the hard oak."[3]

The exceptional durability of white oak is attributable to its special cellular structure which contains a natural sealer called tylosis. Most woods are composed of cell structures that resemble bundles of tubes. When these tubes are severed by splitting or sawing, they are opened to moisture absorption which can lead to decay. When white oak is cut, however, the tylosis in the wood rushes in like a clotting agent to fill any exposed pores thereby sealing out moisture. Research has shown that unstained cedar shingles will last about 15 years in a temperate climate, while the more expensive white oak shingles should last about 50 years under the same conditions. Red oak, a plentiful variety of oak found in Wisconsin, is not suitable for roof shingling.

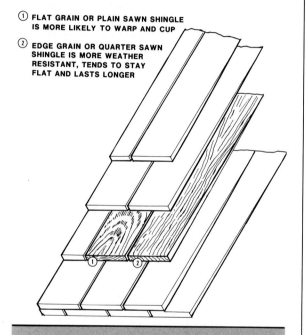

① FLAT GRAIN OR PLAIN SAWN SHINGLE IS MORE LIKELY TO WARP AND CUP

② EDGE GRAIN OR QUARTER SAWN SHINGLE IS MORE WEATHER RESISTANT, TENDS TO STAY FLAT AND LASTS LONGER

Edge grain vs. flat-grained shingles.

Regardless of the wood species used, to reduce the potential for cupping and warping, vertical grain, rather than flat grain shingles should be used if at all possible, and the shingles should be completely free of knots. Cedar shingles are graded according to standards set by the Red Cedar Shingle and Hand Split Shake Bureau. It is recommended that only No. 1 Blue Label grade cedar shingles be installed which are 100 percent clear and 100 percent edge grained. Lesser grades can be used for purposes of economy on secondary buildings such as garages or barns. Avoid using wood shingles wider than six inches to further reduce the potential for cupping and cracking. The length of the shingle is another factor in both the appearance and performance of the roof. Wood shingles are made in lengths of 16", 18" and 24", and the top grade can be installed with respective exposures of 5", 5-1/2" and 7-1/2". Using these exposures ensures an overlap that will yield a minimum of three layers of shingles at any given point. Using longer shingles will increase both the number of layers of shingles at certain points and, according to some professionals, the longevity of the roof. Wood shingles also tend to last longer on the steeply pitched roofs that are common to many older houses because they shed water quickly before it can soak into the wood. Wood shingles should be hand-nailed with hot-dipped galvanized nails. The natural resins in the wood will quickly corrode uncoated steel nails so they should not be used.

Moss or fungi growing on wood shingles are telltale signs that the roof is not drying properly. A simple remedy might be trimming back trees and other nearby vegetation to allow more sunlight to reach the roof, which promotes rapid drying. Fungicides can also be applied to the shingles to stop the growth of damaging plant material. In some cases, the growth of fungi could have been eliminated if the roof, when installed, had been treated with a good quality shingle stain that contained a fungicide. This is particularly desirable on low-pitched roofs where water is more likely to soak into the shingles encouraging the growth of fungi.

SLATE

Slate, the acknowledged king of roofing materials, is a natural stone product that is distinguished from other building stones because it can be readily split into thin sheets. It is an expensive, high-quality material that can often last more than 100 years with very little maintenance. Although the initial installation expense is high, when the cost is amortized over its life, slate may be considerably less expensive in the long run than a conventional asphalt shingle roof. Because of its cost, slate's use in residential construction in Milwaukee has historically been limited mostly to large, expensive houses with a sturdy roof structure designed to carry the extra weight. Slate cannot generally be installed on a house designed to have a wood or asphalt shingle roof because the roof structure may not be strong enough to carry the weight of a slate roof.

A Victorian patterned slate roof at 1843 North Palmer Street.

The color of a piece of slate depends on the dominant mineral in the stone, and the color largely determines its cost. Slate is also classified as either "unfading" or "fading." Red is the rarest, most expensive color and is quarried only in the northeastern U.S. There are about eight different slate colors available commercially including unfading green, which is generally the least expensive, and shades of purple, gray, and black. A slate roof typically contains a mix of several different colors, and is about four times as heavy as a comparably sized asphalt shingle roof.

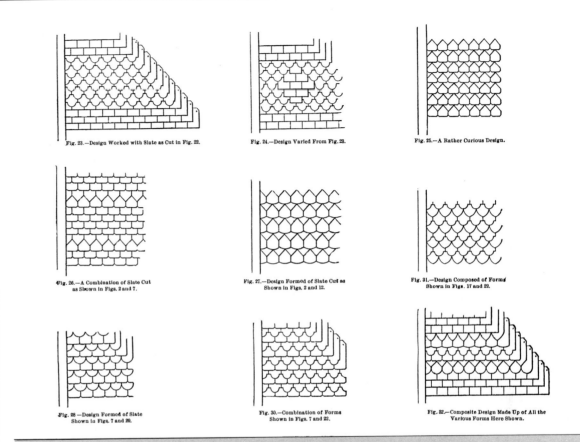

Fig. 23.—Design Worked with Slate as Cut in Fig. 22.

Fig. 24.—Design Varied From Fig. 23.

Fig. 25.—A Rather Curious Design.

Fig. 26.—A Combination of Slate Cut as Shown in Figs. 2 and 7.

Fig. 27.—Design Formed of Slate Cut as Shown in Figs. 2 and 12.

Fig. 31.—Design Composed of Forms Shown in Figs. 17 and 22.

Fig. 28.—Design Formed of Slate Shown in Figs. 7 and 29.

Fig. 30.—Combination of Forms Shown in Figs. 7 and 22.

Fig. 32.—Composite Design Made Up of All the Various Forms Here Shown.

Slate roofers are shown at work in a 1890s line drawing.

Many Milwaukee homes built between about 1875 and 1895 featured roofs with shingles laid in decorative patterns. These early 1890s designs were intended for use on slate roofs, but could also have been executed in wood shingles.

Slate is quarried in the U.S. mainly in Pennsylvania, Vermont, Virginia, and New York. The longevity of slate is legendary. While slate quarried today in the U.S. is conservatively estimated to last between 50 and 175 years depending on the variety, European slate roofs have survived intact for hundreds of years. Perhaps the most famous example is the 1,200-year-old slate roof on the Saxon Chapel at Stratford-on-Avon in England.

Leaking slate roofs are often the result of faulty flashings or a few cracked or missing slates rather than total roof failure. Many slate roofs have been needlessly replaced or covered with other material when repair of the flashings and replacement of a few damaged slates would have been far more economical and aesthetically pleasing. Older slates frequently become dislodged because the steel nails originally used to attach them have completely corroded. Broken or missing slates can be replaced with new or salvaged pieces. To re-attach a few slates to an existing roof, copper tabs called slate hooks are used. Copper nails, which resist corrosion, should be used to install whole new slate roofs or to re-lay entire portions of old slate roofs. Since slate is extremely brittle, a misplaced footstep can easily break a slate, greatly adding to the difficulty of doing repair work on a slate roof. For the repair or installation of a slate roof, it is absolutely imperative to seek out a contractor who is experienced with slate work.

A special style of slate roof found on Milwaukee houses built in the 1920s and

A Cotswold-style slate roof at 2601 N. Wahl Avenue.

1930s is the picturesque Cotswold-style slate roof, which derives its name from the region in England where this roofing method was most prevalent. Unlike a standard slate roof, which is laid in uniform rows, the Cotswold style is characterized by irregular rows of slates that decrease in size by carefully planned increments from the eave to the ridge. The slates are longer, wider, and thicker at the eaves than they are at the ridge. The aesthetic effect of a Cotswold roof has been compared to the orderly beauty of a bird's feathers. Cotswold-style slate roofs are virtually irreplaceable today, and the continued preservation of the surviving examples in Milwaukee is of great importance. Their repair techniques are the same as those used for regular slate roofs.

MINERAL FIBER SHINGLES

Mineral fiber shingles, made of fiber-reinforced Portland cement, are noted for their durability. They are manufactured in several different shapes, sizes, and textures, including styles intended to imitate natural slate. Mineral fiber shingles were commonly called cement asbestos shingles prior to a 1964 name change by the Mineral Fiber Products Bureau, which was itself formerly called the Asbestos Cement Products Association. Some brands of these shingles are still made with asbestos, a material that when airborne presents a health hazard, but is relatively safe when the asbestos fibers are locked into the shingles by a cement base.

The shingles are typically composed of a mixture of 30 percent asbestos and 70 percent Portland cement, which is formed under intense pressure into thin, rigid sheets and

then cut into individual shingles. Mineral fiber shingles are fireproof and will not rot or soften with age. The first mineral fiber shingles were made in the United States in 1905. From the 1920s into the early 1950s, many Milwaukee homes were roofed or re-roofed with mineral fiber shingles, and a large number of those roofs still survive today in good condition.

Asbestos is rapidly being phased out of the manufacture of mineral fiber shingles to comply with regulations set by the Environmental Protection Agency. New types of reinforcing fibers are being substituted for asbestos, but it is not known what effect this will have on the longevity of the shingles. Manufacturers nevertheless are projecting an exceptionally long service life for the new asbestos-free mineral fiber shingles.

Kwasniewski Collection Univ. WI at Milwaukee Golda Meir Library

This 1929 photo of 3461 S. 17th Street shows its original patterned cement asbestos tile roof.

Cement asbestos shingles are considered a permanent material and should not be removed unless there is widespread deterioration, which is rare, or the shingles are completely inappropriate in appearance for the building. A few cracked or missing shingles can usually be replaced with matching or near-matching salvaged substitutes installed by a roofing company that makes a specialty of repairing cement asbestos roofs. These roofing companies will typically keep on hand a stock of salvaged cement asbestos shingles. It is nearly always cheaper to repair a cement asbestos shingle roof than it is to replace it with any other material.

Mineral fiber roof shingles manufactured today to look like slate are often used as an economical, lighter weight substitute for natural slate. The principal drawback to them in the past has been that they tended to fade and

do not have the sheen of slate. New types of mineral fiber shingles have enjoyed wider use in recent years, after falling out of favor in the 1960s and 1970s. Since they are much lighter than slate, they can often be installed on roofs designed for wood or asphalt shingles. Before a simulated slate mineral fiber roof is installed on a house designed to have a wood or asphalt shingle roof, careful consideration should be given to the effect this will have on the appearance of the building.

TERRA COTTA ROOF TILES

2590 S. Superior Street, built in 1870, features a cement asbestos shingle roof that was probably installed during the 1920s or 1930s to replace the original wood shingle roof.

A clay tile roof on a house built in 1926 at 5306 W. Garfield Avenue.

The flat, clay shingle tiles on this 1924 house located at 2533 N. Wahl Avenue were designed to have an appearance similar to slate.

Terra cotta or clay tile, a very durable roofing material that has been in continuous use since ancient times, was used only in a few isolated areas of the U.S. before improved manufacturing techniques made the material affordable and plentiful during the early 1890s. By the turn of the century, the popularity of certain period revival architectural styles created a steady demand for this picturesque, colorful roofing material. The tiles are made in a wide variety of shapes ranging from a flat, thick, plain tile that is installed like slate, to the half-round, interlocking type that includes the popular Spanish and pan (S-shaped) tiles, which are molded with an interlocking roll or rim. Tile roofs are heavier than almost any other type of roofing material and require roof structures specially designed to handle the extra weight. Enough clay tiles to cover 100 square feet, for example, can weigh as much as 1,700 pounds.

The most common types of shingle tile, which were also used for decorative side wall shingling, are square, round butt, hexagon, octagon, scallop, Gothic, Grecian, and Persian. In Milwaukee, clay tile reached the zenith of its popularity during the teens and 1920s when tile was widely used for many fine houses built in the Mediterranean and other period revival styles. Many of these roofs, which were installed with long-lasting copper or lead-coated copper flashings and gutters, are still in excellent condition today. Clay tile roofs are considered to be a lifetime material in the same category as slate.

During the early twentieth century, clay roof tile was made from weathered clay which was exposed to the frost or sun, then allowed to stand for a period of time, tempered by additional kneading of the clay, and finally molded, burned in a kiln, glazed, and fired. Some roof tiles are slip-glazed, like pottery, and have a high gloss surface. Vitrified tiles are glazed by throwing salt on the tile in a fire, creating a vapor which unites chemically with the clay and forms an extremely durable surface. The two most common tile colors in

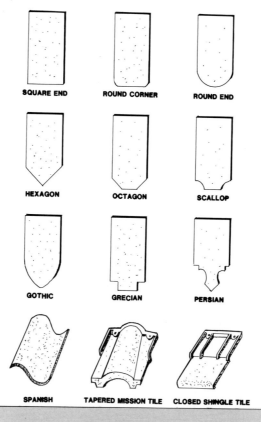

Roof tile shapes.

Milwaukee are red and green. Like slate, flat clay shingle tiles are attached to the roof boards with copper nails. Broken or missing shingle tiles can be replaced with tiles fastened with copper tabs similar to those used to attach replacement slates. Barrel tiles, better known as Spanish tile, are installed without nails by hanging them on wooden cleat strips across the roof. The weight of the tiles alone is sufficient to hold them in place even in the presence of high winds. The wooden cleats may deteriorate over time, but can be

replaced by a roofer experienced in clay tile work. Deteriorated cleat strips can cause barrel tiles to fall from the roof. Roofers who work with clay tile usually have a supply of salvaged original pieces for repair work. New tiles are also available to match many existing patterns.

Roof tiles often have a manufacturer's stamp on the back side. A large amount of the roofing tile used in Milwaukee appears to have been made by the Ludowici Company, which was founded during the 1890s and is still one of the most prominent names in American roof tile manufacture. The company still guarantees its roof tile for 50 years and claims that it should last for more than 100 years. Because some roof tiles manufactured for use in the dry, warm climate of the southwestern U.S. tend to absorb too much moisture to withstand the harsh, freeze-thaw cycles of northern climates, before you purchase new tiles you should check the manufacuter's specifications and installation guidelines carefully, and choose only those tiles that have a proven record of durability in cold climates.

CONCRETE SHINGLES AND TILES

Concrete roof tiles and shingles, first introduced during the 1920s, have become increasingly popular for new construction in recent years, but, unless they were an original feature of a house, their use is generally discouraged for rehabilitating older houses. Concrete roof shingles and tiles are exceptionally thick and heavy, which limits their use to structures with roof framing specially designed to carry the weight. Typical installed weights range

Concrete roof tiles are an original feature of this 1926 house located at 2530 E. Newberry Boulevard.

A new concrete tile roof being installed at 2602 E. Newberry Boulevard.

between 850 and 1,000 pounds per 100 square feet compared with less than 200 pounds per 100 square feet for the lightest asphalt shin-

gles. The flat concrete shingle tiles which imitate wood shakes are not acceptable substitutes for wood shingles on older houses not only because of their weight, but also because of their bulky and rustic look. Concrete shingles designed to imitate slate are generally unconvincing because they are considerably thicker than natural slates. Concrete, half-round, Spanish mission style tiles may be an acceptable looking substitute for clay tiles of the same style and color, but in the long run, clay tiles are probably more durable and colorfast.

METAL ROOFING

Sheet metal tiles, stamped from galvanized steel to resemble Spanish style clay tiles are still being manufactured today. These tiles were installed on many Milwaukee houses and small commercial buildings during the early twentieth century, and numerous examples survive today in good condition. Their cost was considerably less than clay tiles, and heavy roof framing was not required since they are light in weight. Flat sheet metal shingles, both for roofing and side wall shingling, are also still being manufactured today. These shingles typically cost more than the wood

A 1910 copper sheet metal flat tile roof at 2734 N. Prospect Avenue.

shingles that they resemble, but they install faster and are fireproof. Galvanized sheet metal shingles or tiles must be painted periodically to prevent rust. Copper tiles or shingles, a more expensive material, should not be painted and require little or no maintenance. Flat sheet metal tile roofs were probably never common and are relatively rare today.

A "tin roof" is a catch-all phrase that can refer to any one of several different kinds of

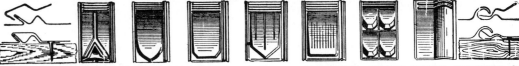

A sampling of the metal roofing shingles available in the early 1900s.

sheet metal roofs. Sheet metal roofs were not really made of tin, but rather of galvanized or terne-coated steel or copper. Some old sheet metal roofs, however, are actually made of sheet steel or iron protected with a plating of tin, which is a shiny, rust-resistant metal. Tin is expensive to produce, however, and it was never used for anything other than for applying a thin plating on sheet steel in roofing applications. Other sheet metal roofs are made of copper. Old metal roofs are rare in Milwaukee because, other than those made of copper or lead, they were usually replaced when they began to leak because of the difficulty of soldering replacement patches on the old material.

A 1917 metal Spanish tile roof at 1218 E. Brady Street.

Sheet metal roofs are constructed of flat sheets held together by three principal methods: flat seam, standing seam, and batten seam. Flat seam metal roofing is usually employed when the roof slope is very slight, such as on a flat roofed porch or the deck on a hip roof. It is desirable in some applications

A standing seam copper roof tops this 1923 Georgian Revival style house located at 3014 N. Shepard Avenue.

because it can be walked on. All the seams are soldered to create a watertight blanket of metal on the roof surface. It is generally used where appearance is a secondary consideration. The standing seam and batten seam are more decorative and are used only on pitched roofs because the seams are not soldered, but joined by rolled lock seams that stand perpendicular to the roof surface. The batten seam is a more stylized version of the simple standing seam with the metal joined over wooden battens to accentuate the joints and form a series of strong vertical lines on the roof. Standing seam and batten seam pitched sheet metal roofs are relatively rare in Milwaukee although many houses have flat seam metal porch roof decks. It would not be appropriate to use this type of roofing on the main roofs of most old houses in Milwaukee.

BUILT-UP ROOFS AND MEMBRANE MATERIAL FOR FLAT ROOFS

A traditional built-up roof covering consists of three, four, or five layers of roofing felt, each layer being coated with hot tar or asphalt. The final or top layer is coated with gravel embedded in the tar or asphalt. Built-up roofing was first introduced in the U.S. in 1840. Although built-up roofing is still in use, flat roof coverings made of monolithic rubberlike membrane materials that are installed like large blankets and are either cemented at the seams with a special adhesive or heated with a torch that bonds the material to the roof surface are more popular. Using a torch around an old building with dry wood sheathing can be a fire hazard, so this latter method should be avoided or very carefully monitored during installation. Because they are a relatively recent innovation, little is known about the longevity of these rubber membrane roofing materials. They are more subject to punctures than other flat roof materials and are not very pleasing to look at, but they are an economical and increasingly popular alternative to built-up hot tar or metal for low pitched or flat roof types. Since there are very few flat-roofed houses in Milwaukee, these products are generally used on houses only to cover the flat decks on top of hip roofs and for porch roofs. This is generally acceptable since these roof surfaces are not usually visible from the street. ∎

FOOTNOTES

[1] **Building Age**, February, 1912.

[2] **Building Age**, February, 1922, p. 55.

[3] Norman Davey, **A History of Building Materials**, London: Phoenix House, 1961, p. 161.

ENERGY CONSERVATION AND INSULATION

ENERGY CONSERVATION AND INSULATION

ENERGY CONSERVATION AND INSULATION

ENERGY CONSERVATION AND INSULATION

ENERGY CONSERVATION AND INSULATION

Like automobiles, houses need periodic "tuning" in order to maintain their peak energy efficiency. Contrary to popular belief, the inherent energy efficiency of older houses is often fairly high because energy-conscious housing design has long been part of our architectural heritage. Many of the basic methods used by architects, homeowners, and builders during the last century to keep a house warm in the winter and cool in the summer are still in use today. Mineral wool and cellulose insulation, for example, were both invented in the late nineteenth century and are still widely used today. This chapter focuses primarily on the architectural and structural aspects of energy conservation in an older house rather than the evaluation of mechanical heating and cooling equipment. The reason for this is that no matter how efficient a furnace or air conditioner is, it will never perform economically unless the house itself is made to minimize heat loss and air infiltration through walls, ceilings, and floors.

People unfamiliar with older buildings often erroneously claim that old houses were originally built as uncomfortable, impossible-to-heat follies that can never be as energy efficient as modern construction. The fact is that studies have shown that, from an energy standpoint, the most inherently inefficient houses standing today in the U.S. were built between 1940 and 1975. Many pre-1940 houses were built to standards of comfort that we would find highly desirable today. One well-known Milwaukee architectural firm in the 1890s, for example, required that the design and construction of its residences had to be sufficient to "heat the entire house to 70 degrees when the outside temperature is 20 degrees below zero."[1] Remarkably, that is still the basic standard for a well-insulated house built today.

Although there are many improvements that can be made to enhance the energy efficiency of an older house, there are no miracles. It is important for homeowners, and prospective homeowners, to realize the inevitable costs that accompany owning and heating any large old house, even a well-insulated one. Tragically many fine old homes, particularly larger ones, have been insensitively altered by homeowners seeking to realize dramatic and often unrealistic improvements in energy efficiency. Energy conservation measures need not destroy or insensitively alter the original architecture of a house. Drastic energy-related alterations such as installing massive solar collectors or blocking up original windows and doors will take a big bite out of your pocketbook to effect and will result in surprisingly little net savings in energy costs. They may also greatly reduce the resale value of your house. It is the job of the modern rehabber to "fine-tune" old houses in order to reclaim some of the original energy efficiency that has been lost over the years because of air leaks, deferred maintenance, or outright damage to the structure. Most of what needs to be done to button-up a leaky old house is surprisingly simple and "low tech," such as caulking, installing storm windows, and adding weatherstripping. Interestingly enough, one of the accidental benefits of a general rehabilitation of the exterior of a house is often an overall increase in energy efficiency. Many homeowners fail to realize that the loss of original architectural features can increase the energy needs of an older house. The removal or deterioration of even minor amounts of exterior wood trim or

siding, for example, not only looks unsightly but can create an easy path for outside air to infiltrate the building and consequently drive up energy costs.

HISTORIC ENERGY CONSERVATION TECHNIQUES

Shutters were often installed on the interior side of windows in the nineteenth century to reduce air infiltration and heat loss.

Today we are rediscovering some of the energy saving features of yesterday's architecture. Shutters, for example, were sometimes installed on the interior side of windows as much to reduce heat loss during cold weather and heat gain during warm weather as to provide privacy. In better classes of construction, interior shutters were made to fold into pockets in the wall on either side of a window. Heavy draperies were also very effective at reducing heat loss through windows and stopping drafts.

Members of the Pretschold family at work about 1917 in their awning shop.

Awnings today can be made of modern fabrics that look similar to those popular years ago.

In the days before central air conditioning, floor plans were often designed to maximize cross ventilation from windows and doors, and features were added to keep interiors cool in the summer. At least one nineteenth century Milwaukee architect, Herman Paul Schnetzky, developed a central ventilation system for houses that consisted of a louvered vent in each room that was ducted to a special flue in the chimney. Large porches, which were often oriented to shield parts of the first floor from the direct summer sun, were another feature that made the interior more comfortable during hot weather. Brightly-colored canvas awnings at the windows added to the architectural character of a house and also greatly reduced heat gain inside the building. If you are considering adding awnings to your older house, avoid using modern, metal awnings, since they bear little resemblance to historic canvas awnings. Let the designs in old advertisements and historic house photographs be your guide in selecting an awning style that is appropriate for your older house. Years ago, awnings were made of cotton canvas which was subject to much more rapid deterioration than today's more durable synthetic, acrylic-based materials. To maintain a period look, however, avoid selecting the shiny, plastic-looking materials that have

The principal factors that determine the appearance of awnings are: color and pattern of fabric, the design of the edge or border, and the size.

become commonplace or the modern "bubble" or "waterfall" style awnings often seen on commercial buildings today.

These exterior blinds with movable slats are hung on special hinges to allow them to be swung shut without removing the storm or screen window.

EXTERIOR SHUTTERS AND BLINDS

Historically, wooden exterior shutters and blinds were an alternative to canvas awnings. They were installed partially for security to keep small animals from getting through open windows in the days before screens were common and partially to save energy because they could be shut snugly over a window to filter out the hot summer sun and to reduce heat and air infiltration during the winter.

Although both exterior blinds and shutters serve the same basic purpose, there is an important distinction between the two. A traditional exterior shutter is made like a small, solid paneled door or, in the case of some 1920s shutters, vertical wooden boards fastened together with a horizontal wooden strip called a "cleat." Various ornamental designs were sometimes cut out of the panels or decorative patterns were stenciled on. Cut-out panel designs were particularly popular during the 1920s. An exterior blind, on the other hand, has movable or fixed horizontal slats called louvers set in a wooden frame in order to regulate the flow of light and air to the interior of the house. Louvered blinds were used extensively from the 1830s through the 1920s, while solid shutters became popular about 1915 and remained in vogue for use on certain period revival style houses through the 1930s.

Exterior shutters.

Before storm windows became common in the 1890s, operable exterior blinds were widely used in Milwaukee. A special window jamb that could be fitted with both exterior shutters or blinds and an exterior storm or screen was a feature of some houses built into the 1920s, by which time exterior blinds and shutters were largely just decorative. Although most original exterior blinds rotted away and were removed decades ago, many houses, especially those built before 1890 were originally equipped with them. Examine the exterior trim and jambs around your windows for telltale scars of the hinges and other hardware that would indicate the house was fitted in the past with shutters or blinds. Any decision to install shutters or blinds on an older house should be carefully planned. Authentic exterior blinds, almost universally misnamed shutters today, are still readily available, but often the modern ones sold today in building supply stores are inappropriate for use on older houses because they do not match the size of old windows and are made of vinyl with fixed louvers. Too often they are installed by misguided owners in an attempt to "Colonialize" or add historic detail to a building that may never have been fitted with blinds in the first place. Even worse, some homeowners screw them to the wall in such a way that it is obvious that they are non-functional.

A blind or shutter panel was typically 1-1/8-inch thick, seldom more than 24 inches wide and made of clear, high-quality eastern white pine. A large window, more than four feet wide, would have been fitted with a folded pair of shutters or blinds hung at either side. During the late nineteenth century, Milwaukee was an important manufacturing center for wooden exterior blinds, shutters and related hardware. Research has shown that many late nineteenth century builders often installed shutters and blinds only on selected windows, usually on the south, east or west sides of a building that received lots of sunlight or wind, and only occasionally on attic windows.

In the nineteenth century, shutters and exterior blinds were always installed so that they could be opened and closed. It was not until the 1920s that shutters were installed merely for decoration by nailing or screwing them in place on either side of a window. Modern, mass produced, stock sized blinds too often are mistakenly installed without any consideration given to the actual size of the window they are supposed to cover. Even if the shutters are merely decorative, they must be sized and mounted on the wall so that they appear as though they could actually close over the window opening if they are to appear realistic.

The best exterior blinds made today, just like those 100 years ago, have movable slats that regulate the flow of air and light. High quality, solid wood panel shutters are also available but, like louvered blinds, they usually have to be custom-ordered from millwork companies that specialize in this type of work. As is the case with most building materials, the prices of shutters and blinds are an indicator of quality and longevity. The best shutters and louvers are made with frames that are pegged together using traditional mortise and tenon joinery (see the **"Doors"** chapter for an illustration). Mortise and tenon frames are considered to be very durable because they have stronger joints than the more common and less expensive method of using glue and dowels which can loosen over time causing the frame to fall apart.

Many companies around the country today offer shutter hardware for swinging shutters. Special shutter hinges that allow the shutters or blinds to close over a storm or screen are also available. Shutters and blinds are typically held in place against an exterior wall with metal "hold backs" or shutter guards, which are also still manufactured today.

ENERGY CONSERVATION TODAY

When buying energy-related building products, beware of "miracle" gimmicks and stick with proven materials. Caulking, for example, is a relatively inexpensive, low-tech item that has been around for years, but its energy-saving potential is tremendous. The advertised promise of a product to deliver big savings on your fuel bill is not necessarily enough to justify its installation in your home, however. For example, you should be wary of any claims that exterior siding and trim made of aluminum, steel or vinyl by themselves will prevent heat loss through an exterior wall. A comparison of the installed cost of the siding with the negligible increase, if any, in energy efficiency, will not add up to any real savings for the homeowner.

Energy conservation projects are often evaluated by what is called "payback," which is the period of time necessary to recoup the cost of the project in energy savings. The payback period can be calculated by dividing the costs of the project by its estimated annual savings. For example, if an energy-related repair costs $100 and results in an annual estimated energy savings of $10 per year, the payback period would be 10 years ($100 divided by $10 per year = 10 years). Most authorities believe that an energy conservation project with an estimated payback period of more than five years

is not worthwhile. This simple method of calculating payback, of course, also fails to take into account the interest you would forfeit by investing your money in an energy conservation project rather than having it in the bank. When the lost interest is accounted for, as bankers and construction professionals would do in computing the cost of a project, the payback period will typically be even longer. Off-the-shelf energy saving products such as computerized setback thermostats are often sold with information that will let you estimate the payback period. If you are contemplating an extensive energy conservation project, such as whole-house insulation that will be done by a contractor, you should ask for an estimation of the payback period. If you are in doubt about a contractor's ability to calculate an accurate payback period, you might consult a heating engineer.

One of the fundamental concepts of energy conservation is that hot or warm air is attracted to cold air. This means that during cold weather, heat is drawn from inside a house toward the cold exterior walls. Insulation is a means to slow down, but not completely stop, the passage of heat through walls, floors and ceilings. All building materials, such as wood siding, brick, plaster and lath, have at least some insulation value and therefore slow the passage of heat. The motionless air inside the hollow cavity of a wall or ceiling has insulation value as well. Insulation materials, whose sole purpose is to impede the passage of heat, are much more efficient than regular building materials at stopping the outside flow of warm air and, therefore, reduce the demand on the heating system which, in turn, saves fuel costs. Conversely, when the outside temperature is

hot, insulation helps to keep the inside of the building cool.

TABLE 1.

Table of R-values for basic Milwaukee building materials.		
Material Description	R-value per inch	R-value for thickness listed
Brick, common (including Milwaukee cream brick)	.20	
Brick, pressed	.11	
Stucco	.20	
Stone	.08	
Gypsum board, 1/2"	.45	
Plywood, 1/2"		.62
Plywood, 3/4"		.93
Concrete block, 8" thick 3 oval cores		1.11
Softwood lumber	1.25	
Wood shingles, average thickness		.94
Wood drop siding, 3/4"		.79
Cement asbestos siding, average thickness		.21
Cement plaster	.20	
Interior air film resistance for a vertical surface		.68
Asphalt shingles, average		.44
Vapor-permeable felt building paper		.06
Outside air film resistance		.17
3-1/2" air space		1.14
Bevel wood siding		.81

The measure of resistance of a building material to heat flow is called an "R-value," and there are standardized lists for the R-values of most building materials. You can determine R-values for your house by analyzing a typical "slice" of the building materials in an exterior wall or attic floor. The larger the R-value, the better, because it indicates more resistance to heat loss. The average uninsulated exterior wall in a wood sided house may have a heat resistance value of R-4.5 while the addition of 3-1/2" of insulation in the hollow space between the wall studs could increase that value to R-17.5. Insulation is purchased according to its R-value. Some types of insulation have greater R-values than others. Generally, the higher the R-value per inch, the greater the cost of the material.

AIR INFILTRATION AND CAULKING

Air infiltration is usually the single biggest energy waster in a house and often accounts for one-third or more of the total heat loss. When air infiltration levels are high, even a well-insulated house may be difficult to efficiently heat or cool. Over the years, the natural aging and settling process of a house will open many small, energy-wasting cracks in interior and exterior walls that allow cold air to leak in, thus forcing the heating system to work harder. Many of the cracks can be successfully sealed with caulking. For the best results, a thorough job of caulking has to be done both inside and out. Reducing air infiltration with caulking has one of the quickest paybacks of all energy conservation projects.

It is important to use a good quality caulk. Common butyl-based caulk available at most hardware stores can fail in an exterior application where there is potential for significant seasonal movement of the joint. For general exterior use, you should choose a high-quality polyurethane sealant, such as Vulkem®, which is available from sealant supply dealers and a few better-stocked lumber yards. Polyure-

thane caulks can also be used on clean masonry surfaces such as concrete block, brick, and concrete. Caulking should not be used as a substitute for tuckpointing masonry joints with mortar, however. (See **"Brick, Stucco and Stone"** chapter.) Caulking is often the best way to seal a gap between masonry and wood surfaces, such as where a brick wall meets a wooden window.

Another fine point on the installation of caulking is the proper use of "backer rods," which are used to help seal cracks that are over 3/8" wide or unusually deep. A backer rod is a soft, or semi-soft, rod that comes in several different diameters. An appropriate size, usually larger than the width of the joint, should be tightly packed into a wide or deep void to serve as a base for the sealant applied over it. Backer rods not only save money on sealant, they also prevent three-sided adhesion of the caulk, which restricts the flexibility of the sealant and would eventually cause the caulk to fail if there is considerable movement in the joint. Backer rods, which are available from better-stocked hardware stores and insulation and sealant supply dealers, also serve as a secondary sealer if the caulk on top of it should fail.

Caulk should be applied to all vertical joints where wooden siding meets corner trim boards and other trim boards around windows and doors. Do not caulk the horizontal joints under each clapboard. Small hairline gaps under clapboards actually serve the necessary purpose of allowing interior moisture to successfully escape the building rather than getting trapped inside the exterior walls where it could condense and cause the decay of the wooden frame or the peeling of exterior paint. In order to get a good, lasting bond, make

sure that any surface to which you apply caulk is dry, clean, and free from peeling paint.

Tightening up the exterior joints of an older house with caulk requires a companion program to seal gaps and cracks on the interior to discourage the situation where airborne moisture passes into a wall cavity from the interior only to be prevented from passing through to the exterior by a tightly sealed and caulked exterior wall. This is a problem because one of the characteristics of warm air is that it captures moisture inside a house and propels it toward colder air outside. Moisture in a house is typically generated by humidifiers, cooking, baths, house plants, and the breath and perspiration of the occupants. When airborne moisture reaches a cool exterior wall, it can condense into a liquid, and collect in droplets inside the wall cavity and cause the decay of the wood framing members and sills.

The central problem with "tightening up" the air leaks in an older house and adding new insulation within wall cavities is that the water vapor that is migrating through the wall has a greater chance of condensing to water inside the wall cavity if the new insulation makes the outside surface of the wall cavity much colder than the surface of the wall cavity on the warm side of the insulation. To prevent water vapor from getting trapped inside an insulated wall in the first place, it is crucial to install a vapor barrier, if at all possible, on the warm or "lived in" side of the wall cavity. Vapor barriers, because they are vital to the longevity of a well-insulated house, are a hot topic of discussion today on the homebuilding scene. Caulking joints on the interior of a house will also inhibit moisture from reaching the wall cavity. As an

added benefit, caulking interior joints will also cut down on drafts.

A common source of air infiltration is the gap around an interior electrical box. Remove the cover plates on switches and receptacles to look for any gaps, but for safety sake, you should first turn off the power at the breaker or fuse box. Gaps around the outside perimeter of a box can be sealed with plaster or drywall compound. Butyl or acrylic caulks can also be used, but never apply any caulk, sealant or insulation to the inside of an electrical box because serious injury or a fire could result. Special ready-made gaskets approved by the Underwriters Laboratories that fit in back of switch or receptacle plates are a safe and quick way to boost energy efficiency around electrical boxes. Air leaks are best detected on a cold, windy day when you can actually feel a flow of cold air. Some people use a lighted candle or stick of incense to detect and then pinpoint the sources of outside air infiltration. Gaps between the back of

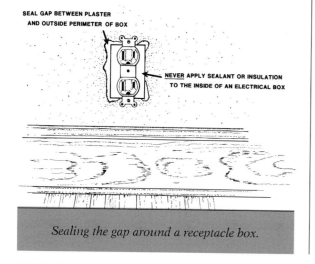

SEAL GAP BETWEEN PLASTER
AND OUTSIDE PERIMETER OF BOX

NEVER APPLY SEALANT OR INSULATION
TO THE INSIDE OF AN ELECTRICAL BOX

Sealing the gap around a receptacle box.

interior trim and walls are other common points of infiltration. Clear, silicone caulks are usually best for applications around natural wood trim.

WINDOWS

Window glass is responsible for more heat loss in a house than any other building material. Discussions about windows frequently include the terms "prime window," which refers to the principal window assembly that is permanently attached to the house, and "storm window," which is a removable extra window installed over the exterior of the prime window.

A single-pane prime window without a storm window may lose twenty times as much heat as an equal area of well-insulated wall. The addition of a storm window can cut the heat loss in half. Properly-fitting storm windows can also greatly reduce air infiltration, and hence drafts, which is vital to the comfort of the occupants during cold weather.

Wooden storm windows are preferable to those made of aluminum for energy conservation as well as aesthetic reasons. A wood frame, besides being historically appropriate for older houses, is a much better insulator than solid aluminum, which rapidly conducts heat away from a building. Another drawback of most aluminum and vinyl storms is that they cannot be easily shaped to conform to the many different types of curved and pointed window tops commonly found in houses built before 1940. In those cases, aluminum and vinyl window installers will usually make the opening fit the replacement storm, for example, by squaring off the top of

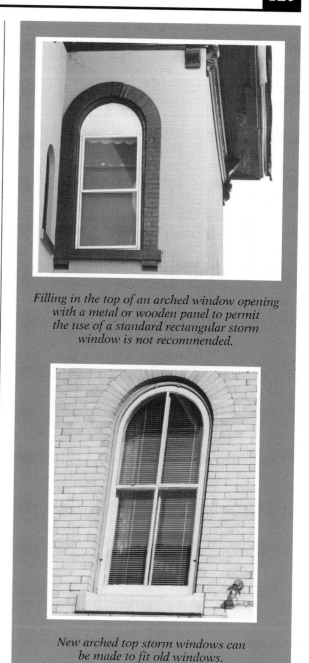

Filling in the top of an arched window opening with a metal or wooden panel to permit the use of a standard rectangular storm window is not recommended.

New arched top storm windows can be made to fit old windows.

a curved window with a solid piece of aluminum or plywood. This results in a clumsy appearance that detracts from the architectural character of the house. Wooden storms, on the other hand, can be made to precisely fit virtually any window shape by local manufacturers. Today it is increasingly popular to use wooden combination storms and screens that can be custom-made to fit older houses and which do not need to be taken down and replaced with screens in the summer, a major drawback of old wooden storm windows. Interestingly, combination storms and screens are nothing new. They were on the market at least by the late 1890s in Milwaukee, although, for some reason, they have only recently become popular.

A modern wooden combination storm and screen window appropriate for use on older houses.

Despite their inherent drawbacks, modern, "triple track" aluminum storm windows which contain a self-storing screen, are useful to reduce air infiltration and will probably be the choice of many homeowners. Although they come in a limited range of factory-applied colors, many homeowners have chosen instead to use a quality, custom-mixed metal paint on the frames so that they can be made to coordinate with a wider range of exterior color schemes.

Inside-mounted storm windows are another way to upgrade the thermal performance of old wooden prime windows. Interior storms are usually custom-made to attach to the window frame or the inside surface of the window trim. One of the advantages is that the storms are completely invisible from the exterior, which is particularly important if you want to preserve the exterior appearance of the molding profiles of multi-paned prime windows. This will create the most authentic historic appearance, if that is important to you. Some manufacturers use plastic glazing instead of glass on their interior storms. Plastic has better insulation value than glass, but is more likely to yellow over time and to scratch from normal cleaning unless you ask for a more expensive scratch-resistant plastic material, such as Margard®.

You should be cautious about replacing your original prime windows with new prime window units if they are in good condition or are repairable. It has become very popular to replace old windows with new prime windows that carry confusing technical names such as "low-e" and "argon gas-filled" or "krypton gas-filled." In recent years, the most popular type of replacement window has a solid vinyl frame and is glazed with what is called "insu-

lating glass," which typically is made of two sheets of glass with a specially sealed air space of about 1/4" in between. The payback period for purchasing and properly installing these window units is very long and often not worth the expense when compared with the cost of improving the energy efficiency of existing wooden windows with storms and caulking. See the **"Wooden Windows"** chapter for a discussion of the techniques to economically and permanently restore even badly damaged wooden windows.

You need to be especially wary of trying to save money by using stock size replacement windows, since these rarely match the size of the old window, necessitating costly alterations to the window opening to make them fit. Having an entire window unit custom made to the exact size of the original opening is the best way to go, but that will significantly increase costs. Installing replacement window units that are smaller than the original opening, as is usually the case, involves extensive disturbance to the interior trim and plaster as well as awkward changes to the exterior siding and trim that can greatly alter the original appearance of the building and can be very labor intensive and costly. In short, the cost of installing replacement windows in stock sizes often carries many extra hidden costs and can greatly compromise the appearance of the building. Money spent replacing original windows to increase energy efficiency can usually be better spent on other projects that will have a much greater impact on the appearance and fuel consumption of the building.

Installing a new, insulating glass prime window is attractive because it does, in fact, have an R-value that can be several times higher

than a single pane of window glass. Do not be overly impressed by these figures, however, because even several times the efficiency of a single pane of glass is still not very much. Windows of any kind are basically an energy luxury in the sense that they lose considerably more heat than a comparable area of well-insulated wall. Insulating glass has been around a long time, and one of the chronic problems is that it is subject to the deterioration of the airtight seal that holds the vacuum or the special inert gases between the sheets of glass that boost energy efficiency. When the seals are broken, as can happen from long exposure to sunlight or repeated flexing and moving, the original high level of energy efficiency is lost and the glass may begin to fog between the layers. The only solution is to replace the whole unit, a task that is not only expensive, but often impossible if you have a window unit that is no longer in production. Some of the more expensive insulating glass, such as "low-e," derives part of its energy efficiency from a tinted coating on the glass that may be aesthetically objectionable for use on a historic house.

If you are really sold on insulating glass, one way to upgrade the energy performance of an old prime wooden window is to substitute a sheet of custom-made insulating glass for the old single thickness window glass. The sash, which is the movable frame that holds the glass, must be slightly modified in order to accept a piece of insulating glass, since the latter is about 1/2" thick compared with 3/16" for a standard sheet of window glass. It is usually not practical to install insulating glass in old true divided light windows with many small panes. In that case, a storm window is the way to go.

After the wooden sash are taken out and the old glass removed, the rabbet, the narrow lip or shoulder in the framing that holds the glass, must be routed deeper. The work can be done with an electric router and a chisel, although some restorers have disassembled the sash and ploughed out a deeper rabbet using a table saw. Insulating glass can be installed in the modified window frame like any other piece of ordinary window glass, but check with the window manufacturer about which glazing compounds are chemically compatible with the seal in the insulating glass.

STORM DOORS

Installing a wooden storm door can improve the energy efficiency of an older original wooden prime door. Historically, the use of storm doors was somewhat limited. Years ago, most homeowners did not want to obscure the exterior view of their finely paneled or ornamented hardwood front door with a storm door. As a result, most houses were built with a vestibule inside the front door. In today's homes these are often called an "airlock" entry. For today's energy needs, however, an appropriate wooden storm door may be desirable, particularly if your old house does not have a vestibule with an inner door.

In terms of energy efficiency, wooden storm doors, like wooden storm windows, are generally preferable to those made of metal. Modern steel security/storm doors that are often ornamented with cast aluminum ornamental grillwork are not historically appropriate for most older houses, so if you opt to install one of these, choose as simple and inobtrusive a design as possible. For Milwaukee houses built before about 1905, you might consider

installing one of the reproduction wooden combination storm and screen doors now available that feature decorative turnings and jig-sawn ornament. These doors feature an interchangeable storm window and screen insert, are energy efficient, and enhance the appearance of an entry as well. Many of these reproduction storm doors are available in oak as well as common softwoods. A hardwood storm door with a stained natural finish, however, is recommended only where the door will be substantially protected from driving snow and rain by a deep porch, since a natural wood finish will not hold up to direct exposure to the weather and will consequently have to be restained and varnished often.

Today's mass-produced wooden storm doors are stocked in standard heights of 6' 8" and 7' 0" and widths of 32", 34" and 36". Other sizes usually must be custom made, which, of course, adds to the price. For most houses built before 1935, particularly when the original wooden prime door is intact, it would be appropriate to install a wooden, so-called "full-view" storm door, which has a single large light that blocks very little of the view of the prime door. Although not as desirable as wooden ones, there are also aluminum storm doors of the "full-view" design available.

For security reasons, a storm door can be installed with fixed-pin hinges that will thwart any attempts to simply remove a locked storm door from the jamb. In place of safety glass in the door, which can be easily smashed, you may wish to substitute an unbreakable, scratch-resistant, clear plastic glazing such as Margard®. (For a discussion about plastic

Queen Anne Style (1885-1905).

Queen Anne Style (1885-1905).

Period Revival (1910-1930).

HISTORICALLY APPROPRIATE WOODEN COMBINATION STORM AND SCREEN DOORS.

Prairie Style (1905-1925).

Arts & Crafts Style (1905-1920).

Full View Style (1860-present).

THREE MODERN STYLE STORM AND SCREEN DOORS
THAT ARE NOT APPROPRIATE FOR USE ON AN OLD HOUSE

safety glazings, see the **"Windows"** chapter.) A storm door should be installed to fit snugly, but not stick in the door jamb. Some home-owners may wish to install a flexible, rope-like "compression bulb" type of weather strip which is stapled or nailed to the door jamb to seal any small gaps when the door is closed. The rope-like bead is flexible and will easily conform to round-top door openings.

WEATHERSTRIPPING

Weatherstripping windows and doors is another effective means of reducing air infiltra-tion. Weatherstripping has been in existence for over a century. Over time, older weather-stripping can lose some of its effectiveness, and new material may have to be installed. There are dozens of weatherstripping products avail-able today, most of which can be installed by the homeowner. Always try to choose products that are the least conspicuous and cause little or no permanent damage to historic materials.

For doors, the installation of bronze or brass, spring-type weatherstripping is still one of the most reliable and durable methods to stop air infiltration. At the bottom of a door, a

Ad from the 1877 Milwaukee City Directory for weatherstripping.

threshold and a door sweep may be installed to block drafts.

For weatherstripping windows there are many "quick fix" plastic seals and putty-like caulks that are used to block drafts. If you want to temporarily seal the inside perimeter of a window for the winter, consider using a removable rope caulk that is simply pressed in place by hand. Spring-type metal weatherstripping can also be attached to the bottom rail of a double-hung window. An alternative is an adhesive-backed, highly-compressible foam weatherstrip. You need to be careful when using many of the do-it-yourself plastic seals and foam strips on movable windows. Some of the products, if installed incorrectly, can actually prevent the window from closing properly. Often, air infiltration can be greatly reduced simply by installing a good-quality sash lock that draws the top and bottom sash together at the middle "meeting rails" to form a weather-resistant seal.

INSULATION

Do not automatically assume that any house more than fifty years old never originally had insulation. During the 'teens and 'twenties, in particular, architects and builders were exceptionally conscious of energy efficient design, and many insulation materials were introduced, such as woven flax insulation mats and insulating quilts which were placed in walls and ceilings. A popular energy conservation measure used in the nineteenth century was back plastering, which refers to lath and plaster which was applied between the wall studs and joists inside the wall to reduce heat loss. Back plastering was common in the better class of residential building into the early twentieth

century, but had fallen out of favor by 1910 as insulating quilts and mineral wools proved to be cheaper and more efficient. In houses that have been back-plastered, it is generally not cost-effective to try to retrofit them with new insulation because the remaining narrow air spaces in the walls and ceilings are too small and too difficult to reach to properly install the new insulation.

Flaxlinum insulation, a tightly compressed, waffle-like mat of flax plant fibers, was introduced around 1914 and remained popular at least until the 1930s. The insulation was made in at least four different thicknesses ranging from 1/4 inch to 1 inch and installed between wall studs during new construction. The R-value of flaxlinum is not presently known, although many years ago a manufacturer claimed the material was a significantly better insulator than a comparable thickness of pine lumber. Flaxlinum is not known to contain harmful chemicals or asbestos, and, because it is believed to be a reasonably good insulation

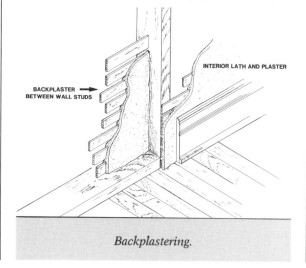

Backplastering.

material, there is usually no need to install additional insulation or remove it unless the walls are opened for other purposes.

Another type of historic insulation material used in Milwaukee between about 1890 and 1910 was a manufactured "insulating quilt" composed of dried eel grass sandwiched between outer layers of heavy duty building paper. Eel grass, a natural product which grows in salt water along the north Atlantic coast, was first used as insulation in America during the late seventeenth century when colonists packed it between the wall studs of frame houses. The excellent insulation value of dried eel grass and its remarkable longevity were rediscovered during the late nineteenth century, and, by the early 1890s, eel grass insulating quilts were a popular product. The quilts, which were installed between wall studs, were two inches or more thick, and, when they are found in place today, it is impractical and usually unnecessary to add extra insulation to the wall cavity.

If you do add insulation, you need to keep in mind that there is a point at which the addition of insulation is no longer cost-effective. This is because insulation has "diminishing returns," which means that although the first inch of insulation may be highly effective at reducing heat flow, the second inch will save only one-third as much as energy as the first. After about the eighth inch of insulation, the gains in energy savings per inch are negligible, and usually the cost of the insulation and its installation will not pay for itself.

Only exterior walls and ceilings that adjoin an unheated space need to be insulated. Interior partition walls and the ceiling

between "lived-in" floors of a building should not be insulated. Some heat loss does occur through basements, but an older brick basement wall has about twice the R-value of modern concrete block basements and is already pretty efficient. Installing good-fitting basement storm windows and insulating along the perimeter beam where the frame of the house rests on the basement wall will reduce drafts and heat loss.

Retrofitting an old house with new in-wall or attic insulation is a major project that requires extra care to avoid damaging the structure. There are three major types of insulation materials commonly used today in residential construction: loose fill, flexible blankets and batts, and rigid panels. When installing any of the loose fill or blanket types of insulation, be sure to wear gloves and a common dust mask to protect yourself from potentially irritating fibers in the material.

Avoid using any wet-mix, foamed-in-place insulation that is poured into a wall or ceiling cavity in a thick, paste-like form and then dries to the contour of the wall cavity. For retrofitting old houses, foamed-in-place insulation has been proven to cause more problems than it does good. This type of insulation subjects the wooden framing to extremely high levels of moisture that can cause problems with decay. Lingering odor problems have also been reported. The first generation of foamed-in-place insulation, called urea formaldehyde, has been removed from the market primarily because of the health hazards associated with the formaldehyde gas that lingers long after the material is in place.

The type of insulation you choose to install in an old house depends to a great degree on how accessible the wall or ceiling cavity that needs to be insulated is. Homeowners should realize that there are several different types of loose fill, blanket, and rigid foam insulation materials, and that each has its own insulation qualities, costs, and uses. Loose fill insulation is made to be poured into wall and ceiling cavities or blown-in through small access holes with special machines. When insulating existing closed walls and ceilings, loose fill insulation is usually the material of choice. Flexible blankets and batts are used when the wall or ceiling cavity is fully accessible, such as might be the case in an unfinished attic or in a room where the interior

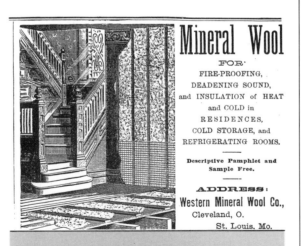

Mineral Wool

FOR

FIRE-PROOFING,
DEADENING SOUND,
and INSULATION of HEAT
and COLD in
RESIDENCES,
COLD STORAGE, and
REFRIGERATING ROOMS.

Descriptive Pamphlet and
Sample Free.

ADDRESS:
Western Mineral Wool Co.,
Cleveland, O.
St. Louis, Mo.

Mineral wool insulation made from molten slag was already a popular material when this advertisement appeared in 1890. Mineral wool was used not only for insulating purposes but also for deadening the transmission of sound between floors. One manufacturer claimed that 40 million pounds of its mineral wool had been installed by 1890.

walls have been stripped of their plaster and lath for some reason. It is never cost effective to strip interior wall plaster or all of the exterior siding and sheathing simply to install new insulation. Such a destructive approach would have to be justified by severe and almost total plaster deterioration or a desire to drastically reconfigure the interior room arrangement. Following is a discussion of the different types of insulation and their uses.

LOOSE FILL

Much of the loose fill insulation in use today is made of several different types of materials collectively called mineral wool, which includes rock wool, slag wool, and fiberglass. Each of these products looks similar, but their physical properties and insulating values can vary considerably. Mineral wool is made, in the simplest process, from molten rock that is passed in front of a high-velocity steam jet. This process converts the liquid rock to soft, thread-like fibers that solidify in a wool-like mass which contains the many tiny air pockets that give the mineral wool its insulation value. Rock wool was originally made from molten granite rock. Slag wool was made from molten "slag," which is a by-product of steel manufacturing. Rock and slag wool can range in heat resistance from R-2.1 to R-3.8 per inch depending on the manufacturer and the material. Slag wool was among the earliest types of loose-fill mineral wool insulation materials and was available in Milwaukee for residential construction at least by 1893. The process of making mineral wool from molten slag was invented about 1875 in Germany. By 1881, at least two mineral wool manufacturing plants were in operation in America, and tests at that

time showed that 2 inches of mineral wool was as much as six times more efficient as an insulator than a 2-inch air space in a wall.[2] During the early 1880s, manufacturing break-throughs improved the quality of mineral wool and reduced its cost. By 1885, mineral wool was used extensively as an insulation material in building construction.[3] It is quite likely that some of Milwaukee's surviving late 1880s vintage homes were built with mineral wool insulation that is still in place today.

Another type of mineral wool which is almost a household word today is fiberglass. Although it is made by nearly the same process as the other mineral wools, it is composed of different inorganic minerals. When fiberglass is used as loose-fill or blown-in insulation, its heat resistance per inch is only R-2.2, but when manufactured in the more familiar roll form, it is commonly rated at R-3.2 per inch.

Cellulose fiber has become one of today's most popular loose fill insulation materials because of its reasonable cost and relatively high insulation value. Made of shredded, recy-cled newsprint or wood pulp and treated with chemicals to retard flammability, cellulose insulation is similar in consistency to loose fill mineral wools. Like mineral wools, cellulose insulation has been manufactured since the late nineteenth century. The R-values for cel-lulose are impressive and range up to about R-3.8 per inch. This value will vary depending on the manufacturer and how the material is used and installed. Cellulose that is blown into a wall will rate a slightly lower R-value than the same thickness materials blown into an open attic floor. Nevertheless, cellulose can rate R-13 in a 3-1/2" wall cavity, which is just

as good as a comparable thickness of fiber-glass batt or blanket insulation.

Machines for blowing insulation into walls and attics can be rented by the homeowner, but the job should really be done by a profes-sional contractor who has a good track record of working with older houses. An insulation contractor should work with the homeowner to determine how to install the insulation with the least damage or alteration to the wood sid-ing, brick or interior plaster.

Installing blown-in insulation involves drilling small holes about every 16 inches near the top of a wall to gain access to the hollow areas between the wall studs. You have the option of drilling the access holes in either the interior plaster or the exterior siding. Exterior access, however, is really not practical if the house is veneered with brick or stone. Because most older houses in the Milwaukee area are built using the so-called balloon frame method (see **"Wood, Siding and Trim"** chapter), there is usually one continuous space between the studs from the foundation to the attic unless interrupted by doors or windows. Often at least some of the insulation can be blown in through small holes drilled inconspicuously in the attic. Ultimately, how-ever, at least some holes will have to be drilled directly into a wall to reach all pockets between the studs and under windows. If access holes must be drilled in exterior wooden siding, it is best to remove one row of clapboarding and then drill holes into the wooden sheathing. The holes should later be plugged and a new piece of matching, wooden siding installed to cover the work area. Some insulation contractors drill directly through the wood siding and then later install wooden

plugs, but this is not desirable because the plugs are often highly visible, even after paint-ing. You should not allow this to be done to your wood sided house.

Drilling holes directly through the exterior siding to permit the installation of blown-in insulation is a poor practice.

Regardless of the type of blown-in loose insulation material you choose, it is essential to create an acceptable vapor barrier on the warm, or lived-in, side of exterior walls. The problem with loose fill insulation is that it usually must be blown into the wall cavity without a vapor barrier, which can be risky because of the potential for creating conden-sation inside the walls that can rot the sills and framing members.

One method of creating a vapor barrier, and perhaps the most cost-effective, is to apply a good-quality, oil based, interior wall primer on all inside walls and ceilings. This can be done as part of an interior renovation. Water vapor cannot easily penetrate the oil-base primer if it is thoroughly applied. Any

type of finish paint, such as latex or oil base, gloss or flat, can be applied over most oil-base interior primers. It is also necessary to pay special attention to sealing points of air infiltration on the interior, such as gaps around electrical boxes and cracks at the trim around windows and doors. In areas of high humidity such as bathrooms and kitchens, you might consider not only using the oil-based primer but also the installation of vinyl wallcoverings which are non-permeable to water vapor. Applying an oil base primer is coincidentally an excellent means of preparing a wall surface for the application of wallpaper. Another way to deal with excessive interior moisture in baths and kitchens is to install a new, high efficiency ventilation fan that is ducted to the exterior, but this is only practical to do if the exterior vent hood can be installed so as not to be visible on a primary elevation.

BATTS AND BLANKETS

Mineral wool insulation, and in particular fiberglass insulation, is commonly made in long, continuous, "blankets," which are 20 feet or more in length. When the insulation is factory-made in shorter lengths up to 8 feet, it is called "batt" insulation. The basic manufacturing process for batts and blankets is the same as for loose fill mineral wools. Batts and blankets are sold in three forms: foil-faced, paper-faced, and unfaced. The facings, which are applied on one side of the batt only, serve as vapor barriers. Unfaced insulation requires the installation of a separate vapor barrier, such as a polyethylene sheet. Both batts and blankets are made in a variety of widths, usually 12, 16 and 24 inches, to fit snugly between studs, rafters, and joists. When installing batts and blankets, care should be taken not to

compress them because this will reduce their R-value rating. This means that a 6-1/4-inch-thick batt rated at R-19 will perform at a much lower R-value if it is crammed into a 3-1/2-inch-deep wall cavity. The R-values for different types of mineral wool batt or blanket insulation will vary and so will the prices. White wool, for example, has one of the best R-values of all batt and blanket insulation, but it may not be readily available to many homeowners. Fiberglass is still probably one of the best insulation materials available in batt and blanket form for its cost.

RIGID FOAM

In recent years, it has become common in new construction to use rigid foam sheets as high-yield insulation material that also substitutes, in most instances, for traditional wooden wall sheathing. There are at least four common types of foam board insulation's now on the market: expanded polystyrene, extruded polystyrene, polyurethane, and polyisocyanurates. Each has different properties and cost. Expanded polystyrene and extruded polystyrene have maximum heat resistant values of about R-5 per inch. Expanded polystyrene is probably the cheapest of the four and is usually white in color. Extruded polystyrene, better known as Styrofoam® brand insulation made exclusively by the Dow Chemical Company, is a widely used material recognizable by its blue color.

Foam boards made of isocyanurate and urethane plastic can have insulation values as high as R-9.7 per inch, but typically the materials will undergo a reduction in R-value after aging. Standard thicknesses range from 1/2 inch to 2 1/4 inches. Manufacturers usually

list R-values at the time of manufacture and after an aging period. Polyisocyanurates have the best insulating qualities of all commercially available insulation products.

The use of rigid foam boards for rehabilitation projects is, of necessity, comparatively limited since it requires the wall cavity to be completely opened up to install the rigid boards. Rigid foam insulation is sometimes applied over old wooden siding as a base for a new layer of siding made of either vinyl or aluminum. This type of application is not recommended because it destroys the architectural character of a house by adding a clumsy-looking layer to the exterior of the building that obscures architectural details,

Installing rigid foam insulation over wood siding is not recommended because it destroys the historic character of the building and can lead to structural deterioration.

results in recessed windows, and increases the potential to trap water vapor in the walls because of the particularly dense nature of the insulation. Another drawback is the fact that carpenter ants are attracted to foam insulation as a nesting place because the material has the same consistency as soft wood, which is the usual nesting place for these insects.

Rigid foam insulation can be useful in combination with fiberglass batt insulation when finishing off an attic space in an old house. Foil-faced foam board can be attached to the exterior wall studs or rafters after the fiberglass batt insulation has been installed between the rafters. The foil facing is a vapor barrier which should be installed facing the inside or lived-in side of the room. Gypsum board can then be installed directly over the rigid foam. However, installing gypsum board over rigid foam insulation using screws or nails often results in wavy-looking inside corner joints, so great care must be taken in attaching drywall over rigid foam.

INSULATING ATTICS

Installing attic insulation is perhaps the single most common and directly beneficial energy conservation project not only because it reduces heat loss, but also because some homeowners want to convert an unfinished attic to living space. There are two different strategies for installing insulation depending on whether or not the attic will be finished and heated.

An unfinished attic that you plan to keep that way can be insulated with mineral wool batts or blankets or loose fill laid beneath the attic floor between the joists. If the attic does not have a finished floor, use mineral wool

batts or blankets with a vapor barrier that faces towards the living space. If you choose to install more than one layer of batt or blanket insulation, only the first layer nearest the living spaces requires an attached vapor barrier. Subsequent layers of insulation should be "unfaced." Although the space beneath an attic floor can be packed with lots of insulation, remember that after about the eighth inch of insulation, there is very little return in energy efficiency. If the attic has a finished floor that cannot be taken-up, and you are not planning to convert it to a living space, blown-in insulation can be pumped into the space between the floor boards and the plaster ceilings of the rooms below. You should never

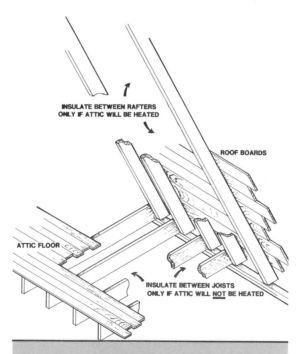

Attic insulation guidelines: insulate between the floor joists only if the attic will not be heated.

insulate between the roof rafters of an unheated attic if you already have insulation under the attic floor.

If you are planning to convert an unfinished attic to a heated, living space, insulating beneath the floor is not necessary or desirable. It is essential, however, to correctly install mineral wool batt or blanket insulation between the rafters, which are the sloping timbers that support the roof. It is particularly important to maintain a continuous air space of at least one inch between the insulation material and the bottom of the roof sheathing boards. Inexpensive plastic baffles, available at most homeowners' supply centers, are stapled or nailed between the rafters to create a permanent air space over which the insulation is subsequently installed. The baffles must provide a clear path for air to circulate from the soffit, which is the boxed-in area that forms the overhang on a roof, to the peak of the roof. If no air space is maintained and the cavity is simply packed full of insulation right against the roof boards, the service life of the roofing shingles can be substantially reduced, the roof sheathing may deteriorate and there can be problems with ice damming on the roof as well. Above all, be sure to install insulation with a vapor barrier facing the warm or lived-in side of the attic. ∎

FOOTNOTES

[1] Architectural specification sheet used during the 1890s by the Milwaukee architectural firm of Rau and Kirsch.

[2] **Scientific American Supplement,** No. 810, December 10, 1881, p. 4941.

[3] **Scientific American.** December 26, 1885, p. 402.

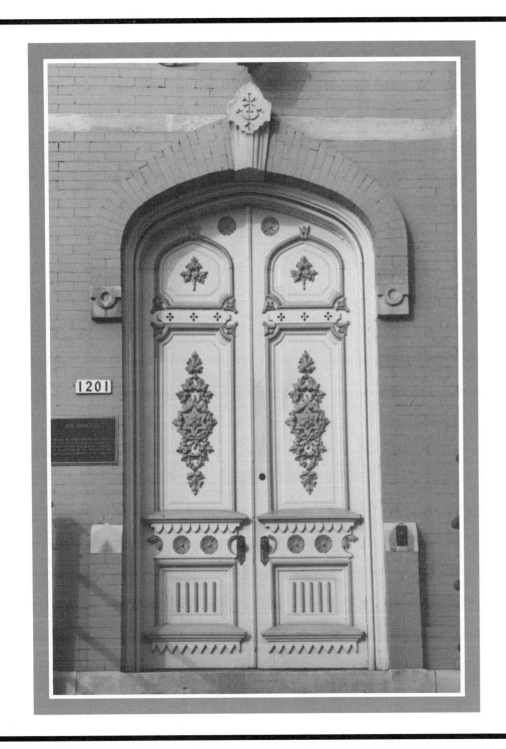

DOORS AND HARDWARE

DOORS AND HARDWARE

DOORS AND HARDWARE

DOORS AND HARDWARE

DOORS AND HARDWARE

DOORS AND HARDWARE

DOORS AND HARDWARE

DOORS AND HARDWARE

DOORS AND HARDWARE

DOORS AND HARDWARE

An elegant, paneled wood front door with finely crafted hardware is often one of the most admired architectural elements of an older house. Paneled front doors are still considered to be a mark of quality in fine homes built today. While new paneled doors of excellent quality are still available, there are very few manufacturers that have a design appropriate for use on a nineteenth or early twentieth century house. New paneled doors are also usually very expensive, making the preservation of an original door highly desirable from both an economic and a historic perspective. Door systems are composed of three elements: the door, its frame, and its hardware.

DOOR FRAMES

The sides of the finished frame within which the door hangs are called jambs. The horizontal member forming the top of the door opening is called a head jamb, and the two upright members forming the sides are called side jambs. Exterior door frames in older houses usually have a wood sill, the horizontal member forming the bottom of the frame. On top of the sill a beveled piece of wood or non-rusting metal called a threshold is usually installed to seal out weather leaks under the door.

Although no longer done in modern construction, historically thresholds were also installed on interior doors to reduce drafts, especially in houses that were originally heated with wood and coal-burning stoves rather than central heating systems. Years ago an interior threshold was an important energy conservation feature because it was a common practice to heat only selected rooms during the winter months. Interior sills should be

retained or replaced in older houses, not only because they still function as draft-reducers, but because they often cover unsightly joints in the finish flooring. Often thresholds are removed in older houses to facilitate the installation of wall-to-wall carpeting which itself then acts as a type of threshold.

OLD DOORS

It is important to retain or accurately replace an original door because its design is usually an integral element in the overall architectural style of a house. Paneled doors were the norm for all styles of houses from the nineteenth century until the late 1930s.

The earliest type of door in common use in Milwaukee was the four-panel door consisting of two short lower panels and two tall narrow upper panels separated by a wide middle or lock rail. This basic four-panel configuration comprised the most prevalent interior and exterior door design in use from 1855 to 1900. When in doubt, this type of door is the one you should consider using if you need a replacement for a missing original front door for almost any house built during this period, unless there is strong evidence of the original design of the missing door.

Doors of this type with round-arched panels held in place with large rolled moldings nailed to the frame were characteristic of the Italianate style which was popular from the 1850s through the mid-1870s in Milwaukee. Doors trimmed with extensive jigsaw decoration and applied moldings were typical of the Victorian Gothic, Eastlake, and High Victorian Italianate styles of the 1870s and early 1880s. Queen Anne style doors of the

1880s and 1890s departed from the four-panel format and are often embellished with a random patchwork of small, raised wooden panels mixed with glazing.

Often the front entrances of larger houses built between 1870 and 1895 had doubleleaf doors, frequently with the upper panels glazed. Entry doors of the later 1890s and early 1900s were often characterized by having only a single broad lower panel surmounted by beveled or leaded glass windows with carved, Neo-Classical style wooden ornaments applied to the rails and panels for decoration. In the early twentieth century fully glazed front doors became common. Paneled doors of various types were popular until the 1940s when flush doors began to assume the dominant spot in the market place that they still hold today.

Since World War II, the flush-surfaced door has become the most prevalent type. It is the most widely available exterior and interior door manufactured today. These doors reflect the machine aesthetic of the modern movement and are not compatible with the handcrafted architecture of older houses. Often these doors are touted for their energy efficiency because they are now usually made of metal with a core of insulating material such as foam or a wood product. Although the central core of a metal-clad door may have a good insulation value, the metal skin is itself very conductive and can bring the overall energy performance of a door down to a very ordinary level. To reduce conductivity, some metal doors are "thermalized" by separating the warm, inside metal surface of the door from the cold, outside surface through the use of a continuous insulating strip called a "thermal

Early Victorian (1855-1875).

Italianate (1860-1875).

Italianate (1870-1880).

Victorian Gothic (1875-1885).

HISTORIC DOOR STYLES IN MILWAUKEE

Victorian Gothic (1875-1885).

Queen Anne (1882-1895).

Queen Anne (1882-1895).

Queen Anne (1882-1895).

Queen Anne (1890-1905).

Queen Anne (1890-1905).

Late Queen Anne (1890-1905).

Colonial Revival (1895-1910).

HISTORIC DOOR STYLES IN MILWAUKEE

Colonial Revival (1900-1915).

Tudor Revival (1900-1915).

Early Twentieth Century (1900-1920).

Early Twentieth Century (1900-1920).

Arts & Crafts (1905-1920).

Arts & Crafts (1905-1920).

Prairie (1905-1930).

Craftsman (1910-1930).

HISTORIC DOOR STYLES IN MILWAUKEE

Colonial Revival (1900-1940).

Georian Revival (1900-1930).

English Cottage (1920-1940).

Tudor Revival (1915-1940).

break" made of plastic or rubber. With the addition of a storm door and weatherstripping, an old solid wood door can usually provide an acceptable level of energy efficiency. Energy conservation should never be used as the sole reason to replace an original front door. See the **"Energy Conservation and Insulation"** chapter for more information about wooden storm doors.

A basic four-panel door suitable for use on many nineteenth century houses.

PANEL DOORS

Panel doors are assembled from vertical members called stiles and horizontal components called rails which frame and support the panels. To allow for the seasonal expansion and contraction of the wood, the panels are designed to float freely without glue or nails in slots cut into the stiles and rails. Never glue wooden panels into the slots during the restoration of a door, or the panels may later crack. Stiles and rails were historically joined with sturdy, mortise and tenon construction, which relies mainly on the strength of the wood rather than on glues or nails. A tenon is

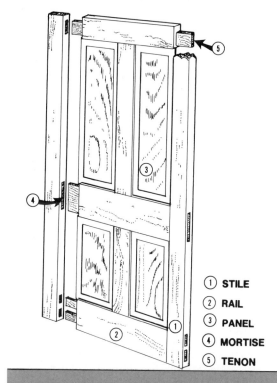

1. STILE
2. RAIL
3. PANEL
4. MORTISE
5. TENON

Frame and panel door construction.

the narrowed end of the rail which fits snugly into a pocket, called a mortise, in the stile. A damaged or deteriorated tenon can cause a door to sag. An alternate method of fabricating paneled doors is through the use of stiles and rails joined with glue and dowels. This is a quicker and less expensive method of making a paneled door, and most paneled doors today are constructed this way.

Older doors were made in a much wider range of sizes and thicknesses than is common today. The standard height of mass-manufactured doors today is 6'-8", and any other height is generally only available on a custom-order basis. Older doors were usually made in heights from 6'-6" to 7'-6" but other sizes were commonly available. Perhaps the most typical height for both interior and exterior doors on the first floor of older houses in the Milwaukee area is 7'-0". Doors on the second floors, where ceiling heights are usually lower than the first floor, are often 6'-8".

In older houses, interior doors are usually 1-3/8" thick and exterior doors are 1-3/4" thick, although exterior doors 2-1/4" thick are not uncommon. Be aware that replacement hardware such as locks and deadbolts may be difficult to purchase new for doors in excess of 2" thick.

Although some exterior doors were made of solid hardwood, many older doors were made of top-grade softwoods such a white pine or cypress that machined easily and would hold a grained or painted finish. High-quality mahogany, which is very stable and weathers extremely well, has long been considered an excellent wood for exterior door construction.

When a hardwood finish such as oak or ash was desired, often only the panels were of solid hardwood construction and the stiles and rails were frequently thickly veneered with the desired hardwood over a softwood core. Softwoods are more stable for door construction than hardwoods, which have a greater tendency to warp and twist over time.

During the 'teens and 'twenties, it was not unusual for exterior doors to be mass-produced in more unusual species of hardwood such as "gum," which has a reddish-brown color and a distinctive grain that accepts a fine, natural finish. Gum wood was principally used as a veneer in door construction, and it should last as long as any of the other more common hardwood veneered doors.

One of the most significant changes in door manufacturing was brought about by the advent of plywood. Plywood is composed of multiple thin layers of wood veneer glued together under pressure to form a thicker sheet. Beginning about 1890, some manufacturers began using flat plywood panels instead of solid wood raised panels in doors. Although it was not possible to machine a beveled decorative edge in plywood panels, the material was less subject to cracking and was stronger than solid wood. Until the early 1920s, the manufacture of door panels was one of the principal uses for plywood. Many early twentieth century houses feature interior doors with large, flat plywood panels often veneered in oak or other hardwoods. Early plywood panels sometimes did not hold up well in wet exterior locations because the glue used to laminate the layers of wood veneer was not waterproof. The development of waterproof glues during the early 1920s paved the way for the manufacture of plywood for use on exterior doors.

Exterior entrance doors for houses were usually finished with faux-graining or had a stained and varnished hardwood outer veneer before 1920, although paint was used on the front doors of some Colonial Revival style houses as early as 1900. Prior to 1880 and after 1920 there was a wider range of finish treatments in use because hardwoods were less commonly used in door manufacturing and the natural wood look was somewhat less fashionable at these periods.

If your exterior door is painted, but made of a high quality hardwood such as oak, ash, birch or cherry, you might want to strip the paint in order to restore a natural finish. Stripping the wood is not advisable, however, if the surface seems to be severely weathered and scarred by many small cracks and splits called "checking." You should also be aware that because of years of exposure to sunlight and weather, the outside face of a completely stripped exterior hardwood door will usually finish to a darker tone than the interior side. Prolonged exposure to water can cause black stains on oak that are very difficult to remove because they usually penetrate deep within the wood. Water stained areas will also show up much darker after stain or sealers are applied.

To properly restore a natural finish on a door, all traces of paint must be thoroughly stripped from the wood. Use chemical strippers that are recommended for removing paint and old stain from the small pores of the wood grain or take the door to a qualified wood stripping company. Many restorers use the combination of a heat plate and chemical strippers to strip hardwoods. (See the **"Wood, Siding and Trim"** chapter for information about stripping wood.)

If a door has a natural wood surface that has weathered, it may be possible to use a stripper that removes only the old, deteriorated varnish or shellac leaving the old stain intact in order to apply a new, clear, exterior sealer. Solvent-based polyurethane sealers have been widely used in recent years for natural wood finishes that are exposed to the weather. Today, new, water-based polyurethanes, which have little of the odor and volatile chemicals associated with solvent based products, are becoming increasingly popular. Water-based polyurethanes dry crystal clear unlike solvent based polyurethanes that have a slight yellowing effect on natural wood. Water-based polyurethanes are new and little is known about their longevity, but they are faster and easier for a homeowner to apply and the brushes can be cleaned with water. Both types of polyurethanes are excellent products, but make sure that any sealer you apply to an outside door is approved for exterior use.

COMMON PROBLEMS WITH OLD DOORS

Several problems can inhibit the proper functioning of older interior and exterior doors. Among the most common complaints are that the doors stick, do not open or close due to swelling or warping, or the lock no longer properly engages the strike plate making the door difficult to keep closed. Loose hinges can cause a door to sag and stick. If the hinge screws cannot be tightened, longer

screws can be substituted or wood plugs, such as wood match sticks (without the heads) can be driven into the holes and the original screws reinserted. If partitions that adjoin the door frame settle or shrink, the frame may move slightly and carry the strike plate with it while the door and lock remain fixed. This will cause the latch bolt to strike the plate instead of entering the hole in the plate making it impossible to lock or latch the door. The only remedy for a strike plate out of alignment is to move it or file the opening in the plate until it is large enough to accommodate the bolt and strike in the lock. Old door frames often show evidence that the strike plate was moved one or more times to compensate for settling. This may leave the jamb area around the strike plate with a rough, unsightly appearance. The disfigured wood can often be filled with epoxy patching compound, sanded and then repainted.

Moisture penetration is the principal cause of warping or twisting in an old exterior door. All sides of a door, particularly the end grain at the bottom, should be appropriately sealed and finished, because even small amounts of moisture penetrating through bare wood can cause the best made doors to warp and twist. It is a practice among some modern carpenters to immediately paint the inside of a freshly bored hole for a lockset in a new door in order to seal out moisture that could otherwise penetrate the door even after other visible surfaces are finished. This technique could extend to the restoration of an old door as well when the hardware is removed.

Stripping off old paint and using epoxy restoration techniques can do wonders to restore the appearance of a gouged or marred old exterior door and jamb. When repairing dents or gouges it should be kept in mind that epoxy must be applied to bare wood, so at least some paint stripping and light sanding may be required to properly prepare the surface for the epoxy, even if you intend to repaint the door. Doors that are severely weathered with multiple layers of peeling paint should be completely stripped to bare wood before proceeding with epoxy repairs or repainting. Doors can be worked on while they are hanging in place, but removing them from the jamb generally makes the job easier. If complete paint removal is necessary, a door can be sent to a commercial paint stripping company. The dip-stripping method may loosen glue joints, however, so it is usually preferable to select a process where the stripper is applied by brush or spray.

Once the surface to be repaired has been stripped to bare wood, epoxy consolidating and patching materials can be applied to repair any cracks, dents, gouges or holes from old hardware that detract from the appearance of the door and jamb. Sand and level the epoxy when dry. The repair should be invisible after painting. Some epoxies can be successfully stained to match the wood around the repair. Epoxy can also be used to rebuild small sections of molding or other missing decorative details on doors. It is sometimes easier and less expensive for restorers to attempt to resculpt a small section of molding from epoxy than to try duplicating a replacement section of molding in wood.

STICKING DOORS

In damp or wet weather, or if the humidity is particularly high inside a house, wood doors may absorb moisture which will cause them to swell and possibly stick or rub in the door jamb. Sticking points are often distinguished by worn areas in the paint or stain on the edges of the door. Doors may also stick in the jamb due to the settling of the house's foundation. If a sticking problem is seasonal, you may wish to wait for dry weather when the wood will contract and then paint or seal any bare wood on the door where moisture or water vapor is penetrating.

Planing the edges of a door may be necessary to remedy sticking caused by settling or shifting of the building. Planing is also a second-choice option to deal with a swollen door. Doing a proper job of planing the edge of a door takes a combination of skill and sharp tools. Many homeowners have made the mistake of using a dull-blade small plane on the edge of a door which creates a marred, ragged edge that not only looks unprofessional but often does not completely cure the sticking problem. Removing too much wood is another common pitfall. Improper planing can result in unnecessary air leaks and new weatherstripping may have to be installed on exterior doors to correct the problem. For most planing jobs, the door should be removed from the jamb, unless the area that needs attention is only a few inches long and near the top of the door. In order to do a proper job of planing a door edge, a large, long-bed plane such as a "jack plane" or an even longer so-called "jointer" plane has to be used in order to achieve a smooth straight edge. Many carpenters today use small, hand-held electric planers that produce remarkably smooth, straight edges on a door.

Whenever the edge of a door requires extensive planing, there is always the possibility that the hardware might have to be removed and then set deeper into the edge of the door. On some old doors, it may be easier to plane the hinge edge because hinges are easier to remove and reset than are old mortise locks on the other edge of the door. Many carpenters years ago, however, installed mortise locks so that about 1/16" could be planed from the lock edge without having to remove and remortise the lockset. Be aware that the lock edge of any door is beveled slightly to prevent the door from banging against the jamb as it is closed.

Used doors at a salvage dealer.

SALVAGED DOORS

Old wooden doors were typically well constructed and frequently outlast the life of the building in which they were originally installed. As a result, there is a good supply of salvaged doors available to restorers. It may be difficult, however, to find a door that is in perfect condition, fits precisely and is hinged

ONE THAT GOT AWAY. This photo, taken just before the demolition of a Milwaukee house in the 1930s, shows a richly-carved door, probably dating from the 1860s or 1870s that would be a restorer's dream today. Salvaged doors such as these are difficult to locate today and command premium prices.

on the required side. Keep in mind, however, that epoxy materials can be used to patch a myriad of imperfections such as lock holes or hinge mortises that are out of place. It is advisable to purchase a used door that is slightly larger than the actual opening so that you can trim the door down for a precise fit. If too much cutting is required, however, it can sacrifice the appearance and structural integrity of the door, so try to find a door close in size to the original. Removing more than one inch from the width of a door is not recommended. Before purchasing a used door, be sure to check it thoroughly for any warping by sighting down its edges and also examine the bottom edge of an exterior door for decay.

GETTING NEW HISTORIC STYLE DOORS

High-quality reproductions of historic style wood doors can be purchased by mail order from millwork companies specializing in historic woodwork. Before selecting a reproduction door for your house, do some research by looking at other houses similar to yours in the city that retain their original doors so you can find one of appropriate design.

Local millwork manufacturers are also capable of making custom, reproduction doors from your detailed shop drawings or clear, descriptive photographs. Because of limitations in the sizes and styles of mail order, historic style new doors, custom fabrication may be the only route to go in some cases if authenticity is very important. Wood doors with round-arched panels and moldings, such as might be found on an Italianate style house, for example, will probably have to

Lisbon Storm and Screen Company.

be custom-made. Admittedly, it is easier for most homeowners to shop for a door from a catalog than to have detailed drawings made for a custom manufacturer to follow. Shipping costs, however, can significantly boost the price of a mail-order door.

Reproduction doors are generally expensive, as is all specialty millwork, whether it is of modern or historic design. Be sure the doors are made from clear, straight-grained lumber that has been properly dried. Using quality wood is vital to reduce the potential for warping and twisting. See the **"Wood, Siding and Trim"** chapter for a discussion about the selection of wood. Don't be afraid to ask a millwork manufacturer about the quality and species of the wood used to make the door.

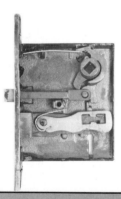

A typical cast iron mortise lock, shown here with its side panel removed, is surprisingly simple and inexpensive to have repaired by an experienced locksmith.

"Hanging" a door, which is a trade term for installing it, is a job for an experienced carpenter. Close tolerances must be observed, and many carpenters have special tools and

jigs that speed the installation and accuracy of the job. Installation of old-style mortise locks in a new door is also time consuming and not a job for an amateur. Some carpenters make a specialty of hanging doors.

HARDWARE

The unmistakable soft, golden glow of properly refinished brass and bronze decorative door hardware attracts attention like few other architectural details. In years gone by, exuberant hardware designs were also executed in other metals as well such as cast iron and steel. Hidden from view, but no less important, are

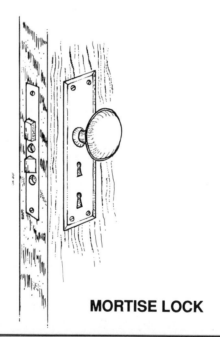

MORTISE LOCK | **RIM LOCK**

A mortise lock is installed in a pocket, called a mortise, cut into the edge of a door. A rim lock is mounted on the surface of the door.

the mechanisms that latch and lock the door. Collectively, the lock assembly, door knobs and trim plates (also called escutcheon plates) are called a lockset. The fact that many interior and exterior locksets still function well after 100 years or more of service is a testament to the quality of their design and construction. Old locksets that do not operate properly generally need only surprisingly minor, inexpensive repairs to make them function like new.

TYPES OF LOCKS

There are two general types of older door locks: rim locks and mortise locks. A mortise

lock, by far the most common type in older houses, fits into a pocket, called a mortise, cut into the edge of the door. Rim locks, also called box locks, are surface mounted, often made of cast iron, and were generally used in basements, attics or other areas of secondary importance in a house. High quality reproduction Colonial brass rimlocks were installed in some costly Colonial Revival style homes built during the teens and twenties. Inoperable old mortise locksets or rim locks can usually be repaired at small expense. Many lock malfunctions stem from a worn-out spring or a broken piece of metal called spring steel inside the lock which can be easily replaced by a qualified locksmith. Although locksmiths do make house calls, it is usually quicker and much less expensive for a homeowner to remove the lockset and take it to a locksmith's shop.

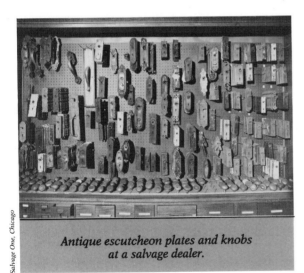

Antique escutcheon plates and knobs at a salvage dealer.

Salvage One, Chicago

The type of key used to open an old mortise or rim lock also tells something about its internal structure. An old style, so-called "skeleton key" is used to open a lever tumbler locking mechanism. On the other hand, the more complex cylinder-type locking mechanisms use the familiar blade-like keys that hang on our key rings today. There are three basic types of skeleton keys (traditionally called bit keys) that are used with old lock sets: the round key, which has a solid, round shank; the barrel key, which has a tubular shank with a hole in the end to fit over a guide pin in the lock; and the flat shank key, which has a wide, flat, knife-like blade with small notches. Local locksmiths can make new skeleton keys to fit old mortise or rim locks. If you do not have an original key to duplicate, you can remove the lock set from the door and take it to a locksmith's shop to have a new key custom-made to match the pattern of the lever tumblers.

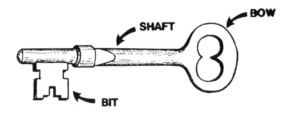

A typical bit key.

Generally, the old locks that provided the best security cost the most, which, incidentally, is also a general rule of thumb to follow when trying to evaluate the quality of a new lock set. The locking mechanism in an old lever tumbler mortise lock set for an exterior door is usually much more sophisticated than a mortise lock set intended to be installed on an interior door. The difference in complexity between mortise locks for interior and exterior doors is an important fact to keep in mind if you are trying to find an antique replacement for a missing, original skeleton-type key. You may be lucky enough to find an antique bit key that will operate a lock set on an interior door, but it is very unlikely that you will find, by chance, a key for an exterior door lock set, since these locks were made to satisfy much higher standards of security. When looking for any replacement skeleton keys, remember that many keys may close or "throw" the deadbolt in an old lock, but most will not easily open it, if at all. It is not unusual to hear the story of a homeowner who thought he found an appropriate replacement skeleton key for an old mortise lock, only later to find that the key would not open the lock after he was locked in a room with no other way out.

DEADBOLTS

A deadbolt, in the simplest terms, is a barrel bolt security lock that is operated by means of a key on either side of a door, or by a key from the exterior and a lever or turn button on the inside. An old mortise-style lock on an exterior door usually has a sturdy, built-in deadbolt, but if it does not work, it can usually be repaired by a local locksmith at a very reasonable cost. To increase the security of an older door, homeowners often install a second, separate, heavy-duty deadbolt made of hardened steel although this alteration should be thoughtfully undertaken. Deadbolts are designed to be installed on prime entry doors that are usually at least 1 1/2" thick, but not on storm and screen doors, which are much thinner in construction.

According to the Milwaukee Code of Ordinances, deadbolt locks are required on all tenant-occupied single family and duplex rental units in the city. This code rule does not apply to owner occupied units in duplexes and single family owner occupied homes. An old mortise lockset that has a built-in, operable deadbolt with a bolt that extends at least 1/2" beyond the edge of the door will comply with the code rule for rental properties, and it would then not be necessary to install a new, separate deadbolt.

There are two principal types of deadbolt locks: a surface-mounted rim lock that installs on the inside surface of a door and the mortise-style lock that is installed through holes drilled in the face and edge of the door. For most older doors, a traditional style mortise deadbolt is recommended because it is strong, readily available, and installs with less alteration to the inside trim and door jamb. Installation of a bulkier, surface-mounted deadbolt generally involves chopping out a piece of the interior door casing, which is often objectionable for aesthetic reasons.

It is a common practice to install a deadbolt that requires a key to open it from either side in order to prevent an intruder from smashing a pane of glass in a door and reaching inside to open the lock. Deadbolts that operate only with a key, however, can present a safety hazard in the event of a fire because time spent looking for a key to open the lock can delay or even prevent escape from a burning house. If you choose to fit all your entry doors with deadbolts that open from the inside only by key, always have at least one emergency deadbolt key readily available inside the house. Children in the household should know exactly where emergency keys are located. If an entry door is solid wood and does not feature any glazing, it is often recommended to install a deadbolt with an interior turn button. In situations where a door is glazed with ordinary window glass (not beveled or leaded), such as might be found on a plain rear entry door, it may be prudent to substitute a sheet of scratch resistant, unbreakable clear plastic such as Margard® (see **"Windows"** chapter) in place of the existing glass and then install a standard deadbolt with an interior turn button.

Price generally indicates the quality of a deadbolt. The most expensive deadbolts for residential use are smooth in operation, exceptionally strong, and highly resistant to being picked open. If you plan to use an existing lock on a door along with a new deadbolt, try to purchase a deadbolt that can be rekeyed to match the existing key lock. It is much safer and more convenient to use only one key to open a door. Ask a locksmith about the brands of deadbolts that are compatible with the type of key used in an existing lock. A locksmith can change the key pattern on most old and new locks for a modest price.

DOOR HARDWARE MATERIALS AND FINISHES

Brass and bronze have long been considered the premium metals for use on the visible parts of door hardware because each can be cast in fine patterns and buffed to a beautiful finish or plated with another metal such as silver or nickel. Door knobs made of glass, wood, and pottery were in fashion at various times during the late nineteenth and early twentieth centuries, but traditionally they were intended for installation on interior doors. If you find an old exterior door fitted with this hardware today, it probably is not original to the door, and brass, bronze, or iron hardware would be more appropriate.

Silver plated brass and bronze door hardware was fashionable from the 1840s into the 1870s for use in very costly homes. Some of the finest nineteenth century hardware was silver plated by a method known as hand-plating or close plating. A sheet of rolled silver was soldered to the brass article and then finely polished. Because of the thickness of this plating, it had good wearing qualities, but the process was labor-intensive and very costly. Electroplating has long been the standard method of plating metal. Electroplated finishes are very thin and can deteriorate over a period of years, but some metal finishing companies are capable of replating old hardware at reasonable prices with excellent

NASHUA LOCK CO.,
NASHUA, N. H.

MANUFACTURERS OF

Builders' Hardware,

FINE CASTINGS

—IN—

Bronze, Brass, & Iron.

Full Line of Samples and Goods may be found at

36 Pearl St., Boston, and 148 Lake St., Chicago, Ill.

As this 1885 advertisement indicates, fine quality ornamental brass and bronze hardware was particularly fashionable during the last quarter of the nineteenth century.

results. Although silver plated lighting fixtures can be found in Milwaukee houses, it is doubtful that any original silver plated door hardware survives today.

During the 1870s nickel plate over brass became a very fashionable finish for better-quality hardware. Nickel plating, which resembles silver but is somewhat grayer, became a symbol of quality and was so well known throughout the country that the celebrated New York, Chicago and St. Louis Railroad was nicknamed the "Nickel Plate Road" in 1881 because of the abundant nickel-plated trim used in its passenger cars. Nickel plating had faded in popularity by the turn of the century except for use in bathrooms. Many nickel plated finishes have held up well over the years, but those that are deteriorated should be replated rather than stripped to expose the solid brass base metal underneath, as has mistakenly been done by some restorers. Both nickel plate and silver plate tarnish unless the surface is sealed with a clear lacquer.

A very popular and common finish used in Milwaukee between 1885 and 1915 was copper plating. The warm, soft glow of burnished copper appealed to both the Victorian sensibilities of the late nineteenth century and the aesthetic yearnings of the followers of the Arts and Crafts movement in the early twentieth century. Copper electroplated on iron or steel will have often worn down to the base metal after years of use, requiring replating. A solid copper piece or copper deeply plated over higher quality base metals may only need refinishing to bring out its warm reddish luster. Copper will quickly tarnish if not sealed in lacquer after refinishing.

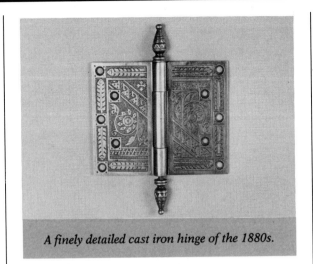

A finely detailed cast iron hinge of the 1880s.

The taste for rich ornamentation during the late nineteenth century produced a myriad of specialty finishes on hardware that today are often hidden by layers of paint and varnish. Excellent quality ornamental hardware was made in iron or steel with a finish known as the Bower-Barff process, which was named after the two Englishmen who developed it during the mid-nineteenth century. The process, which is not known to be in use today, created a lustrous soft-black or bluish-black finish that never needed painting by treating the metal with high temperature gases in a special furnace. Although the surface was somewhat rust-resistant, it was not rustproof and was best suited for interior applications. Exterior iron hardware finished by the Bower-Barff process, which was very common, is often found today in a corroded condition. The Bower-Barff process cannot be duplicated at present nor can it be convincingly imitated with plating techniques or paint. Deteriorated iron hardware originally finished by the Bower-Barff process should probably be painted a flat black.

Cast iron was a material that was extensively used for making door hinges. They were cast in a variety of very pleasing decorative patterns at low cost and were commonly used in even the most modest late nineteenth century houses. Hinges made of lesser grades of cast iron have occasionally cracked with years of use because the material is inherently brittle. As a result, older doors will sometimes be found with only one original cast iron hinge and a later, simpler, usually poor-fitting, replacement hinge. Reproduction cast iron hinges are available today and salvaged originals can be found, with some searching, at antiques and salvage dealers. Although cast iron is difficult to plate because of its porous surface, some old, high quality, cast iron hinges were successfully plated with bronze. Cast iron hinges had faded from popularity by the turn of the century as new, plain steel hinges proved to be much stronger, relatively inexpensive and easy to plate with bronze and brass. Milwaukee was a leader during the late nineteenth century in the production of so-called "thin wall" cast iron, which was a strong, high-quality metal that was vital to the production of thin pieces of finely detailed ornamental building hardware. This type of iron was better suited to accept a plated finish of brass or bronze than the coarser, rougher grades of ordinary cast iron.

HEMACITE

"A striking illustration of...American genius," according to a writer in 1888, was the production of molded, decorative door hardware from a newly invented substance called "hemacite." It is an unusual, historic hardware material popular during the 1880s that is

rarely found today. Hemacite was probably used for both interior and exterior doors in less expensive construction as well as utilitarian and secondary installations such as second floor bedrooms and carriage barns. The material was actually a mixture of blood from slaughtered cattle, sawdust, and some chemical compounds which was molded into door knobs under hydraulic pressure of 40,000 pounds per square inch. Hemacite was the invention of Dr. W. H. Dibble, a well-known, Jersey City, New Jersey dentist who patented his discovery in July of 1877. Hemacite hardware can still occasionally be found in old buildings today. Restorers and some antique dealers might mistakenly identify hemacite as wood. Unlike wooden door knobs, however, hemacite was usually finely detailed. Early tests of hemacite hardware indicated that it was water resistant.

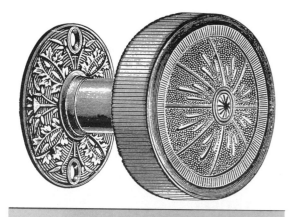

An illustration of a hemacite door knob dating from the late 1880s.

The natural color of hemacite after molding is ebony black, but it was also integrally colored seal brown, leather and terra cotta.

Hemacite hardware was sometimes plated with bronze, brass or nickel. Hemacite hardware was reputed to be exceptionally durable and "suitable for interior and exterior house trimmings as well as a vast variety of other useful articles." Because hemacite was transformed into an extremely fine powder before molding, it was capable of reproducing exceptionally fine details in finished hardware.

By the late 1880s, hemacite was most popular for door knobs and shutter and drawer knobs. At that time, one hundred different styles of door knobs were offered by the manufacturer along with a guarantee that the product would last as long as the door.

If you find hemacite hardware today, you should preserve it, particularly because of its interesting history. From a practical standpoint, there is probably little restoration that can be done to hemacite beyond a good cleaning or perhaps the removal of old paint. Nothing is known about the reaction of hemacite with modern cleaning chemicals and paint removers, so it is advisable to first make a small test cleaning patch on an inconspicuous area of the hardware.

REFINISHING OLD METAL DOOR HARDWARE

Brass, copper and bronze acquire a natural, brownish patina with age that some restorers may actually wish to preserve, although a polished finish is more dramatic. In its simplest form, restoring a gleaming finish to tarnished copper, bronze and brass hardware involves polishing the metal with high-speed cloth and wool buffing wheels to which fine abrasive

buffing compounds have been applied. Wire buffing wheels, steel wool, and sandpaper are not recommended for use in restoring fine metals such as copper, brass and bronze. With patience and persistence, homeowners can do a fine job of polishing brass and bronze hardware, but for a like-new appearance, professional metal finishers or silversmiths may need to be consulted.

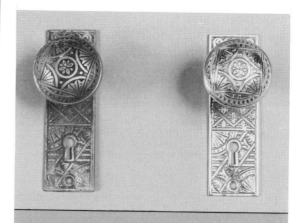

Bronze door hardware before refinishing on the left and after polishing and lacquering on the right.

Metal finishing craftspeople typically go through a series of steps to clean and polish metal that few homeowners can properly and safely duplicate. The process begins by removing any paint on the hardware by immersing it in a caustic bath of hot alkalis and then transferring the metal to a mild acid bath for deeper cleaning. Polishing follows by using buffing compounds of various aggressiveness to remove tarnish and minor imperfections. Metalsmiths frequently use very fine files to remove small scratches before buffing begins. After the initial buffing, the metal is soaked in another acid bath to remove any buffing com-

pound that may have been caught in the depressions of a decorative surface. Final polishing is done with a very soft finishing buff and fine grit buffing compound. To keep copper, brass and bronze from quickly re-tarnishing, the finished surface can be sealed with clear lacquer which is sprayed on and then baked in an oven to make the coating harder and more durable. An expert lacquer finish will not detract from the beauty of the bare polished surface and should last for years to prevent re-oxidation, depending on the wear the hardware is subject to.

Corrosion on cast iron and steel hardware can be removed by sandblasting or special cleaning acids used by "de-rusting" specialty companies. Both methods are acceptable from a preservation standpoint. It is vital to remove all rust from iron and steel because corrosion can continue to eat away at metal even under a thick coat of paint. After cleaning, iron and steel hardware must be quickly primed and painted in order to prevent the formation of new corrosion. Use a good quality primer for clean metal, and top it with an appropriate finish, which is usually flat or low-gloss black. Two-part epoxy paints are considered the best to use for exterior iron and steel hardware.

Some old steel and iron hardware was originally plated with bronze and brass. Over the years, this thin plating tends to wear away in spots and tarnish. Iron and steel hardware in otherwise excellent condition can be successfully replated today. Because of increased governmental restrictions on the chemicals used by plating companies, there are fewer plating firms today than in the past and fewer still that will be willing to do small plating jobs. Plating companies can be found in the local Yellow Pages.

REPLACING MISSING HARDWARE

To replace missing historic hardware, restorers can hunt for salvaged originals, purchase reproductions, or have copies custom-made from an original that may exist elsewhere in the building. It is generally preferable to use salvaged original hardware, but it may be difficult to find an exact match for the existing hardware pattern in an old house. Keep in mind that the volume of hardware patterns available at the turn-of-the-century was staggering. In 1899 the Yale and Towne Co., a major hardware manufacturer that is still in business today, needed a 900-page catalog to illustrate its complete line of door and window hardware. Many restorers choose instead to use antique replacement hardware that is reasonably close in vintage and design to the original hardware in the building, but not an exact match. Modern reproduction hardware, which is available from many vendors around the country, varies significantly in price according to quality. Bronze reproductions made in America are generally tops in terms of both quality and price. At the other end of the scale is the plethora of brass reproduction hardware made in the Far East, which is much less expensive, but typically also lacks the fine detail and meticulous finishing qualities that are associated with the antique, American-made hardware they were copied from. In between are various intermediate grades of reproduction hardware.

Door hardware such as escutcheon plates, knobs, doorbell push buttons, and hinges can also be custom-reproduced from an original by small foundries. This option is not as economi-cally infeasible as many people think and merits serious consideration in cases where the original hardware is particularly distinctive and it is impossible to find matching pieces any other way. Two general types of casting processes, sand casting and the lost-wax method, are used to reproduce hardware. Sand casting is relatively inexpensive and quick. Essentially the original is pressed into foundry sand to make a mold for molten metal to be poured into. The price is usually very affordable even when only one or two copies of an original are needed. Sand casting does not lend itself to the reproduction of very fine detail, but it is a good method to copy common decorative cast iron hinges or simply patterned brass or bronze items. Low cost reproduction brass hardware available as stock items is generally made by the sand-cast method.

Lost-wax casting, in low production runs, involves making a rubber mold from an original piece which is then used to make a duplicate of the hardware in wax. This wax "positive," which is a finely detailed copy of the original, is then coated with special clay and baked in an oven to dry the clay and simultaneously melt away the wax inside it leaving a hard, hollow mold into which molten metal is poured. Because the wax mold literally disappears, this process is called the lost-wax process. After the metal cools, the clay mold is broken away to free the casting which is then finished with grinding wheels, files, and finally buffed and polished. Lost-wax casting is used where reproduction of fine detail in premium metals, such as brass or bronze, is particularly important. To begin the process of custom-duplicating hardware, contact an artisan who works in cast metals or a small foundry. ■

Pouring molten metal into molds at a foundry. Cast bronze, brass, and iron hardware is made in this manner.

WOODEN WINDOWS

WOODEN WINDOWS

WOODEN WINDOWS

WOODEN WINDOWS

WOODEN WINDOWS

WOODEN WINDOWS

WOODEN WINDOWS

WOODEN WINDOWS

WOODEN WINDOWS

WOODEN WINDOWS

Countless wooden windows in Milwaukee area houses are well into their second century of reliable service. When properly restored and maintained, older window units are remarkably smooth in operation, preserve the historic character of the building, and can compare favorably with the energy efficiency of equivalent modern window units. Even severely deteriorated old windows can often be successfully rejuvenated with modern materials at a fraction of the cost of total replacement. Homeowners unaware of basic window rehabilitation techniques may needlessly replace repairable, original wooden window units with expensive, modern substitutes that are out-of-character with the style of their building and perhaps inferior in quality and durability to the old wooden windows.

Historically windows were an important component of the design of a house, and much attention was paid to their size, configuration and detailing by architects and builders. Other than being functional, windows were one of the major decorative elements that gave a house its architectural character. As a result, there were different styles of windows for each different architectural epoch. It is very important to maintain the same type of window your house was built with. Installing windows different in appearance from the originals can seriously compromise the design integrity of your old house. Although almost any style of window can be duplicated today, it is usually cheaper and easier to retain and restore the ones you have. This is especially true if your windows are unusual or particularly ornate or require a type of craftsmanship to fabricate that is not generally available today.

WINDOW TERMINOLOGY

The two most common types of traditional operable windows are vertical sliding and hinged. The most prevalent type of wooden window in older houses, the double hung, is composed of two windows, each called a sash, that slide up and down in separate channels. Sash that are hinged on a side and swing open like a door are called casement windows. Although most casements are made of wood, some early twentieth century casement windows were made of steel or iron. A window that cannot be opened is called a fixed window.

The frame of a sash is constructed of horizontal rails and vertical stiles. The two over- lapping rails in the center of a double hung window are called meeting rails, and they are specially beveled to form a weather-tight seal when they are fastened together with a sash lock. Muntins are the thin pieces of wood that divide the glass in some sash into smaller panes. The boards on the top and sides that frame the opening in the wall are called jambs. The sill is the bottom member of the frame and is sloped on the outside to deflect run-off water away from the building.

An old double-hung window is typically equipped with a counterbalancing system of ropes and pulleys that make it easier to raise each sash and hold it in a stationary position.

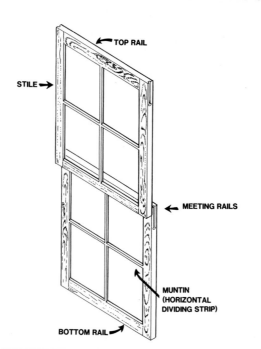

Double-hung window.

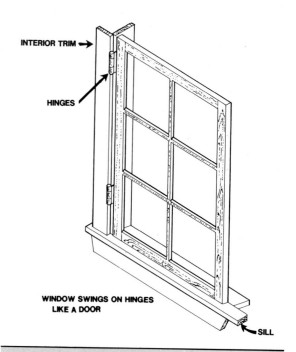

A casement window.

Previous Page: Window at 2734 E. Bradford Avenue.

Nearly all double-hung windows manufactured through the 1930s operate on a similar system of pulleys and iron counterweights. Typically, pulleys are built into the top of each side of the window jamb and carry a rope or chain connected to an iron weight at one end and the window sash at the other end. The weights are hidden out of sight in a pocket in the wall behind the jamb.

Although windows manufactured today typically utilize different systems, the pulley and counterweight system of balancing double-hung sash should not be discounted as inefficient or outdated. It is a long wearing, reliable system that, in many ways, is superior to modern counterbalancing systems. Compression sash guides are perhaps the most common components used today to hold moveable sash in place. They are also used to retrofit older windows and employ hidden springs that force a metal channel against the edge of the sash to hold the window open in any position as well as to act as a weather seal. Compression guides tend to lose their tension over time and periodically must be replaced. Most modern balancing systems must be replaced or repaired with each manufacturer's specific replacement parts, if they are still available. Because window companies change the design of their windows periodically, finding replacement parts for a particular model could be a problem in the future.

The quest for invention, coupled with a fascination for emerging technology during the late nineteenth and early twentieth centuries, produced some remarkable improvements to such traditional building products as the pulley and counterweight sash balancing system.

By the late 1880s, hardware manufacturers had introduced a spring-loaded sash balancing system that operated much like a modern retractable tape measure. It was installed at the top of the window unit in place of sash pulleys. Counterweights were eliminated and a flat, metal tape was substituted for traditional sash cord. Although this sash balance was smooth-operating initially, it was never very popular and apparently had a limited service life. Historic nineteenth century spring-loaded tape balances should be retained if possible. Broken balances might be repairable.

REPAIR VS. REPLACEMENT

Old wooden window units have several inherent advantages over modern replacement units made of aluminum or vinyl. The decorative exterior moldings that are a hallmark of many older wooden window frames cannot be economically duplicated in aluminum or vinyl. Older wooden windows were typically constructed of high quality, very durable lumber that is very difficult to replace today. Old wooden windows are generally homeowner-serviceable because wood is much easier to work with and infinitely more repairable and paintable than aluminum or vinyl. Aluminum and vinyl windows are made in a limited number of factory colors that may not be compatible with the color schemes that best enhance the architecture of older houses. Replacement parts for century-old wooden window systems including pulleys, counterweights and sash cords are still available today. Modern window units, on the other hand, often require the manufacturer's specific replacement parts, which may not be available in the future as

designs change and companies go out of business.

Windows are natural energy wasters, but we really can't live without them. Even modern, so-called high-efficiency window units still lose about five times as much heat as a comparable area of well-insulated wall. An original wooden window in proper working condition and fitted with a storm window will yield about the same energy efficiency as a modern, so-called "insulating glass" window unit. The basic restoration of a wooden window and the installation of a proper storm window will often increase its energy efficiency to a point where installing replacement windows is not cost effective. See the **"Energy Conservation and Insulation"** chapter for a more extensive discussion about heat loss through windows. Another drawback of high-efficiency window units is that the shapes of traditional wooden muntins often have to be enlarged to an awkward-looking size and shape in order to accommodate modern "insulating glass" which is much thicker than standard window glass.

Too often the decision to replace an original wooden unit is made before all of the repair options are considered. Careful planning is essential if a window restoration project is to be sensitive to the historic character of a house and make the best use of the homeowner's budget. The cost of installing modern replacement window units can quickly consume a budget, making it necessary to delay other projects and dampening a homeowner's enthusiasm for the rehabilitation process.

6 over 6 Colonial style window.

2-over-4 Italianate style window (1855-1875).

2-over-2 arched Italianate style window (1865-1875).

1-over-1 round head Italianate style window (1865-1875).

HISTORIC WINDOW STYLES IN MILWAUKEE

Pointed Victorian Gothic windows (1870-1885).

Arched top Victorian Gothic window with a hood mold (1870-1885).

Victorian Gothic window (1875-1885).

Queen Anne window (1882-1895).

*Queen Anne window
(1882-1895).*

*Landscape sash
(1885-1910).*

*Colonial Revival lattice
window (1890-1910).*

*9-over-1 Arts and Crafts
window (1900-1920).*

HISTORIC WINDOW STYLES IN MILWAUKEE

*4-over-1 Arts and Crafts
window (1900-1920).*

*Prairie style window
(1900-1920).*

*Leaded Tudor Revival
casement window (1915-1930).*

*Leaded Tudor Revival
window (1915-1930).*

A lunette window.

A frieze window.

An ocular window.

ORNAMENTAL WINDOW TYPES

An eyebrow dormer.

A lobed cameo window.

Piano windows.

Queen Anne gable sash.

An oriel window.

A Palladian window.

ORNAMENTAL WINDOW TYPES

Craftsman gable sash.

A boxed oriel window.

A bay window.

There are four distinct categories of work that can be done to a window unit depending on its condition.

1. **Routine Maintenance.** Windows that are structurally sound can usually be restored to working order and an acceptable level of energy efficiency with only minor repairs. Common, inexpensive projects include replacement of broken sash cords or glass, scraping and painting, installing new glazing compound, and replacement of broken sash locks.

2. **Structural Repair.** A lack of routine maintenance over the years can lead to serious deterioration and decay of the window unit. The presence of decay in a window unit does not mean it should be replaced. Modern wood epoxy restoration techniques can economically rejuvenate even severely damaged and decayed window units.

3. **Replacement of Sash Only.** The original moveable sash may be missing or damaged beyond repair, but the frame with its pulleys, counterweights, and exterior moldings may be intact. In this instance, new, wood replacement sash can be installed in the existing frames at a cost that is usually less than total replacement of the entire unit.

4. **Replacement of the Entire Unit.** As a last resort, when damage to the original window unit is too severe to permit consideration of any other alternative, new window units made to the exact dimensions of the old one and preferably made of wood to duplicate the look and material of the old units should be installed.

REMOVING SASH

For repairs more extensive than painting or inserting a new bead of glazing compound, the window sash should probably be removed from its frame. The lower sash can be withdrawn from the frame by simply prying off the interior stop moldings. Care must be taken to remove the stops without damaging either them or the window frame. Loosen the stop initially by working from the sash track side with a small pry bar so that any pry marks will not be visible. When the stop is loosened, it can be pried free from the front by using a pry bar buffered from the frame with a putty knife. Work up and down the stop in small increments. Ease the window out of the frame and detach the sash cords that are knotted in the sides of the sash. Never remove nails from a piece of finish trim, such as a window stop, by pounding them out from the back side. This will create large, unsightly nail holes on the finished surface that will have to be patched. Instead, use carpenters' nippers to pull the nails through the wood from the back side or else just cut them off.

The top sash in a double-hung window unit is held in place by a pair of thin, rectangular strips called parting stops that are set into grooves in the sides of the frame. In order to remove a parting stop without breaking it, the top sash must be lowered to the window sill. If the sash is stuck in place with layers of paint, as is often the case, carefully run a utility knife, thin putty knife, scraper or trowel down the seam between the stop and the window sash to break the paint bond. Also score the seam between the parting stop and frame and clear the track below the top sash of excessive paint buildup and dirt so that the sash will slide up and down easily. Grasp the bottom of the sash and wiggle it back and forth with a downward pressure to get it moving. Do not pound on the meeting rail of a stuck top sash to get it to slide down, as this may break its joints. When the sash moves an inch or so, it can be pried and pulled down from the top. With the sash seated on the sill, the parting stop can be carefully pried out by grasping it with the fingers of both hands and wiggling it out, working down from the top. The parting stop should never have been nailed or glued in place unless an earlier, improper repair was made. With one parting stop removed, the sash window can be withdrawn from the frame and the sash cords detached.

GLASS REPLACEMENT

Replacing window glass is a job that is always safer and easier when done with the sash removed. The window glass sold today, which is machine-made, may differ from the variety that was originally installed in an older house. In the nineteenth century, much of the clear window glass was made from hand-blown hollow cylinders that were subsequently cut, reheated, and flattened into sheets. This process imbued the glass with a wavy, slightly irregular surface that subtly distorts the image seen through it — a quality some restorers actively seek to preserve. Hand-blown window glass is still made for restoration projects, but it is costly and suitable mainly for buildings constructed before 1850. Some hand-blown glass may have a very slight curvature called a crown that is evident when looking down an edge of a larger pane of glass. The crowned side of the glass was typically installed facing the exterior for the

best appearance and to reduce the risk of breakage when the glass was being fastened to the sash. During the nineteenth century, window glass was regularly imported from Europe because glass manufacturing there seemed to be more advanced than it was at many American glass companies. American makers often graded their glass as AA, A, B, and stock sheets. Glass that was graded "AA" had the least imperfections and cost the most. Foreign glass makers had their own grading standards.

Manufacturing mouthblown window glass in the nineteenth century.

Old windows were typically glazed with either single strength or double strength glass. Single strength glass sold today is 3/32-inch thick and double strength is 1/8-inch thick. Because much old window glass was handmade it was not always of uniform thickness making it sometimes difficult for restorers

looking at the glass today to determine its strength. In the past, many builders limited the use of single strength glass to single panes no larger than 24 by 30 inches.

When thicker and sturdier glass was required for use in doors or large windows, plate glass was installed. Plate glass was not "blown" like regular historic window glass, but was made by pouring molten glass to a uniform thickness on a special iron table. When the liquid glass cooled into a flat, solid sheet, the surface was ground and polished to a fine finish. Cutting plate glass is usually a job for an experienced professional. Most historic and modern plate glass has a slight greenish tinge when viewed from the edge. Builders of the past who wanted a top-quality plate glass sometimes specified "French Silvering Quality," which is nearly silver-white when viewed from the edge. This grade of glass, because of its exceptional quality, is particularly worthwhile to preserve.

Window glass that is not cleaned regularly can acquire a hazy, cloudy, exterior surface after many years that cannot be restored with regular glass cleaners. Glass in this condition is too often replaced, or, worse yet, used as an excuse to remove the entire window unit and replace it with a modern substitute. A recommended, much less expensive, approach is to try using a professional glass restoration product such as X-19 Glass Cleaner and Restorer manufactured by American Building Restoration, a Milwaukee area firm. The liquid chemical is reportedly a blend of wetting agents and detergents that will remove haze and atmospheric pollutants. Before using any restoration chemicals, be sure to read all of the instructions thoroughly.

Removing old, rock-hard putty is one of the most time-consuming jobs in window restoration. Traditional putty is made from linseed oil and a material called whiting (calcium carbonate). A small amount of white lead or zinc oxide was sometimes added to the mixture to make the putty more durable. Putty could be made, according to one old recipe, from a mixture of 18 pounds of raw linseed oil and 100 pounds of dry commercial whiting. After mixing, the putty was allowed to age for two days. It was then mixed again with a little more raw linseed oil to obtain the proper working consistency. This type of classic hard putty, which can last a lifetime in a window, has been superseded today by glazing compound, which is a more elastic, softer material. Hard, old putty can be removed from a wooden frame with a small chisel, but care must be taken not to cut into the wood because doing so will result in a poor-looking reglazing job. Hardened putty can be softened by heating it with a soldering iron or a special iron made for such purposes. Using a heat gun will probably cause the glass in the frame to expand rapidly and break, unless the glass is shielded with an insulating material such as fiberglass. After the putty and glass are removed, the frame can be sanded, patched, and repainted. Although a belt sander works well to remove old paint, it can also create lead dust from the pulverized paint. Belt sanders must also be used very carefully to avoid unsightly gouging that can hamper the performance of the window when it is reinstalled. Disc sanders are particularly difficult to control and should be avoided if possible. Standard pad sanders have a tendency to cause a slight rounding of the narrow, flat surfaces on a window sash and should be used only with great care.

HOW TO REMOVE WINDOW SASH FOR REPAIRS.

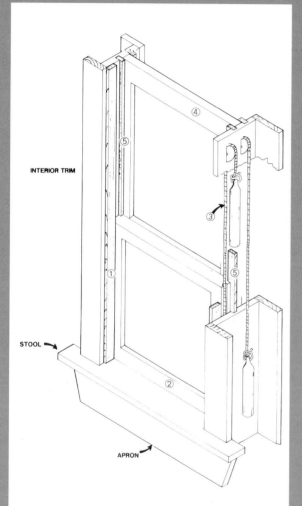

INTERIOR TRIM

STOOL

APRON

① STOP
② LOWER SASH
③ SASH CORD OR ROPE
④ TOP SASH
⑤ PARTING STRIPS

Remove the wood "stops" that guide the lower sash.

Pull the lower sash out of the window and rest it on the stool.

HOW TO REMOVE WINDOW SASH FOR REPAIRS.

Disconnect the ropes or chains that are attached to the sash.

Move top sash down until it seats on the sill.

Remove the wooden parting strips that are friction-fit into grooves in the window frame. Remove the remaining sash from the window unit and detach sash cords.

Before applying any putty or glazing compound to a wooden sash, the rabbet, or recess in the sash that holds the glass, should be painted with primer or coated with linseed oil. Dry, unprepared wood will quickly absorb the oils in glazing compound causing it to prematurely peel off. The paint or oil should be dry before the window is glazed. It is best to wait a few hours between priming and glazing if possible.

Measurements for replacement glass must be very precise. Glass that is too loose in the frame will not be weathertight. If the new pane is a little too large, it may be impossible to cut it down to size. Cutting a ribbon of glass 1/8-inch or smaller from an oversize pane is very difficult and seldom successful. Replacement glass should be cut about 1/8-inch smaller than the actual dimensions of the opening. This creates a margin of 1/16-inch between the edges of the glass and sides of the rabbet to allow for imperfections and expansion and contraction.

Before installing the glass, a thin bead of glazing compound no more than 1/8 inch thick should be applied to the rabbet on which the glass rests. This step is essential to promote a weathertight seal and, to a lesser extent, to protect the glass from breaking during installation. Using light, even pressure, the glass should be eased into the bed of soft, well-kneaded glazing compound until only about 1/16 inch of compound remains between the glass and the wood. This process is called bedding the glass.

Glass is held in place with small, triangular pieces of metal called glazier's points that are pushed or driven into the sash with a putty knife. If you are doing extensive reglazing work, you might consider using a special glazing stapler that can greatly increase the speed and accuracy of setting glazier's points. Reputty the sash after the glass is firmly secured. For a proper-looking job, the glazing compound should not project beyond the edge of the rabbet. Keep in mind that the imperfections in a sloppy putty job will be magnified by the finish coat of paint.

PLASTIC GLAZING MATERIALS

Clear plastic glazing, which is impact resistant, can be substituted for glass in windows and doors where security and safety are overriding concerns. The best plastic glazing materials are virtually unbreakable and difficult to distinguish from glass. Using the appropriate plastic glazing material in windows can eliminate the need for installing non-historic materials such as glass block, metal bars or grates, or, even worse, completely closing up a window or door opening.

Two major types of plastic – acrylics and polycarbonates – are commonly used for glazing purposes. Acrylic, the more common and less expensive plastic glazing material, is widely known by the popular Plexiglas® brand name, although there are other brands as well. Acrylics are impact resistant but not unbreakable, being about 15 to 30 times stronger than glass of the same thickness. Polycarbonates, best-known by the popular Lexan® brand name, are virtually unbreakable, being more than 200 times stronger than glass. It is also easier to cut polycarbonate material with power tools than it is to cut acrylics. Polycarbonates are the material of choice where maximum security is desirable. Both acrylics and polycarbonates are easily scratched unless purchased with an optional abrasion-resistant clear coating. Margard® is the brand name of scratch-resistant Lexan®. Polycarbonates treated with abrasion resistant coatings are similar in optical quality to standard window glass and should be used where both security and appearance are important concerns. Clear plastic tends to yellow with long exposure to ultraviolet light from the sun. Some plastics, however, are offered with a special coating to inhibit yellowing. Yellowing is also minimized when plastic glazing is installed on the north side of a building or in a protected area such as under a porch roof.

There is generally a considerable cost savings per square foot if plastic glazing is purchased in the standard 4 by 8-foot sheets stocked by plastics distributors and glazing companies. Common thicknesses used for glazing are 1/8, 3/16 and 1/4-inch. It is important to get the correct thickness, because if the plastic is too thin to span the size of the opening, it will distort and bow. Usually 3/16-inch plastic is recommended for windows up to about 24 inches in width, but wider windows should be glazed with 1/4-inch material for the best appearance and durability. To install 1/4-inch-thick plastic in a typical window, the recess or rabbet in the frame that holds the edge of the glazing material may have to be deepened with a router and the corners squared with a chisel. Because this is a difficult and tricky operation, it should be done by an experienced carpenter or woodworker. In most applications, plastic glazing should not be installed with screws over the outside face of a window frame because it looks unprofessional and some of the acrylic glazings may

tend to crack if screws or holes are bored near the edges of the material.

Compared to glass, plastic glazing has a high rate of expansion and contraction when subjected to temperature fluctuations. The larger the sheet, the greater the potential for movement. As the plastic moves in a window or door frame, it can break the glazing seal, causing the glazing compound to crack and fall out. Monofilament caulk, a professional-grade material, is probably the best material for sealing plastic glazing. It can be tooled reasonably well to provide a finished appearance similar to that of standard glazing compound.

EPOXY REPAIR

The use of modern, high-quality wood epoxies, as described in the **"Wood, Siding and Trim"** chapter, has made possible the professional, permanent restoration of wood window sash and frames that, in the past, would have had to be replaced. The areas most vulnerable to deterioration in a typical double-hung window unit are the sill and the bottom rail of the lower sash that rests on it. Usually the rest of the unit is found to be in good condition.

Relatively few sills are deteriorated beyond the point of lasting restoration through the use of wood epoxies. Begin by removing loose paint, caulking, putty, and any fillers that may have been applied in previous repair efforts. Any rotted areas should be consolidated with a liquid epoxy that must thoroughly penetrate the deteriorated area. Drill small holes to channel the epoxy into the wood if necessary. Epoxy paste filler should then be used to level

the surface, filling all cracks and other defects that would provide a path for water to collect inside the wood. When the epoxy cures, the surface can be shaped and sanded. Apply a quality, paintable wood preservative to the repaired surface to increase the adhesion of new primer and paint.

Repairing a decayed sash rail requires more time and attention to detail, but is still a relatively simple procedure. Often the tenons on the bottom rail that attach it to the side stiles are completely rotted away. In this case, new wooden dowels must be glued into the rails taking the place of the missing tenon. Epoxy patching material can then be packed around the dowel ends to form a new connection and to replace any missing or rotted wood.

Begin by carefully disassembling the damaged frame. Remove any old metal brackets, screws or nails that may have been used in earlier efforts to repair the sash. If a joint is solid, leave it alone. Drill two new holes exactly where a decayed tenon used to protrude. Drill the holes deep enough so that the dowels will be seated in sound material. Liquid epoxy consolidant should be used to glue the new dowels in place.

With the dowel ends protruding from the rail at least equal to the width of the stile, reassemble the joint and pack epoxy compound into the joint wherever the wood material is missing. Use pipe clamps or bar clamps to hold the sash square and to its precise dimensions while the epoxy sets. This is important because if the sash is glued with a warp or twist in the frame, it will not function properly when reinstalled. When the epoxy cures, the joint can be shaped with files, rasps,

and sandpaper. When painted, the repair should be virtually invisible and have lasting structural integrity.

SASH CORDS

Replacing sash cords requires a minimal investment in materials, and the labor spent can be particularly rewarding when it results in a window that can once again glide almost effortlessly to an open position. Having both the upper and lower sash functional and easily moveable in their tracks also facilitates

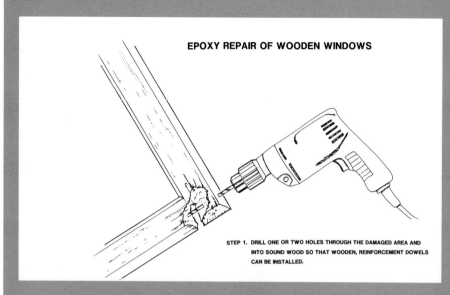

EPOXY REPAIR OF WOODEN WINDOWS

STEP 1. DRILL ONE OR TWO HOLES THROUGH THE DAMAGED AREA AND INTO SOUND WOOD SO THAT WOODEN, REINFORCEMENT DOWELS CAN BE INSTALLED.

Inserting new dowels.

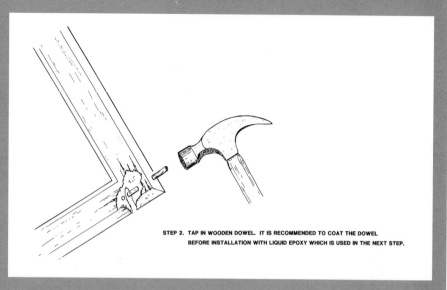

STEP 2. TAP IN WOODEN DOWEL. IT IS RECOMMENDED TO COAT THE DOWEL BEFORE INSTALLATION WITH LIQUID EPOXY WHICH IS USED IN THE NEXT STEP.

Attaching the rail to the stile using the new dowels and epoxy filler as glue.

EPOXY RESTORATION OF WOODEN WINDOWS.

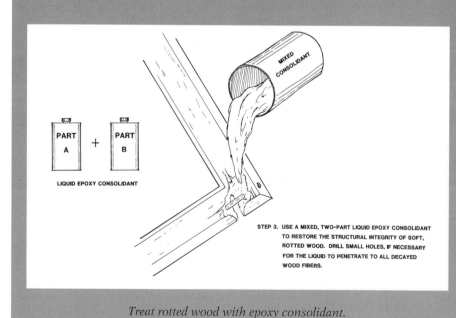

MIXED CONSOLIDANT

PART A + PART B

LIQUID EPOXY CONSOLIDANT

STEP 3. USE A MIXED, TWO-PART LIQUID EPOXY CONSOLIDANT TO RESTORE THE STRUCTURAL INTEGRITY OF SOFT, ROTTED WOOD. DRILL SMALL HOLES, IF NECESSARY FOR THE LIQUID TO PENETRATE TO ALL DECAYED WOOD FIBERS.

Treat rotted wood with epoxy consolidant.

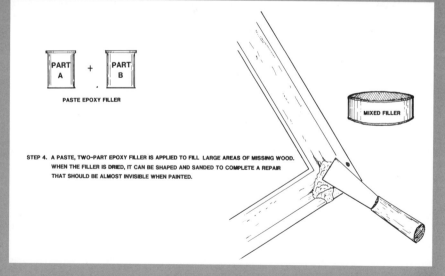

PART A + PART B

PASTE EPOXY FILLER

MIXED FILLER

STEP 4. A PASTE, TWO-PART EPOXY FILLER IS APPLIED TO FILL LARGE AREAS OF MISSING WOOD. WHEN THE FILLER IS DRIED, IT CAN BE SHAPED AND SANDED TO COMPLETE A REPAIR THAT SHOULD BE ALMOST INVISIBLE WHEN PAINTED.

Apply epoxy filler; shape and sand smooth; prime and paint.

cleaning and painting the windows from the interior.

For the best results, always buy sash cord that is clearly marked and sold for this purpose. Sash chains can be substituted for cord if a more permanent material is required. There is some evidence that "flat" sash chain is the most durable. It is made in stainless steel and aluminum. The cord or chain is attached to the side of the sash window and loops around a pulley in the top of the window frame and hangs down to hold the weights hidden in the weight pocket. When the bottom sash and both of the interior stops are removed, the weight pockets on either side of the frame will be accessible through a small "door" found on the face of the jamb near the sill. Usually one small screw secures this door in place.

Feed each length of replacement sash cord from the pulley at the top of the window down to the weight in the pocket. The rope or chain will drop easier if it can be weighted with a small nut or a screw. All four ropes or chains for a double-hung window are the same length. Use enough rope or chain so that the weights will allow each sash to retract into a closed position. Too little or too much cord will interfere with the correct performance of the window.

If cord is used, examine the knot that was tied around the sash weight and duplicate it with the new cord. It is important to tie a proper sash cord knot so that the weights will hang perfectly vertical and not scrape on the sides of the weight pockets as the windows are moved up or down. There are three sash knots illustrated in this chapter. Years ago carpenters were particularly careful to tie proper

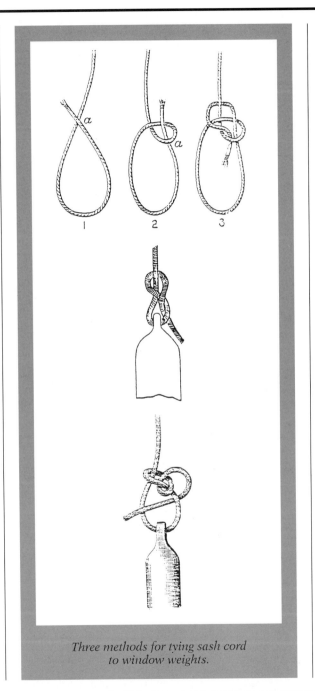

Three methods for tying sash cord to window weights.

sash cord knots so the windows would operate with a minimum of noise. Reinstall the top sash first when the new ropes are in place and properly knotted. Pull the top sash down to the sill so the parting stop can be slipped back into its groove. Do not nail or glue the parting stop in place. Reinstall the bottom sash and replace the interior stops.

SCREENS

Installing a screeen.

Window screening was reportedly first marketed in America in 1857. Wire screening, however, was not widely available until the late 1870s. Most Milwaukee houses probably were not fitted with removable, full window exterior screens until the 1890s. Interestingly enough, the combination storm and screen window was invented in the late 1890s as an alternative to the fall and spring chores of putting up and taking down separate storm or screen windows, but it did not catch on. If your older house still has a good set of older storms and screens, consider keeping them. A new, exact-size, wooden replacement storm or screen window can be made at a reasonable cost by local manufacturers to replace deteriorated or missing units.

Most of today's window screens are made of thin strands of fiberglass, steel, copper or aluminum wire. Steel rusts over time, and fiberglass is vulnerable to tearing. Many fine, older houses in the city were fitted with screens in windows and doors made from bronze or copper wire. These screens have an almost unlimited service life and may last longer than the wooden framing around it. Bronze and copper screening are premium materials that are still available today. Bronze is considered slightly more resistant to rough usage than copper, but is also more expensive.

HARDWARE

Old windows are often equipped with sturdy, fine quality hardware such as ornamental sash lifts and sash locks that should be preserved whenever possible. Missing or broken hardware can be replaced with high-quality reproductions or architectural salvage dealers often have a supply of old pieces if an

A 19th century hasp type lock.

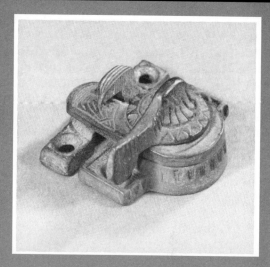

A 19th century hook type lock

VARIOUS TYPES OF SASH LOCKS

A closed cam lock.

A modern open cam lock.

exact match is required. The most difficult to replace are old sash locks made of cast iron because the material is inherently brittle, and fewer of them have survived over the years. Cast bronze or brass sash locks are more durable, but considerably more expensive. A sash lock is a particularly important window accessory not only as a security device, but also to reduce air leaks by drawing the top and bottom sash together at the meeting rails.

LEADED GLASS

Leaded glass windows, also called art glass windows, are among some of the most distinctive and admired architectural features of homes built before 1930. Most homeowners today recognize that leaded glass windows are valuable and attractive and should be preserved. The repair or reconstruction of old leaded glass is usually beyond the skill of a homeowner and should be done by a competent stained glass craftsworker.

In recent years, there has been a renaissance in the leaded glass trade, but still there are relatively few people in the business who are familiar with the fine points of restoring old leaded glass windows. Many stained glass studios today work primarily in the production of new, custom leaded glass windows and consequently may not be sufficiently familiar with the techniques used in restoring old windows to produce acceptable repairs.

One of the crucial steps in restoring leaded glass is color matching pieces of replacement glass to the original glass. Some leaded glass studios maintain large inventories of glass and can produce perfect, or nearly perfect, color-matched repairs. A very small studio, on the other hand, with a correspondingly small glass inventory, may not be in a position to offer a customer an acceptable, color-matched repair.

Leaded glass windows are typically constructed of small pieces of clear, colored or beveled glass joined together with H-shaped lead or zinc strips which are called "cames" or simply "leading." Zinc was most popular during the early twentieth century, but before that lead was used almost exclusively in the construction of art glass windows. Because lead is relatively soft, you can virtually make an impression in it with your fingernail, which you cannot do with zinc which is much harder. Repairing or rebuilding windows with the harder zinc leading requires more labor and is consequently more expensive.

Molten solder (a combination of lead and tin) is applied to each joint in the leading to unite all the individual pieces into a single panel. After soldering is completed, a special compound, referred to as "cement" in the leaded glass trade, is worked into both sides of the panel to fill up any minute differences in size between the thickness of the glass and the width of the channel in the leading. Cementing keeps the glass from rattling, makes the panel stronger, and keeps out the weather. Over time, cementing can deteriorate and fall out, which not only makes the window weaker but also decreases its energy efficiency. Years ago, "cement" was actually a mixture of Portland cement, whiting and other ingredients, but today it is common for stained glass studios to use a commercial grade glazing compound instead. If you examine an old leaded glass window, you can usually see the cement at the edge of the leading.

There are two major problems inherent with older leaded glass windows: broken, cracked or missing pieces of glass and general deterioration of the leading. Many older leaded glass windows have both of these problems. Leaded glass craftsworkers can often spot-replace a cracked or missing piece of glass without removing the entire panel. This type of repair, which can be done at the job site, does not require any replacement of the original leading or soldering but can be done only when the leading is in good condition.

Extensive deterioration of the leading, indicated by a badly bowed panel, is an almost inevitable problem with older leaded glass that can often be remedied only by a complete releading job in which the window panel is removed from its frame, disassembled, and then rebuilt using new leading. Leading deteriorates for a variety of reasons including vibrations from the constant movement of the window panel in a door or movable window sash, exposure to sunlight and water, poor solder joints, and vandalism. Some leaded windows require only spot-repair of both the leading and glass. Often, however, all of the leading in a panel needs to be completely replaced rather than spot-repaired. New leading should always match the old in terms of size, profile, and color. Using a different style of leading to rebuild an old window will drastically alter the original appearance. Leading is usually silver-gray in color, but by using special chemicals, it can be blackened if that is determined to have been the original finish. ■

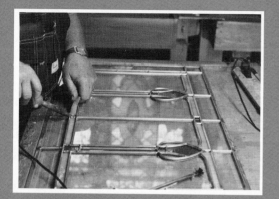

The glass is fitted ino the new cames.

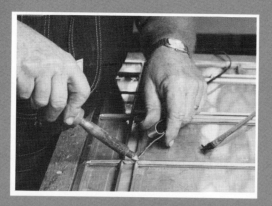

The joints are soldered.

After soldering, the window is "cemented" using a commercial quality glazing compound to fill the tiny gaps between the glass and the leading.

MAKING OR RESTORING A LEADED GLASS WINDOW

A mixture of fine sawdust and whiting is then sprinkled on the window to clean the window surface of the glazing compound and to stiffen and reduce the stickiness of the glazing compound.

A stiff brush is used to finish the cementing process. The glazing compound is allowed to stiffen for a day or two before installation.

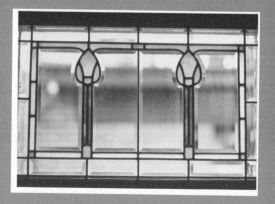

The completed and installed window.

PORCHES

PORCHES

PORCHES

PORCHES

PORCHES

PORCHES

PORCHES

PORCHES

PORCHES

PORCHES

The wooden porch reached the zenith of its architectural development in Milwaukee between 1850 and 1930. The legacy of porch building during that era is unequalled in the history of American residential architecture. Most houses built in Milwaukee before 1930 featured prominent front porches, many of which were brilliant essays in craftsmanship and design. Some are small and utilitarian, such as the door porch or the porch hood intended only to keep one dry until the door was opened, while, at the other end of the spectrum, there are the expansive Victorian verandahs that were designed as spacious outdoor rooms with elaborate roof structures, impressive columns, and ornate railings.

Time has taken a heavy toll on Milwaukee's once abundant stock of wooden porches. Many have been removed over the years. Porches of pre-1900 vintage are rarely found completely intact. Often the original porch roof structure survives, but the original posts, railings and decorative woodwork may have long ago been replaced by clumsy new parts of inappropriate design, thus stripping the house of style-giving architectural details. The architectural style of a house, in fact, is often most evident in the detailing of its porch. As a result, one of the most drastic alterations that can be made to an older house is to remove an original wooden front porch and replace it with a poorly designed modern substitute, or worse yet, no porch at all.

Authentically rebuilding or restoring an original front porch is one of the most important steps that can be made to reclaim the period appearance of an older house. Featured in this chapter are three designs for porches representing the Italianate, Queen

Milwaukee County Historical Society

1020 E. Kewaunee Street about 1900 with its original porch.

1020 E. Kewaunee Street today with the porch removed.

Anne, and Colonial Revival styles that could be adapted for use on the many Milwaukee houses that have lost their original porches.

Broadly speaking, porches served the twofold purpose of sheltering entrances and providing covered outdoor living spaces. Since the early part of this century, we have used the term "porch" to describe any roofed, open space attached to a house. Before about 1900, however, most Americans used the term "verandah" and, to a lesser extent, "piazza" to describe any porch that was large enough to

use as an outdoor living space. A "porch" during that era referred only to the small covered area sheltering a doorway.

Although by the early twentieth century American designers had dropped "verandah" and "piazza" from their vocabulary as old-fashioned terms, these words provide an interesting insight into the historical design antecedents for the American domestic porch.

The roots of porch design are ancient. The word porch is derived from the Latin term

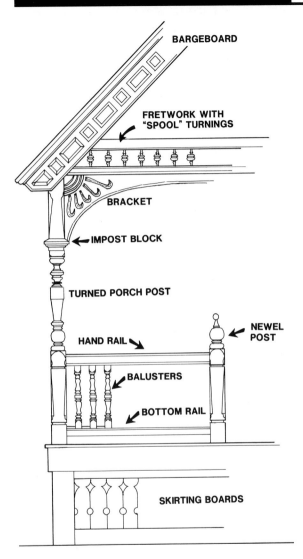

Historic porch with components identified.

BARGEBOARD

FRETWORK WITH "SPOOL" TURNINGS

BRACKET

IMPOST BLOCK

TURNED PORCH POST

NEWEL POST

HAND RAIL

BALUSTERS

BOTTOM RAIL

SKIRTING BOARDS

temple. The portico, as it came to be called during the Renaissance, was a feature of many classically designed public buildings and churches and occasionally was used to aggrandize the main entrance to a mansion or palace. Early American architects were greatly interested in classical style architecture and sometimes incorporated a portico into their

In 1979 this was a good example of a modest Victorian cottage embellished with a simple, but elegant original front porch.

designs, as Thomas Jefferson did at Monticello. Porticoes were popular domestic architectural features for costly houses from about 1815 to 1860, and then were revived again about 1895 and remained in use into the 1920s. Porticoes in Wisconsin were usually intended more as impressive architectural embellishments for a main entrance than as

Removal of the porch during a 1980s remodeling robbed this house of its architectural character. Money is often spent on insensitive remodeling projects when the same funds could have been used to preserve historic architectural details.

"porticus," which describes a covered entry supported by classical columns, such as would be seen on the front of a Greek or Roman

An 1870s Victorian Gothic style porch.

An 1870s Victorian Gothic style porch.

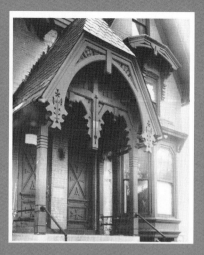

An 1870s Victorian Gothic style porch.

An early 1880s Victorian Gothic style porch.

"LOST" MILWAUKEE PORCHES

These photos, taken during the 1960s, recorded some fine examples of Milwaukee wooden porches that have since been demolished. "Lost" porches such as these are an excellent design source for recreating or restoring a porch today.

An 1880s Queen Anne style porch.

An 1880s Queen Anne style porch.

An 1890s Queen Anne style porch.

An 1890s Tudor Revival style porch.

living spaces and were often monumentally scaled. When a more intimate covered outdoor living space was desired adjacent to a living or dining room, a small scaled portico, popularly called a "piazza," was used. "Piazza" was the term used in the mid-nineteenth century, particularly on Italianate houses, for a living porch before the term verandah came into common use in the 1880s.

The word "verandah" comes to us from India where the Hindi term "varanda" refers to a roofed, open gallery or balcony. Large, wraparound "varandas" used as outdoor living spaces were popular residential features in central and southern India because of the hot climate. British colonists living in India adopted the "verandah" and took it back to Britain and to their colonies where it was "Anglicized" and incorporated into their late nineteenth century domestic architecture. Americans, in turn, adopted the verandah as a fashionable and practical architectural feature and adapted it to the materials and lifestyles prevalent in this country. Because of Milwaukee's typically narrow lot sizes, the rambling, wrap-around verandah found on Queen Anne houses in other parts of the country could not often be built here, and most houses just have a deep front porch.

At the turn-of-the-century, a spacious front porch was used during warm weather as a casual living, dining and recreation space much the same as back yard decks and patios are now. To make a porch more comfortable during warm weather, it was sometimes screened-in, or rolled bamboo or wicker shades were installed to regulate sunlight. The ingenious, demountable screen systems were installed on the inside of the porch posts to preserve the architectural appearance of the posts, railings, balusters, and other woodwork from the street or yard. Leafy plants in hanging pots suspended around the perimeter of the porch ceiling also served as a practical, yet fashionable, sun screen.

Beginning in the 1920s, many open porches were permanently enclosed to create sun rooms. Others were converted to year-round rooms. Some of the porch conversions were done sensitively, but others drastically altered the original appearance of the house. Today there is a trend by some homeowners to convert their enclosed front porches back to open air porches.

An unusual example of a restored porch at 1843 N. 2nd Street that includes a small, open deck area.

The popularity of large front porches declined after World War I as life styles and, consequently, architectural styles, began to change. By the 1940s, the typical front porch for a new home often consisted of little more than a concrete pad called a stoop. The porchless trend continued until the 1970s when the covered front porch was revived as a popular architectural feature in new construction. The front porch on a modern house is often largely ceremonial since its role as a family living space has long since been usurped by the rear patio or wooden deck.

BASIC MAINTENANCE

The ingenious designs seen on the surviving wooden porches in the city's older neighborhoods are testaments to the creative abilities of the carpenters and architects who worked in Milwaukee in years gone by. One inherent problem associated with many of these intricate designs, however, is that moisture tends to collect in key structural areas creating conditions ideal for insect infestation and the decay of the wooden members of the porch. Water is often trapped beneath the bases of porch columns and newel posts, at the joints between handrails and porch posts, and at the joints between the balusters and the bottom rails they are fastened to. These points are some of the first to decay on a typical wooden porch, making it unstable, even though the rest of the structure may be perfectly sound.

Another major factor contributing to the demise of otherwise solidly built porches is poor foundation construction. Insufficient foundations that do not extend below the frost line have caused many porches to sag and pull away from the house over the years. In the process, joints have opened up allowing water

to penetrate the wood and create conditions that lead to decay.

A long-term maintenance strategy is necessary to protect both old wooden porches and new ones built today. Perhaps the key point to keep in mind is that, in order to be durable and long-lasting, porches must be built and maintained to shed water. The first line of defense is to keep the roof and gutters watertight and to keep as much decay-causing moisture off the porch as possible by quickly removing snow from the railing and floor. It is vital to caulk the tops of all joints between handrails and posts and any open joints on decorative woodwork such as trim on newel posts. When original handrails and decorative woodwork become structurally unstable, they should be carefully disassembled and any deteriorated pieces should either be replaced in kind or treated with structural epoxy compounds before being reinstalled, primed and painted.

In spite of the decay causing moisture problems inherent in much porch design, many older porches have survived in excellent condition partly because they were built of superior quality wood that is not readily available to builders today, such as cypress or redwood, which each have a very high natural resistance to decay (see the **"Wood, Siding and Trim"** chapter). Porches rebuilt or extensively repaired with lesser quality lumber may be subject to much more frequent maintenance and repair.

Some sources of deterioration are difficult to spot, such as the excessive moisture rising from bare earth beneath a porch that leads to the decay of the floor framing and paint peel-ing from floor boards. The lattice work or skirting boards enclosing the area under a porch should be designed with generous openings that will promote a good circulation of air to carry off some of the moisture. When air circulation is poor or design dictates skirting boards or lattice work with small openings, you should consider creating a vapor barrier under the porch by laying overlapping sheets of plastic over the earth and then covering them with a thin layer of crushed stone. Installing a vapor barrier beneath a porch can be done as a retrofit measure to protect an existing porch or as part of a preventive maintenance plan during construction of a new porch. Be sure to pitch the plastic away from the building so any surface water that collects under the porch can drain away from the foundations.

Maintenance of the porch roof and flashings includes regular inspection of the porch ceiling for any obvious signs of leaks. Gutters should be maintained (or installed if they are missing) to properly drain water away from the porch foundation. An old flat porch roof now covered with rolled roofing may not be watertight, and this may be a warning sign that a deteriorated and leaking old tin roof was hastily covered. Derbigum or rubberized membrane roofing are the materials most commonly used today on flat-roofed porches. This is a much better material than rolled roofing.

Because many older porches have not been properly maintained over an extended period of time, they may now need extensive rebuilding. The following sections can be used as a guide to reconstructing all or part of an older porch.

PORCH FOUNDATIONS

One of the most common repairs that needs to be undertaken on an old porch is to repair or replace the porch deck and its foundations. There are several ways to build a porch foundation. To be stable in this climate, all porch foundations must extend below the frost line, which would be a minimum of 48 inches deep in southeastern Wisconsin, according to the State of Wisconsin's Uniform Dwelling Code. A typical porch foundation system consists of a poured in place concrete pad, called a footing, usually between 12 and 20 inches in diameter, located directly beneath each porch column. This system directly transfers the weight of the porch to the ground. It is vital that the bottom of each concrete pad rests on undisturbed, hard-packed earth, and not on loose soil or fill. Dirt and stone fill can continue to settle for decades causing the porch foundation built on top of it to slowly sink as well. As a result, in some cases foundations may have to be dug much deeper than 48 inches below the surface in order to reach undisturbed, load-bearing soil. Be particularly careful not to build a porch foundation on top of the recent backfill that may surround an older house as a result of repair work on the foundation or the installation of underground utilities.

There are three general methods for building a footing. Perhaps the most familiar type is a wooden post, usually made of pressure-treated yellow pine, secured in a poured concrete footing. To resist the tendency for the concrete to crack from the movement of the wooden post imbedded in the middle of it, the concrete is usually poured between 12 and 20 inches in diameter. To tie the post and the

THREE TYPES OF PORCH FOUNDATION PIERS

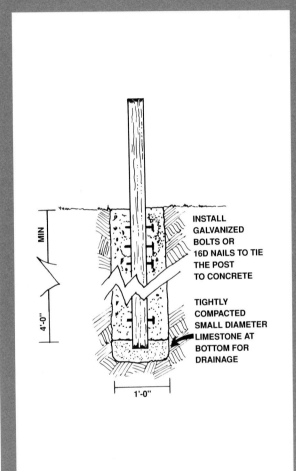

INSTALL GALVANIZED BOLTS OR 16D NAILS TO TIE THE POST TO CONCRETE

TIGHTLY COMPACTED SMALL DIAMETER LIMESTONE AT BOTTOM FOR DRAINAGE

4'-0" MIN

1'-0"

Wood post imbedded in concrete.

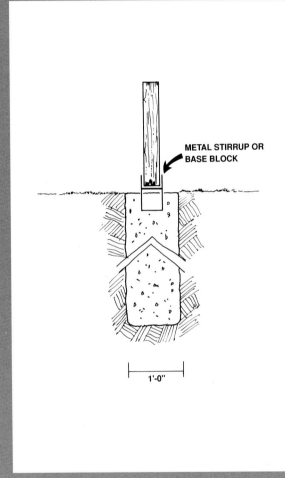

METAL STIRRUP OR BASE BLOCK

1'-0"

Wood post set on metal stirrup or base block.

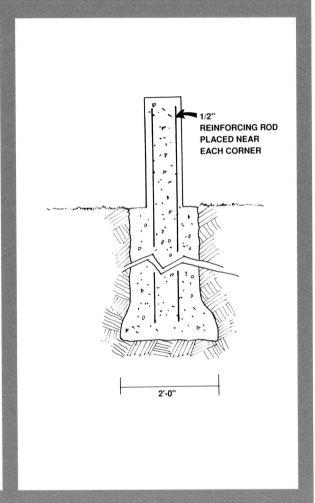

1/2" REINFORCING ROD PLACED NEAR EACH CORNER

2'-0"

Monolithic poured concrete pier (footing flared at bottom if possible).

concrete together, a few protruding galvanized bolts near the bottom of the post should be installed. Builders years ago sometimes used several large, 16 penny galvanized nails driven in half their length for the same purpose. To drain water away from the bottom of the wooden post, it can be placed atop a few inches of small diameter, tightly compacted crushed stone in the footing hole before pouring concrete around it. This method of constructing a foundation is relatively quick and somewhat simplifies later phases of construction. Any wooden porch post that is buried in or placed directly on top of soil should be pressure-treated. Never place the cut end of a treated post in contact with the ground because it may expose untreated wood fibers in the center of the post to damaging levels of moisture. The wood fibers in the center of a post are susceptible to damage because the liquid used to pressure treat the wood often does not soak in all the way to the middle of a 4 by 4 or 6 by 6 post.

Another method, preferable to the one just described, involves pouring a concrete footing to the top of the ground and placing the wooden pressure treated post in a special metal stirrup that is set into the top of the wet concrete before it dries. This way, no part of the wooden post extends below ground and the stirrup allows air to circulate around the post bottom keeping it dry to prevent premature decay. This type of foundation should last longer than the previous method and is easier to repair later if the post rots or the foundation settles unevenly.

Wooden, pressure-treated posts, either set directly into a concrete footing or resting on top of one in a metal stirrup, are both accept-able construction methods. However, for a very strong and decay-proof foundation, you might want to consider eliminating the wooden post altogether in favor of constructing a concrete pier or column all the way up to the bottom of the porch floor framing.

To build a typical concrete pier, a round, ready-made cardboard form or a square plywood box is suspended with bracing over the footing hole and then both the footing hole and wooden box pier form are filled with concrete. For extra strength, reinforcing bars, usually 1/2-inch in diameter, should be inserted near each corner of a pier while the concrete is still wet.

To provide a means for later attaching floor joists to the concrete piers, drill small holes in the sides of the forms at appropriate places and insert 1/2-inch-diameter foundation bolts, called J-bolts, while the freshly-poured concrete is still wet. The floor framing lumber can then be bolted directly to the finished piers once the concrete has cured. Building 8-inch-square concrete piers is generally sufficient to support a porch floor that stands four feet high or less above the surrounding grade level. If you prefer round columns, a paper concrete form tube with a 10-inch diameter would be a good choice. Building a plywood form box for a porch pier is a job for someone with experience in concrete work because the box must be reinforced and tightly fastened at the joints so that it won't burst open when the heavy wet concrete is poured into it.

FLOORS

After the foundation work is finished, floor framing can begin. Most porch floor units are made up of horizontal wooden planks set on edge, called joists, to which the finished wooden porch flooring is nailed. Porch floor joists, which are typically set parallel to the house, are nailed at each end to a perpendicular-running plank called a skirting board. Metal stirrups, called joist hangers, are used to reinforce the connection between the joist and the skirting boards. As a unit, the joist assembly is bolted to the foundation posts and attached to the side of the house with long, heavy lag screws. In order to prevent decay, at least two large washers should be used with each lag screw between the joist and the house in order to create a small gap that will allow air to circulate between the brick foundation and the joist and quickly dry out any decay-causing moisture that collects there.

Porch floors are commonly built to slope away from the house in order to drain runoff water away from the building. Although one architect's specification of the early 1880s required a porch floor to slope or pitch one vertical inch for every five feet of horizontal run, a slope of 1/2" for every five feet of horizontal run would be sufficient today to drain runoff water away from the building. Although some pitch to a porch floor is usually desirable, too much pitch can make pedestrians feel uncomfortable and could even create unsafe conditions when the floor is wet and slippery.

Older porch floors were typically made of 7/8" thick (actual measurement) tongue and groove boards, known as "center matched strip flooring," which was installed by "toe nailing" each strip into the joists through the tongue of each board to eliminate any nail heads from showing (and rusting) on the top

of the floor. The tongue and groove system unified the entire floor into one strong, rigid mass. Today's center-match porch flooring is only 3/4" thick and cannot be used to spot replace boards in porches constructed of the 7/8" flooring used years ago. For an exact match in a patching job, a few small pieces of 7/8-inch tongue-and-groove flooring could be made by a carpenter with a small thickness planer and a few standard router bits.

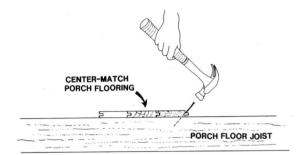

CENTER-MATCH
PORCH FLOORING

PORCH FLOOR JOIST

Installing center-match porch flooring. No nails are visible on the finished floor because each strip is "blind-nailed" through the tongue.

Much of the center-match flooring available today is made of Douglas fir, which is exceptionally strong and has relatively good decay resistance. However, before installation, all wood porch flooring should be coated on all sides with a good quality paintable wood preservative. To prevent premature peeling or paint failure, old time carpenters frequently recommended that the undersides of the floor boards be primed before installation. This is still a recommended practice today, and can be done after the coat of wood preservative is applied. To keep water out of the joints between the floor boards, common building specifications of years ago often called for the

joints between each strip of flooring to be coated or packed with pure white lead during the initial installation. White lead was the thick, heavy, paste-like compound that was used as a base for most oil paints years ago, but it is no longer made today. As gaps appeared between the porch floor boards over time due to shrinkage, they would also be filled with white lead or possibly wood putty. Today, if gaps open up at the floor board joints, it is a good idea to fill them with a high quality epoxy or caulk suitable for this purpose and then prime and paint. This will help prevent the rotting of the "tongue" in the tongue and groove boards.

The new center-match flooring available today that is made of pressure treated lumber is highly resistant to decay, but because the material has a high water content, it can shrink and warp considerably after installation as it slowly dries out. This will create unsightly gaps. For these reasons, pressure treated center-match flooring is not highly recommended. Some pressure treated lumber can be purchased kiln-dried to a relatively low moisture content, which will eliminate the shrinking problem to a large extent, but be prepared to special order this material and to pay a premium price.

Using center match strip flooring for a front porch creates the finely finished appearance that the builders, homeowners, and architects of years ago found both attractive and highly desirable. A porch floor made of common deck plank lumber laid with small drainage gaps between the boards is not a recommended alternative because it looks crude and out of place on a reconstructed or restored covered historic porch. This type of

flooring was designed for use on open outdoor patio decks, not on porches.

SKIRTING

Lattice work, sawn slat skirting boards, and framed diamond-mesh wire screening have all been used to enclose the area beneath a raised porch. Original nineteenth century wooden lattice and skirting boards are relatively rare because they are prone to decay from long exposure to moist earth and the foundation plantings that often surround the porch. Wooden slat skirting boards were often highly ornamental and were very important to the appearance of a porch because the Victorians did not plant flowers and shrubs to conceal the foundations of a porch the way we do today.

If you want the highly refined and decorative look of patterned skirting boards, you must make them yourself from planks of wood with a jig saw, since they are not manufactured for sale anymore. This is not particularly difficult to do and can add a great deal of design interest to a house. Remember that the bottom end grain of a skirting board acts like a wick to soak up decay-causing moisture from the soil beneath it, so it is very important to keep it out of contact with the ground. Pressure-treated wood with relatively few knots is a good choice of material to use for skirting boards. Cedar lumber which is graded "#3 and better" is another possible choice since it also has a good natural resistance to decay, is relatively economical, and holds paint well. On the other hand, common, untreated pine construction lumber, even if painted, is highly vulnerable to decay when used for porch skirting. To improve the durability of any wooden skirting, the individual

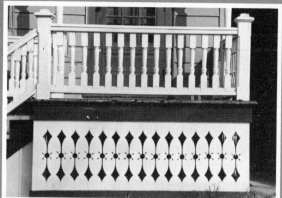

A FEW OF THE DOZENS OF HISTORIC SKIRTING DESIGNS FOUND IN MILWAUKEE

boards should be thoroughly coated or soaked with a quality wood preservative, including the cut ends of pressure-treated lumber, and then primed and painted before installation.

Diagonal and rectangular lattice work is made today of cedar and also in relatively inexpensive, pressure-treated, preassembled sections, measuring 2 x 8 or 4 x 8 feet in size. Lattice must be nailed or screwed to the back of a basic, flat, four-sided wooden skirting frame typically made of 1 x 6-inch lumber. Attaching lattice to the posts supporting the floor joists without a board enframement will not replicate the finely finished appearance of a historic porch, since it will look crude and the porch supporting structure will show through it. Although restoration purists have tended to rule out the use of many synthetic materials, lattice work made of PVC plastic is generally considered acceptable because it replicates the historic appearance of wood lattice and will not decay if installed in contact with the soil. The drawback to its use, other than its limited availability, is that PVC plastic lattice is presently made only in white, which may not be compatible with the overall color scheme of many older houses.

STAIRS

Historic wooden porches in Milwaukee always had wooden steps. The use of poured concrete or brick steps is generally not appropriate unless the entire porch deck was originally made of brick and concrete, which was not common until the early 1900s, and then usually only for fairly expensive houses. Wooden porch steps are built with relatively few pieces of lumber, but the building codes that regulate their construction are particu-

larly demanding. For this reason, stair building is generally a job for experienced carpenters. The state's uniform building code allows a maximum of 3/16-inch variation between the heights of adjacent steps. Research has shown that our legs quickly adapt to a precise rhythm when climbing stairs, and the foot in motion instinctively clears the top of a stair tread by as little as 3/8 of an inch. A variation in height between adjacent steps of 1/2 inch, for example, can easily cause someone to stumble and fall. About 3,800 people die each year in falls on stairs, and many more people are injured. The safety implications of properly building stairs cannot be overstated.

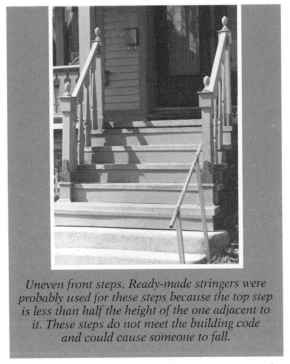

Uneven front steps. Ready-made stringers were probably used for these steps because the top step is less than half the height of the one adjacent to it. These steps do not meet the building code and could cause someone to fall.

The basic components of a staircase are the stringers, risers, treads, balusters, abutment

walls, handrails, and newel posts. The stringers are the sloping structural members that provide the main support for the treads, risers, and other parts of the staircase. There are usually stringers located under both sides of a typical stairway and one under the center as well if the stairs are very wide. A riser forms the vertical face of each step, and a tread is the technical term for what most people call a step.

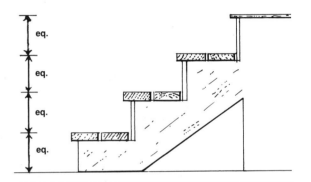

All steps should be of equal height. No step should exceed 8 in. in height, and there can be no more than a 3/16 in. variation in height between adjacent steps.

Any successful stair building project begins with properly cut stringers, which almost invariably have to be custom-cut for each porch in order to conform to building codes and to produce a safe and professional-looking job. Avoid using ready-cut stringers, since these are intended primarily for use with backyard decks where the ground level at the bottom of the steps can be graded to produce a consistent step height. Rarely can ready-cut stringers be properly used when building

steps between an existing porch deck and an existing concrete sidewalk because the top and bottom steps will usually have to be cut more than the allowable 3/16 of an inch to fit. In some attempts to use ready-cut stringers to fit existing front porches, we have seen as much as a 4-inch difference between the height of one step and the one adjacent to it. Keep in mind that good carpenters, as a rule, do not cut new stringers from tracings of an old set of stringers being replaced, because often changes in the height of the sidewalk or grade over time have made the bottom riser height unequal to the others. A good carpenter would re-measure and make the rise of each step equal in height. Another building code rule to remember is that the rise or height of a step must not exceed 8 inches. Steps with a rise greater than 8 inches have been found to be difficult to climb and potentially dangerous. Risers are most commonly between 7 and 7 1/2 inches high.

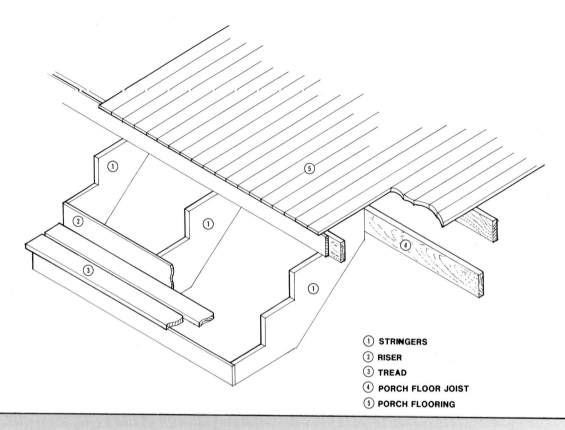

① STRINGERS
② RISER
③ TREAD
④ PORCH FLOOR JOIST
⑤ PORCH FLOORING

Typical wooden porch stair construction.

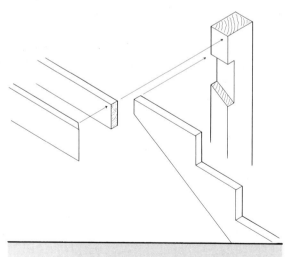

One method of attaching a stringer to a foundation post.

POSTS AND COLUMNS

Wooden porch posts and columns are among the most distinctive architectural elements a house can have. There are several different types of porch posts that were commonly used in traditional porch building: solid turned posts; solid square posts with applied ornament; built-up square or rectangular box columns; and turned hollow columns.

The type of post that is right for your porch depends on the style and construction date of the house. All of these post types have been in use continuously throughout the years, but each has enjoyed a particular period of popularity at different times. The earliest surviving residential architecture in the city dates from the Italianate and Victorian Gothic eras (1850 to 1880) when square solid posts with applied ornament were most popular. Solid, turned, highly ornamental round posts came into

An 1870s High Victorian Gothic style porch with square posts that have been trimmed with applied moldings.

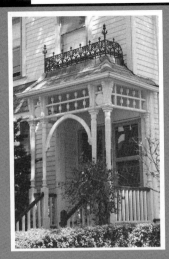

An 1880s or 1890s Queen Anne style porch with solid turned posts.

An early 1900s porch with hollow Classical columns.

A c. 1915 Craftsman style porch with box columns.

THE FOUR BASIC TYPES OF PORCH POSTS

favor during the 1880s and are most closely identified with the Queen Anne style. Although solid turned posts were used extensively in various forms until about 1910, hollow, classical columns became popular during the 1890s when there was a resurgence of interest in classical design, and they have remained in use to the present. Built-up square box columns were common between 1910 and 1930 when the Arts and Crafts, Prairie, Craftsman, and Bungalow styles were in vogue, and there was a demand for large section square posts. During the 1920s and 1930s, many late nineteenth century porches, particularly on Queen Anne style houses, were modernized by replacing the original turned posts or solid square posts with tapered box posts meant for the Bungalow and Craftsman

style houses of that era. These large box columns often give Victorian-era houses a heavy, ponderous appearance, and homeowners should give some consideration to replacing them with the correct style of post.

Classical style columns are perhaps the easiest to recognize because of their timeless design, which was pioneered by the ancient Greeks and Romans. Consisting of a turned base, a shaft and a capital, the classical column is one of the architectural triumphs of western civilization and has been consistently admired throughout history. A porch fitted with classical columns and capitals is a delight to the eye and a mark of distinction for a house. Most other column types, square or round, are based on the classical column. The ancient Greeks

and Romans meticulously refined the proportions of their columns into a near science. Most classical wooden porch columns of the nineteenth and early twentieth centuries were proportioned according to the ancient formulas. One of the characteristics of a properly designed column is that the shaft tapers slightly towards the top and is subtly enhanced with a visual correction called "entasis," meaning "to stretch" in Greek, which is a slight swelling or bulging in the shaft below its midpoint. The purpose of this is to make the columns appear straight, which they would not if the shaft was a uniform diameter from top to bottom. When the principles of entasis are properly applied to a column, the resulting visual harmony reflects one of architecture's most significant achievements. Some design-

ers, particularly in the early twentieth century, greatly exaggerated entasis to create special design effects. Remember the importance of entasis when searching for replacement columns. Modern aluminum replacement columns, for example, are a poor choice for an older house because they usually cannot be made with entasis and, as a result, have a very non-historic and top-heavy appearance. Today there are numerous manufacturers of reproduction wooden columns and porch posts. Construction methods, wood types, guarantees, and prices vary, but for either solid-turned or stave-built hollow columns, all-heart redwood is considered the premium material in terms of price and quality.

Traditionally, a solid-turned porch post or newel was made from a single block of wood. Years ago when construction lumber was milled from large diameter trees, it was relatively easy to find a stable, clear piece of turning stock 6 inches square and 8 to 10 feet long. Today, however, with most construction lumber milled from small diameter, relatively young trees, it is difficult to find solid, quality lumber in that dimension that will not split as it dries. Most manufacturers today, for the sake of stability and economy, make their solid porch posts from stock that is made by gluing together several pieces of smaller dimension lumber into a large block. After a post made from glued-up stock has weathered, it is not uncommon for the glue lines to show through the paint slightly. It is vital that waterproof glue is used to hold together any outdoor woodwork made of glued-up stock. Some woodwork made for interior use is made of glue that is water soluble and thus should not be used outside. Because most porch posts were originally made of high

quality material difficult to find today, many restorers make the effort to restore them with structural epoxies or by fitting in new pieces of wood to replace rotted sections. (See **"Wood, Siding and Trim"** chapter.) Since porch posts tend to decay where they contact the porch floor and where railings are attached, the posts usually have to be removed in order to cut out rotted wood to install new pieces or to do a thorough job with epoxies. Since epoxy restoration can be highly successful and much less expensive than buying new posts, it should be seriously considered as an alternative to replacement.

Adequate ventilation is vital to extend the life of a solid post or a hollow wooden column. A notch or vent in the column base and top venting through the center of the cap of a hollow column into a soffit creates an air flow that keeps the inside of the column dry and greatly reduces the possibility of decay.

Although Italianate and Victorian Gothic style square wooden porch posts can be successfully reproduced by experienced carpenters or woodworkers, the construction of large, turned, Queen Anne style porch posts is a job for a well-equipped millwork shop that specializes in wood turnings. Replacement posts for Italianate and Victorian Gothic style houses must be carefully designed in order to recapture the intent of the original builders. As a rule, these posts should be made from impeccably straight, nominal 6 x 6 lumber, which actually measures 5-1/2 inches square. Do not use the more common 4 x 4 posts which are actually 3-1/2 inches square because they are too thin and will look spindly compared with the originals. All porch posts should be placed on a cast aluminum base

block which lifts the bottom of the post up off the porch floor and allows air to circulate under the post to keep it dry and prevent the conditions that lead to decay and insect infestation. Aluminum base blocks are available at many building supply companies, but caution should be exercised in installing aluminum on concrete porch decks because of a possible chemical reaction that will lead to the deterioration of the aluminum.

Admittedly, it can be difficult to locate good quality 6 x 6 lumber suitable for use in making reproduction porch posts. Much of the common pressure treated lumber available today is unsuitable because it has unsightly knots and tends to split along the grain as it shrinks and dries. Redwood and cedar are excellent choices, but they must be dried to a moisture content of around 19 percent before installation to prevent the problems caused by excessive shrinkage. Quality post blanks may have to be special ordered. Some builders choose to use 4 x 4 lumber veneered with high quality clear boards to build out the post to the required dimensions. This is acceptable, but be aware that if the work is not expertly done and the casing boards are not sufficiently dry, there is the possibility that the corner joints may open up. Built-up cased posts are also difficult to chamfer correctly. Chamfered corners are a common characteristic of most Italianate and many Victorian Gothic style posts.

To finish a post, various moldings are carefully mitered and nailed to it including, at a minimum, the base block, also called a plinth, a necking molding near the top, and the capital or bracket work applied at the top. This arrangement of moldings is actually a reinter-

Doric

Tuscan

Ionic

Corinthian

FOUR COMMON TYPES OF CLASSICAL PORCH COLUMNS

pretation of the elements of a classical column and is intended to dress-up a plain post. Although copies of original moldings cannot generally be purchased "off the shelf," they can be made by a millwork shop or woodworker who owns a good selection of router bits or old molding planes. Stock molding profiles can also be substituted to simulate a period appearance. The central portion of the post shaft, above the level of the handrail, is often "chamfered," which means the outside corners are cut away or beveled at a 45 degree angle. This can be done with a router equipped with a chamfer bit that cuts a 3/4-inch long bevel. Smaller or narrower bevels probably will not look authentic. Study drawings of porch posts from pattern books or go to look at surviving original posts to understand exactly where the

post should be chamfered and how the moldings should be applied.

Some original square porch posts feature reeding and small, chip-carved sunburst or floral patterns located immediately above the level of the hand rail. "Bull's eyes," the name for round, concentric moldings cut with a special tool in a drill press, were another popular type of decoration. Several firms around the U.S. are again making bull's eye cutters to replicate nineteenth century designs, so, although this would definitely be custom work that might require some shopping around, it may be possible to get even this type of decorated post made today.

The base block area can be a troublesome spot for deterioration because water tends to

get trapped between the post and the back of the block. Caulking the top of the joint to seal out water is usually only a temporary solution. You may want to consider cutting a 1/4-inch-deep rabbet or recess around all four sides of the bottom of the post to the height of the base block molding which is then nailed into it. Water will then roll over the faces of the block rather than getting trapped behind it.

Fitting like a crown at the top of a classical, round column, a capital may simply be a round-turned piece of solid wood, as is typical of the Doric style, or it can be a florid essay in Gothic, Corinthian or Ionic style carving. Although some of the capitals used to top porch columns were individually carved of solid blocks of wood, most were actually cast

DETAILS OF PORCH CORNICES AND FRETWORK
USED WITH SQUARE SOLID WOODEN POSTS (1870-1885)

EXAMPLES OF SPINDLEWORK USED WITH SOLID TURNED POSTS (1885-1900)

in molds using a composition material consisting of a paste of wood fiber, cement, and other reinforcing fibers. When it is painted, composition is virtually indistinguishable from handcarved wood. Composition ornament weathers well if it is maintained, but because it is susceptible to damage from thawing and freezing, many old column capitals have deteriorated or have been completely removed. Luckily, several manufacturers are again making replacement column capitals in a full range of styles and sizes so that it should be possible to replace almost any classical capital with a new duplicate.

NEWEL POSTS

Newel posts are the upright members that support the handrails of a stairway or the railing section of an upper deck. The solid turned newel and the box, or built-up, newel are the two general types of newel posts. Historically, most older porches were built without handrails on the stairs. Today, however, a handrail on the stairs is a necessity desired by most homeowners and usually required by law. The state uniform dwelling code, in fact, requires a handrail on any staircase of more than three steps.

Rather than have a staircase with railings, until the 1930s it was very common for steps to be abutted on either side by low wooden or masonry walls. The tops of these ornamental walls formed shelves where flower urns or flower boxes were sometimes displayed, but the real purpose was to make the stairs look more solid and to architecturally integrate them with the foundations of the porch. Although many of the wooden abutment walls

A stoop with turned newel posts.

have rotted away and have been removed, careful consideration should be given to rebuilding them if there is evidence that they once existed. Since stairs with abutment walls never had handrails, adding them can be problematic. Probably the best way to add a handrail is to simply install a freestanding pipe rail or simple wrought-iron picket hand rail on the stairs. This is functional, economi-

cal and inobtrusive enough that it won't compromise the original design.

For porch stairs with railings, a sturdy, well-anchored newel post is the key to a safe, strong handrail. In terms of durability, solid, turned newel posts are generally preferable,

A porch with abutment walls flanking the stairs and a pipe hand rail.

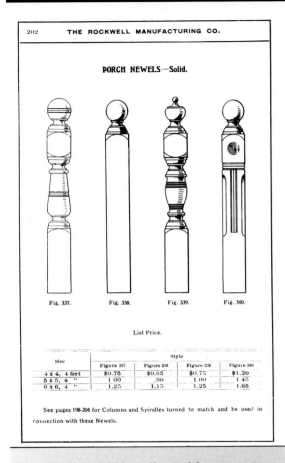

PORCH NEWELS—Solid.

Fig. 337.   Fig. 338.   Fig. 339.   Fig. 340.

List Price.

Size	Style			
	Figure 337	Figure 338	Figure 339	Figure 340
4 x 4, 4 feet	$0.75	$0.65	$0.75	$1.20
5 x 5, 4 "	1.00	.90	1.00	1.45
6 x 6, 4 "	1.25	1.15	1.25	1.65

See pages 198-204 for Columns and Spindles turned to match and be used in connection with these Newels.

These newels would be well-suited for use on Queen Anne style houses built between 1880 and 1910.

although they may not be suitable for all architectural styles. Attaching a newel post to an exterior staircase has always been a problem for builders. A newel nailed directly to the top of a porch step is subject to decay at the bottom and will generally be weak since it can easily pull loose. Bolting the newel to the inside of the stringer and cutting the treads to fit around the newel is a much better con-

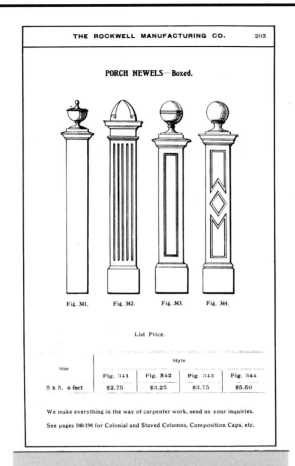

PORCH NEWELS—Boxed.

Fig. 341.   Fig. 342.   Fig. 343.   Fig. 344.

List Price.

Size	Style			
	Fig. 341	Fig. 342	Fig. 343	Fig. 344
5 x 5, 4 feet	$2.75	$3.25	$3.75	$5.50

We make everything in the way of carpenter work, send us your inquiries.

See pages 180-194 for Colonial and Staved Columns, Composition Caps, etc.

These boxed newels would be appropriate for use on houses built between 1895 and about 1915.

struction method. Washers should be used to create a tiny gap between the newel and the stringer so that water does not get trapped in the overlap. Still another method, and probably the best, is to bore a hole in the bottom of the newel to fit over a pipe that protrudes from a concrete footing beneath the stringer. Some builders may choose to bolt the wooden stringer to the pipe as well. A 1-1/4-inch out-

side diameter galvanized metal pipe should be sufficiently strong, although black pipe, used for gas lines, is a stiffer material. If you choose to use black pipe, it should be coated with a galvanizing compound before installation. The newel should fit snugly on the pipe. Secure the newel to the pipe with a wood screw that penetrates the wall of the pipe through a pre-drilled hole. Gap the bottom of the newel and porch step by about 3/32-inch. This will allow air to circulate under the bottom of the newel. The base of the newel should be soaked in a good quality, paintable wood preservative and then primed and painted before installation.

Hammann's perfection railing post anchor, patented in 1903, was designed to eliminate some of the problems of attaching a railing post to a flat porch roof.

Attaching a wooden railing newel post to a flat porch roof deck requires special care because leaks can occur at the attachment point resulting in the decay of the roof sheathing as well as the bottom of the newel post. Historically, builders nailed the railing post to the wood sheathing on the flat roof and then installed metal roofing and carefully soldered flashing around the post base. The flashings were often attached to the decorative base

blocks around the bottom of the post, but these tend to cup and pull away from the post, allowing a clear path for water to penetrate the roof sheathing and soak the post base, causing harm to both the roof and the post. To address the inherent problems of installing roof railing newel posts, in 1903 the now vanished Wm. Hammann Co. of Milwaukee patented a "perfection railing post anchor." The T-shaped metal anchors, which were used in pairs, eliminated the need for special flashing around the post base and allowed air to circulate between the post base and the metal roof, helping to keep the post bottom dry and prevent decay. Similar anchors are still available today.

RAILINGS

Turned spindles are perhaps the best-known type of balusters used in the construction of railings on historic porches, but many other types of railings were also used depending on the budget of the original owner and the intended design effect. In terms of selecting new porch balusters, cost does not always indicate the quality or appropriateness of the design. Using reproductions of the square baluster stock of the 1880s and 1890s may be more appropriate for the restoration or reproduction of a Queen Anne style porch than installing the more expensive, Colonial style turned spindles that are so readily available in the marketplace today.

Many restorers are surprised to learn that many of the city's earliest porches were intentionally built without railings. Influenced by the simple, clean architectural lines of ancient buildings in Greece and Italy, architects and designers deliberately excluded porch railings from many of the city's Italianate and Victorian Gothic style houses. Sometimes these porches were later "modernized" during the 1880s and 1890s with the addition of railings, as elaborate porch balustrades with turned spindles became the fashion of the day.

If, through research, you believe your house originally did not have a porch railing, you may still add an appropriate style balustrade that will conform to local building codes and look historically appropriate. Many of the original Italianate and Victorian Gothic

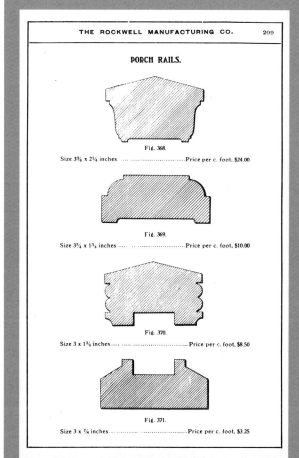
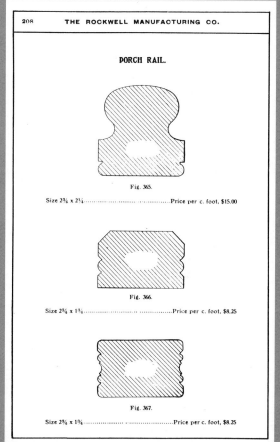

At the turn-of-the-century, Milwaukee's Rockwell Co. offered these standard porch railings in their catalog. A bottom rail, such as #371, however, would tend to collect water and rot and should probably not be reproduced if longevity of the railing is what you want.

style porch balustrades were made of decoratively sawn boards set between a handrail and a footrail. Appropriate designs for simple, Italianate style porch balusters are illustrated in this chapter, and other acceptable designs can be selected from old pattern books and millwork catalogs.

Today, building codes require porch railings to be built to a height of at least 36 inches above the porch deck. The top of a handrail on a staircase must measure between 30 and 34 inches above the top of any tread. These heights, however, are typically much higher than historic porch railings would ever have been. Although newly built porch railings on an older house have to conform to current building codes, existing porch railings built years ago before the adoption of the code are allowed to remain, and, for that reason, should probably be preserved or repaired. When it is necessary to bring a handrail up to code height, it should be done, as much as possible, in a way that will preserve the original scale and appearance of the porch. One way to add height to an old railing is to add an extension, for example a horizontal pipe or dowel on brackets, to the old railing. This added member, if relatively thin, should be fairly inobtrusive and not detract too much from the original appearance. This technique can also be used to add height to new railings without making them look too out of scale.

With the revival in interest in historic design, many architectural spindles are again being mass produced at reasonable prices. The old house restorer must take care to choose spindles that are scaled for the restoration of traditional porches. Many modern porch spindles are made from blanks of wood that are 1-1/2 inch square or less, resulting in

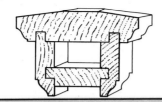

Design for a boxed handrail where a massive appearance and substantial thickness are desired.

very thin spindles. Traditional spindles were made from lumber blanks that were between 1-3/4 to 4 inches square. Using spindles that are too skinny for the restoration or rebuilding of a historic porch will give the structure a skimpy, cheap, non-historic look. When in doubt, buy thicker rather than thinner spindles. They will look better and last longer. In addition to what can be found at building supply stores, there are now many firms nationwide that specialize in mail-order, custom and semi-custom, architectural wood turning aimed at the restoration market. Their advertisements can be found in preservation-related magazines. Porch spindles can also be custom-made in local wood-turning shops to duplicate an original design. This is the way to go if you want to replicate an historic porch design authentically or just need to replace a few damaged spindles without replacing the whole railing or, perhaps, to add a handrail to some porch steps, where there never was one. Consult the Yellow Pages under "Wood Turning" for millwork shops to contact. The least expensive turnings made today are mass produced in pressure treated yellow pine, while the finest custom turnings are made of all-heart redwood, but there is a wide variety of woods and quality levels in between.

Many people make the mistake of spacing spindles too far apart. A typical turn-of-the-century porch featured 1-3/4-inch square spindles spaced 3-1/2 inches apart when measured from center to center, while 2-1/2-inch diameter

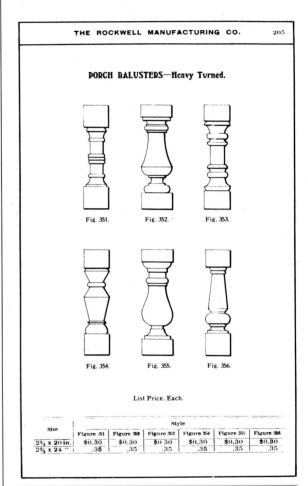

These porch balusters would be appropriate for use on Italianate style houses of the 1870s as well as the bold, Colonial Revival and Neo-classical porches common in the first decades of the twentieth century.

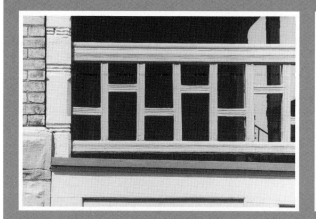

Queen Anne fretwork railing (1885-1890).

Turned balusters (1890-1910).

Classical balusters (1895-1920).

HISTORIC PORCH RAILING DESIGNS

Arts and Crafts railing (1905-1915).

Arts and Crafts railing (1905-1915).

Arts and Crafts/Craftsman railing (1905-1915).

Harp style railing (1915-1930).

Square picket railing (1895-present).

Craftsman railing (1910-1930).

HISTORIC PORCH RAILING DESIGNS

Victorian wrought iron railing (1885-1895).

Iron picket railing with scroll work (1900-1915).

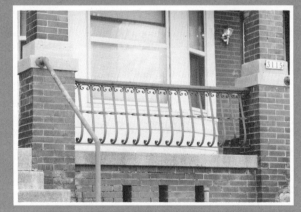

Iron harp style railing (1900-1915).

spindles were often spaced up to 4-1/2 inches apart when measured from the center of one spindle to the center of the next. It does take more spindles to duplicate the appearance of a traditional porch railing correctly by spacing the spindles closer together, but the design effect is well worth the additional cost. A railing with the spindles too widely spaced looks flimsy and cheap.

Handrails and footrails were usually attached to newels and porch posts with nails or screws. A modern, more reliable alternative, however, is the combination of a special nutlike fastener called a Tite Joint® and a common metal dowel screw. The Tite Joint® fastener is concealed in a small hole drilled in the bottom of a rail and works with a dowel screw inserted in the spindle to literally bolt the two pieces of wood together. You may prefer to install a galvanized metal washer between the two pieces of wood to be joined in order to create a small gap that will allow air to circulate to quickly dry out moisture that could otherwise lead to peeling paint and decay. It is important to make the handrail and footrail thick enough so that they don't look flimsy. This is done by constructing the top rail of two components, a beveled handrail mounted on a subrail to which the balusters or spindles are attached. The footrail should be made of at least 2-inch-thick stock.

PORCH DESIGNS

The following section includes drawings of porch designs that could be used on Milwaukee houses built between 1870 and 1910. ■

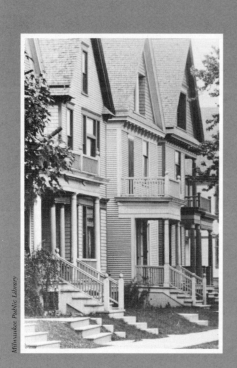

Milwaukee Public Library

| *Continue the porch railing down the steps.* | *A free-standing stair railing.* | *A matching railing at the sidewalk steps.* | *A pipe rail.* |

FOUR WAYS OF PROVIDING A HANDRAIL AT A SET OF EXTERIOR STAIRS

This drawing of an Italianate style frame house (c. 1875) shows no railings on the porch or stairs, which would have been typical for that period. Today, railings may be required by the building code.

The same house with scrollsawn, wooden railings.

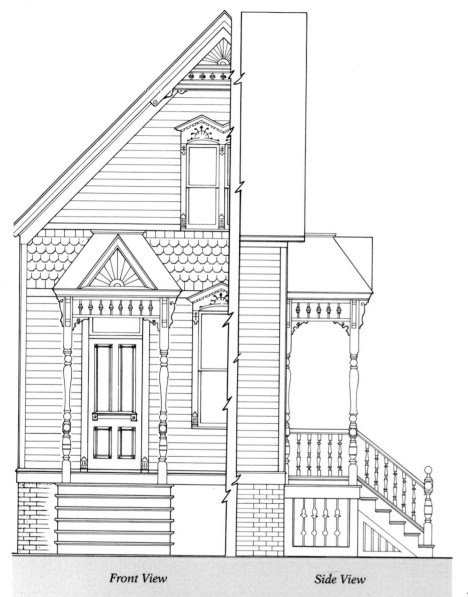

Front View

Side View

A Queen Anne style door porch suitable for use on many
houses built between 1885 and 1900.

A turn-of-the-century Colonial Revival style house and porch
of a type that is very common in Milwaukee. The flat porch roof was
often not intended for use, and the balustrade was purely ornamental.

ADDITIONS, GARAGES AND OUTBUILDINGS

ADDITIONS, GARAGES AND OUTBUILDINGS

ADDITIONS, GARAGES AND OUTBUILDINGS

ADDITIONS, GARAGES AND OUTBUILDINGS

The rehabilitation of an older house for comfortable, modern living may include the construction of an addition, a deck, a detached garage, or a small outbuilding. Although these new structures can greatly enhance the useful life of an older building, care must be taken because if the new construction is poorly planned, it can obscure or detract from the original architectural qualities of the house. All accessory structures and additions should, as a rule, reflect the architectural style, scale and materials of the main buildings on the property. When an addition or outbuilding is badly designed or reflects an architectural era different from the house, it looks like an unwelcome intruder on the property. It would be out of place, for example, to build a reproduction of an 1890s, frame, carriage house in the backyard of a 1920s, brick, Mediterranean Revival style house. An inappropriate addition or outbuilding can actually detract from the resale value of a property, particularly in older neighborhoods where the houses are often prized primarily for their interesting architecture.

A new, compatibly designed garage or house addition does not necessarily have to be prohibitively expensive or even hard to build. It should, however, be designed in accordance with a few general stylistic principles in order to ensure that the structure will look authentic and complement your property. Homeowners and contractors often have a sincere desire to reproduce historic designs, but, in practice, have difficulty in detailing a new structure to look authentic. The design of a house addition or new period-style garage is usually a job for a professional architect or architectural design consultant who is skilled in historic preservation design. For a garage, a home-owner may bypass the custom-design process and instead purchase stock plans for a reproduction carriage barn or other small outbuilding from the many mail order companies that specialize in this type of work and advertise in building and shelter magazines. The design of a house addition, however, is usually unique, and custom plans will probably be necessary to make the new structure adapt to the needs of the owner and to complement the architectural style and configuration of the existing house.

ADDITIONS

There are several general guidelines to remember when designing an addition:

* Preserve the overall historic character and appearance of the main building from the public right-of-way by making the addition as inconspicuous as possible.

* Echo the historic materials and details of the main building in the addition. Let the designs of the past be your guide and avoid using modernized versions of historic details.

* Reflect the floor heights, roof shape, massing, and window and door types of the main building in the addition to the greatest extent possible.

* Design the addition so that it does not destroy important historic architectural features of the main building.

In order to preserve the historic appearance, details, and materials of the main building, an addition should be designed to hide as

The Gustav Pabst house, 3030 W. Highland Boulevard, as built in 1898.

The Gustav Pabst house as it looks today after the construction of an insensitive modern addition in 1976.

little as possible of the original building. If it is large, set the addition apart from the main building and utilize a small link, such as an enclosed breezeway, to join the two. It is best to keep the size of an addition small in relation to the size of the original building and orient it so that any distinctly modern features such as skylights and decks cannot be seen from the street. Additions to the rear of a building usually present the least disturbance to historic fabric and appearance. Even in the

Previous Page: A house with a matching carriage barn under construction at the turn of the century. (Photo courtesy of the Milwaukee County Historical Society)

case of rear additions, homeowners should still consider salvaging any old, architecturally distinctive, reusable materials that are removed to make way for the addition such as original windows, doors, ornamental wood-work, or brick.

Whether a very visible addition will be compatible with the historic character of a building is often difficult to assess until it is actually finished, but building an addition that is markedly different in style from the original building can destroy much of the his-toric architectural significance of a property. A new addition that is visible from the street should generally have the same type of foun-dation material, exterior wall finish, trim, and window and door types as the original house as well as a similar roof type and slope, the same floor and ceiling heights, and a related composition of windows and doors. Even additions that are not visible from the street will be much more pleasing if designed with these concepts in mind.

Designs for additions that feature "modern-ized" or noticeably redesigned architectural details are seldom successful from an aes-thetic point of view. It is often better to try to work with or copy traditional architectural details rather than attempting to make a mod-ern design statement.

It is important to choose the correct materi-als for an addition so that it will complement an older house. The chapters in this book on **"Wood, Siding and Trim,"** and **"Brick, Stone, Mortar and Stucco,"** identify some of the important differences between modern and historic building materials that every owner of an old house should know before

These before and after photos illustrate that modernized versions of historic architectural details are seldom successful.

Before remodeling

After remodeling

starting construction on an addition. It may be difficult, for example, to find wooden win-dows to exactly match the profile and size of older, existing windows on a building, and this fact could have a significant impact on both the cost and appearance of the finished addition.

Searching the ads in building and home remodeling magazines will give you an idea of the variety of reproduction building materials available today. Years ago, using salvaged materials was often the only alternative for many homeowners who wanted to replicate old construction details in a new addition.

Today, the use of quality reproductions of historic building components is a good choice for finishing an addition when salvaged materials are unavailable or impractical to use.

When designing and finishing any addition, pay special attention to details such as doors, windows, and trim. Know the style of your house thoroughly and what materials are appropriate for it. Just because a manufacturer says its product is based on an authentic design, that does not mean it is right for your house. For example, many mass-produced, and fairly costly, Victorian style building products intended for the new home construction market are historically inaccurate and would look out of place on an addition to an authentic Victorian house.

The task of finding good quality, new, historically designed building parts is not as difficult as it once was because now more than 2,000 manufacturers offer products suited for use on old and reproduction style buildings. Many modern building products can also be easily adapted to fit the style of an older house. New window units, for example, can be ordered from some large manufacturers with factory-applied, traditional, flat exterior trim boards. Do not necessarily expect a contractor, architect or other design professional to be up-to-date on sources of historically designed materials. Do your homework by collecting catalogs and trade information from as many manufacturers as possible.

Most older houses in Milwaukee are built on raised masonry basements, and, if this feature is part of your house, an addition to it should be constructed on a raised basement as well. The footing, which is a slab of concrete upon which the foundation wall is built, must be a minimum of 48 inches below the level of the finished grade. New foundation walls beneath an addition can be made of modern materials such as poured concrete or concrete block, but the exterior surface of the foundation wall above the ground level should be veneered with brick, stone or stucco to match the foundation of the house. Be sure to specify to the mason contractor in writing that mortar joints in new masonry will be sized and tooled to match the old masonry and that new mortar will be tinted to a color as close as possible to the original. The size, style, and color of mortar joints are major factors in the overall appearance of any finished masonry wall. These are important details that, if specified in a contract, should not necessarily add to the cost of the project. See the **"Brick, Mortar, Stone and Stucco"** chapter for more information on basement construction.

It is also important to give some consideration to the type of structural materials that will be used in constructing the addition. For example, roofing materials are fastened to roof sheathing which has traditionally been comprised of boards that are about 7 1/2 to 12 inches wide. A popular type of roof sheathing widely used today in new construction is called oriented strand board or OSB, for short. OSB is one of several products on the market today collectively known as reconstituted wood panels, which are made from wood chips, particles or strands held together by glue. While there is nothing wrong with using OSB for lightweight asphalt or fiberglass shingle roofs, since it is less expensive than plywood or roofing boards, it would be better to install traditional roof boards or good quality plywood roof sheathing on your addition if you are using a heavy type of roofing shingle, such as architectural grade asphalt or fiberglass shingles, clay tile, or slate.

Similarly, the gable roof of an addition can be framed by using either traditional wooden rafters or else modern factory-made roof trusses. For do-it-yourselfers who are inexperienced at cutting rafters, ordering custom roof trusses may be quicker and result in a better quality roof. It should be kept in mind, though, that many roof truss designs restrict usable attic space, and there have been some problems with wood shrinkage in the trusses as they dry out, resulting in the "rising truss" phenomenon that sometimes causes finished interior drywall ceilings attached to the bottom chord of a truss to separate from the walls at corner joints. This problem does not affect the structural integrity of a roof, but it results in an annoying cosmetic defect. Shrinkage in roof trusses can be alleviated by having them built with better quality heartwood from a tree (see **"Wood, Siding and Trim"** chapter), which tends to shrink less than the so-called juvenile wood and sapwood that is contained in much of our construction lumber today. Check with your builder, architect, or truss manufacturer to discuss other precautions that can be taken to avoid the rising truss problem.

If your house has an old slate, clay tile or cement asbestos roof and you want the roof of your addition to match it, using salvaged roofing tiles may be practical. Although slate roofing is still being quarried and clay tiles are still being made, salvaged materials will probably be less expensive and may better match

The Robert Machek House, built in 1893-94 at 1305 N. 19th Street, as it looked before the construction of a large addition.

The addition, seen at the far right, captures the detail and massing of the original house.

Detail of the Machek House addition illustrating how it is set off from the house slightly and connected by a recessed passage.

the weathered appearance of the historic roofing material on the house. Some local contractors make a specialty of salvaging old, high quality roofing materials. The **"Roofing Systems"** chapter contains information on the most common types of historic roofing materials.

Illustrated is an example of an historic house, the Robert Machek House, that has had an addition made to it. This addition illustrates a number of the points that were discussed:

- The addition is visibly distinct from the historic building because it is joined to the house by means of a small link or passageway. By attaching the addition in this way, little of the historic fabric of the house had to be destroyed.

- Every effort was made to copy, rather than redesign, historic architectural details.

- The roof pitch of the addition is the same as the house.

- The foundation and wall treatment are the same as those used on the house.

- The garage doors were made to look like historic carriage barn doors.

- Historic, half-round rain gutters were installed.

SUNROOM ADDITIONS

The sunroom, a bright, airy room with extensive glazing in the walls and often in the ceiling as well, is becoming a popular addition to make to an older home. Historically called a conservatory, the sunroom, in one form or another, was popular in America from the mid-nineteenth century into the 1930s. In northern climates, the sunroom or conservatory was originally intended as a warm, sunny retreat and a place to raise house plants to

brighten interiors during long dreary winters. By the 1920s, the sunroom had become an informal sitting room. It was fenestrated with banks of windows and was almost a universal feature of both large and small houses, even modest bungalows, where it was often located at the front of the house where it also served as a foyer.

Relatively few Victorian houses in Milwaukee had conservatories, and, of the ones that did, most have disappeared. Since sunrooms are again a popular feature, you might want to add one to your Victorian house. Today there are several firms offering sunroom kits that are faithful reproductions of historic designs used on the better-class houses of the late nineteenth and early twentieth centuries. You may want to do some research to determine if your house originally had a sunroom or a conservatory, although most did not. The sunroom was usually located off the dining room or the rear parlor,

and its outline may appear in the building "footprint" that is drawn on the old city fire insurance atlases that are kept at the Milwaukee Central Library.

The new, historic-design sunroom kits may also be appropriate for use on homes that may never have had a sunroom. If it will be visible from the street, you should avoid building one of the modern curved glass or shed roofed sunroom kits that are widely marketed today. All sunroom kits are costly, and it would be smart to shop carefully and assess the impact that the sunroom will have on the overall appeal and livability of the house. Like any other addition to an older house, the job of custom-designing a sunroom for an older house should be reserved for a design professional who is familiar with historic preservation guidelines.

CARRIAGE BARNS AND REPRODUCTION GARAGES

Today's standard garage designs probably will not appeal to the property owner who wants a new garage to complement the architecture of an older house, particularly if the garage is going to be highly visible from the street. The alternative to the generic-looking modern garage is a custom built structure based on the design of a historic carriage barn or of the garages of the early motor car era.

The majority of Milwaukee's surviving carriage barns and early twentieth century garages were built of wood, although there are masonry garages and even a few brick carriage barns. Brick garages and carriage barns would be exceptionally costly to duplicate

today and every effort should be made to preserve the original surviving examples. Preservation of the few remaining historic wooden carriage barns and the many old frame garages is often more problematic, and homeowners may have little choice but to replace a seriously dilapidated structure.

Before you begin to design a new detached garage or accessory building, familiarize yourself with the following applicable building codes:

- The roof overhang of these structures may not be located closer than 18 inches from any adjoining lot line or closer than four feet from any alley line when access to the garage is from the alley.

- The total area covered by an accessory building cannot exceed 1000 square feet.

- The height must not exceed 17 feet when measured from the garage floor to the high point of the roof. An accessory building is allowed to be up to 24 feet in height when it is built on a property that is designated as a city landmark or in a landmark district.

- The height of the exterior walls is limited to a maximum of 10 feet, except in the gable ends.

- Exterior walls may be a maximum of 12 feet tall, except in the gable ends where they can be taller, if the structure is built on a property that has city landmark status.

Carriage barns are considerably different in overall proportion and massing than automobile garages. It is important to understand the differences between carriage barns and garages in order to select a design that is appropriate for your house.

Carriage barns, usually called stables years ago, were built in Milwaukee from the 1840s until about 1910. They were functional structures that were usually located at a rear corner of the lot and divided on the interior into three principal spaces: a large room for the family carriage, another space containing stalls for the horses, and a large hayloft on the second level. Because of the need for a hayloft, these were fairly tall structures that could visually hold their own on the lot and not be dwarfed by the tall Victorian houses of the day. Owning and maintaining a horse and carriage in the city was an expensive, laborious proposition, and, according to research of old city insurance maps, less than half of the Victorian houses in Milwaukee ever had a carriage barn. Among the problems inherent in keeping a horse in the city, other than the need to purchase feed and exercise and groom the horse daily, was the waste problem. Experts at the turn of the century estimated that the average horse produced about twenty-two pounds of manure a day, and some urban residents probably avoided owning a horse because it presented a serious sanitation problem on a small city lot. Not only was it problematic to get rid of the manure, but stables smelled and attracted flies and rodents.[1] Owning a horse and a carriage was not a necessity for most families because they could either rent a carriage when they needed one or board a horse and carriage at one of the many commercial livery stables located throughout the city. The 1895 Milwaukee city business directory lists 70 livery stables, and there were probably many others in addition

to that number that were unlisted. Most city-dwellers, however, relied on Milwaukee's extensive streetcar system for transportation. In the city's working-class neighborhoods, small sheds or barn structures were fairly common and usually sheltered a few chickens, a cow or other farm animals and, occasionally, a mule and a wagon. Automobiles began replacing horses for transportation just after the turn of the century, but some Milwaukeeans kept horses and other farm animals in their stables through the early 1930s.

There are relatively few original carriage barns remaining today in the city to serve as models because they had limited service lives for several reasons:

- Many carriage barns were built without a proper masonry foundation, and the wooden framing members, which often rested directly on hard-packed soil, were prone to decay. The presence of animals and animal waste in the barn accelerated the decay process.

- Carriage barns, although many were finely detailed, were treated as utilitarian structures for the storage of animals and wagons and were less likely to receive proper painting and maintenance than houses.

- Many carriage barns were actually larger than necessary for storing automobiles and were subsequently replaced with smaller garage buildings when the automobile came into general use, thus freeing up yard space for recreational use and admitting more light and air to the backyard.

Automobile garages were a new building type invented about 1905. Initially the word garage referred to a commercial structure where autos were stored, refueled and serviced. In a sense, the commercial garage was a livery for automobiles and, in fact, it was commonplace for an early twentieth century commercial stable to store and service automobiles in addition to maintaining a horse and carriage boarding and rental business. An automobile house, on the other hand, originally referred to a small, private, car storage building constructed as an accessory to a house. By 1910, however, the term garage became synonymous with either a commercial or private building dedicated to storing cars. Garages were originally modeled on the carriage barns they were rapidly supplanting in functional importance. Since they did not require horse stalls, however, garages required less floor area and also did not have to be as tall as a carriage barn, since they did not require a second story for storing hay and oats. The garage was, for all intents and purposes, essentially a truncated carriage barn with a low roof.

In order to understand the evolution of the first garages, it may be helpful to know something about the early history of the automobile. The first production automobiles introduced around 1900 were affordable only by the affluent. Nevertheless, the automobile rapidly increased in popularity. In 1904 an estimated 21,000 automobiles were manufactured in America, and by 1905, there were reportedly 1,492 automobiles in Wisconsin alone. That number increased to more than 20,000 by 1911 and had surpassed 100,000 by 1916; 200,000 by 1919; and 300,000 by 1921.[2] The majority of these cars were Henry Ford's

Model T, which had made the private auto affordable for the average American. The years around 1910 marked the turning point from the horse and carriage era to the automobile era for most middleclass Americans. Coincidentally, in 1911 the first hardware specifically made for garage doors was reportedly introduced.[3]

In the early years, cars were seldom used in winter because of cold weather starting problems and poor road conditions. Many early car owners, unsure about the mechanical reliability of their vehicles, also owned a horse and carriage and stored their autos in carriage barns. **Horseless Age**, the first magazine written for "automobilists," reported in 1906 that in terms of storing a motor car, "A dry, well-lighted and ventilated stable or barn will answer, but on the whole a house specially built for the purpose is money well invested."[4] It quickly became apparent, however, that the humid environment caused by a horse inside a carriage barn could promote corrosion of a car's mechanical parts, and this created the urgent need for a separate building to shelter only the automobile. The writer in the **Horseless Age** article cautioned against building a haphazard shed for storing a car because "generally such a place is too dark and unclean for the housing of delicate and expensive machinery."[5]

As the ownership of the private automobile became widespread by 1915, many new houses began to be built with a detached garage.[6] Garage building soared in the 1920s, and in 1923 it was estimated that more than 3,000 private garages would be built that year alone.[7] In the 1920s, the attached garage appeared, although it did not become com-

mon until after World War II. Although it would be wrong to build a reproduction Victorian carriage house style garage to go with most houses built after 1910, almost any house built after that date could be properly fitted with a detached garage.

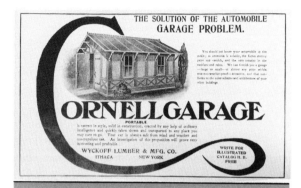

A 1907 design for a manufactured panelized wooden garage.

Some of the first private garages were "portable" and made of panelized wood or steel construction so that an owner could quickly and easily set up a shelter for a car. Milwaukee's Milcor Company was a national manufacturer of prefabricated steel garages that were popular between about 1915 and 1930. The garages were made of smooth steel panels that formed both the roof and walls. A decorative floral motif metal ornament was typically featured in the gable end above the doors. Some of these garages, usually the one-car size, still survive in Milwaukee today, and the remaining examples should be preserved by keeping them well painted so that they won't rust. Rusted steel can be prepared for priming and painting by first sanding and scraping off the corrosion or sandblasting it with a relatively gentle abrasive, such as glass

An advertisement for metal garages.

beads. See the **"Fences and Retaining Walls"** chapter for information about preserving metal. The application of creative color schemes to the remaining steel garages could

do wonders in terms of making them attractive, recognizable historic buildings.

A c. 1920s prefabricated metal garage.

Early twentieth century building codes partly determined the appearance and placement of a garage or carriage barn on a residential lot. Although the old codes are no longer in force, they can aid in the design and location of a new reproduction garage or carriage barn on your property if authenticity is your goal. For example, the 1914 Milwaukee building code required that all stables and carriage barns used to house animals had to be at least 15 feet away from any residence. A cupola or rooftop ventilator was required for any barn or stable used to house a horse, mule, or cow. Recognizing the potential for fire from the home storage of oil and gasoline, before the mid-1930s any freestanding automobile garage located closer than 10 feet to a house had to be built with walls made of fireproof, solid masonry such as brick, concrete block, terra cotta, or a combination of these materials.

DESIGNING A CARRIAGE BARN GARAGE

Average-size carriage barns in the city were remarkably similar in floor size to today's two-car garages, and many of the old designs are easily adaptable for modern use. Included in this chapter are several designs for carriage barns that were typical of the late nineteenth century and the early years of the twentieth century.

Several firms around the country today sell mail-order plans and working drawings for reproduction carriage barns and small outbuildings. Not all of these designs are suitable for use in Milwaukee, however. It is advisable to avoid the Colonial, eighteenth century style designs such as the so-called "Saltbox," which would look out of place with the city's late nineteenth and early twentieth century architecture. The best models for a new period style carriage house are often the well-preserved surviving original structures and the published designs of carriage barns found in old magazines and pattern books that can be adapted and built to modern standards to accommodate today's automobiles.

The first step toward recreating a historic carriage barn is getting the overall proportions and massing correct. The typical city carriage barn, which had a distinctive, but simple, silhouette, was a one-story, gabled structure with a minimum sidewall height of nine or ten feet and a steep roof pitch, which usually measured between nine and twelve inches of vertical rise for each foot of horizontal run (see **"Roofing Systems"** chapter). In contrast, the proportions of a modern garage create a markedly different silhouette because

the sidewalls are built with a minimum exterior finished height of about seven feet and the low roof has a pitch that is about half as steep as that of a carriage barn. The steep roof pitch and tall sidewalls of a carriage barn were necessary to create a loft space which was used for the storage of hay and feed. A dormer with a hayloft door provided the means by which to hoist bales of hay into the loft. The largest private carriage barns, built as accessories to the city's finest houses, were rambling, 1-1/2 to 2-1/2 story structures that often included living quarters on the second floor for grooms and chauffeurs.

If you are seeking to recreate the look of a historic carriage barn, you will need to use a steep roof pitch and tall sidewalls. You cannot simply add "Victorian" details to a standard modern garage if you are serious about building an authentic carriage barn garage because the proportions will be too low to look correct. Perhaps the most serious flaw in many mail-order carriage barn plans is that they also lack the proper height and proportioning.

For many years, one of the difficulties involved in building a reproduction carriage barn has been that the requisite steep roof pitch and tall sidewalls will produce a building height greater than the 17 feet maximum allowed by Milwaukee's building codes. This code was reportedly written to eliminate the possibility that an attic space above a garage could potentially be converted to an illegal apartment. Recently, however, the local building code has been amended to allow the construction of a carriage barn or garage of up to 24 feet in height (excluding finials or cupolas on the roof) on Milwaukee properties with City landmark status. If your property does

not have City landmark status, however, and you want to create an accurate looking carriage barn with the proper roof pitch and sidewall height, it will probably be necessary to request a variance from the building code from the City's Board of Zoning Appeals. Although this is a time-consuming process, you should not hesitate to pursue a variance if an authentic appearance is important to you.

Carriage barns were usually roofed with wood shingles, sometimes stained red or green, although slate was used on the most expensive masonry structures. Today, asphalt shingles will probably be the material of choice for roofing a new carriage barn or re-roofing an old structure. The roof color should match the roofing on the house, unless the roofing on the house is of an inappropriate modern style or color. The Yankee or standing rain gutter was typically used to drain water off the roof of a carriage barn, but today, a much better choice would be the half round gutter, which is also called an eaves trough. See the **"Roofing Systems"** chapter for detailed information about the selection and installation of shingles and gutters.

Carriage barns almost always featured a large and sometimes very ornamental louvered cupola or ventilator at the peak of the roof which served to exhaust heat and fumes and circulate air inside the building for the benefit of the animals. Several firms today make wooden and metal cupolas that are appropriate for use on a historic carriage barn. Authenticity and quality vary, but the relatively inexpensive, short, boxy cupolas sometimes sold off the shelf at large building supply stores are not recommended. Local sheet metal workers can also custom build a

HISTORIC CUPOLA DESIGNS

metal roof for a cupola according to the original designs illustrated in this chapter. Regardless of the source, a cupola is one of the distinctive stylistic features of a carriage house, and you should definitely incorporate one into your design.

A wooden carriage barn can be painted to match the house it was built for, but a simpler coordinating color scheme is historically correct as well. Color possibilities are limitless, and it is advisable to consult one of the many books now available on historic paint colors. Do not expect to find, however, extensive information on painting carriage barns and outbuildings. Research indicates that many nineteenth century carriage barns were either painted in dark, rich colors or else white, gray or tan. The following colors, for example, would be authentic for a simple, wood sided stable or carriage barn of the late 1890s: walls, dark green; wood roof shingles, stained dark red; window sash, black; and trim, light green or cream.

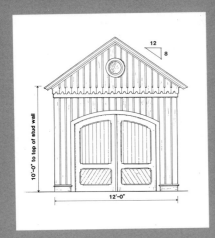

An 1855-1875 period carriage barn.

An 1875-1885 period carriage barn.

An 1880-1890 period carriage barn.

SIX HISTORIC DESIGNS FOR CARRIAGE BARNS THAT COULD BE USED AS MODELS TO DESIGN A REPRODUCTION CARRIAGE BARN STYLE GARAGE

An 1890-1910 period carriage barn.

An 1895-1910 period carriage barn.

An 1900-1910 period carriage barn.

A wooden carriage barn suitable for houses built between 1860 and 1875.

A brick carriage barn suitable for houses built between 1870 and 1880.

A wooden carriage barn suitable for houses built between 1870 and 1885.

PHOTOGRAPHS OF HISTORIC CARRIAGE BARNS IN MILWAUKEE

A wooden carriage barn suitable for a Queen Anne style house built between 1885 and 1895.

A shingled carriage barn suitable for houses built between 1885 and 1900.

A concrete block carriage barn suitable for houses built between 1900 and 1910.

A carriage barn suitable for houses built between 1890 and 1905.

A carriage barn suitable for houses built between 1895 and 1910.

A carriage barn suitable for houses built between 1895 and 1910.

PHOTOGRAPHS OF HISTORIC CARRIAGE BARNS IN MILWAUKEE

A carriage barn suitable for houses built between 1900 and 1910.

A brick carriage house for a mansion built in the early 1900s.

A brick carriage house for a mansion built in the Chateauesque style.

DESIGNING A HISTORIC GARAGE

With the advent of popularly-priced automobiles, carriage barn building rapidly gave way to the first generation of one- and two-car detached garages designed specifically to store automobiles. By 1910, a garage, rather than a carriage barn, was likely to be built as an accessory building with a new house or to be added to an older property as a replacement for a carriage barn.

Many early twentieth century garages were not markedly different in size and proportions from today's modern garages except that they often had higher side walls, although some garages built to service large homes or mansions contained second story chauffeur's quarters. There are, however, major differences in detailing between old garages and today's garages. Garages from the 'teens through the 'twenties, for example, often featured decoratively-sawn rafter ends called "show rafters" that were designed to complement the Craftsman and Arts and Crafts style houses of the era. When the rafter ends were concealed by a boxed-cornice, the fascia board was often trimmed with a crown molding that added visual interest to the roof line.

Half-round gutters were commonly used (see the **"Roofing Systems"** chapter) rather than today's standard K-style gutters, which are more boxy. Garage gutters were also commonly installed to rest on notches cut into the rafter ends. These gutters require skilled installation in order to ensure that water will properly drain to the downspout. Some garages had dormers to add interest to the roofline and give them a more cottagey look, but the cupola, which was then functionally obsolete, was not a typical garage roof feature.

Front Elevation of Garage.

This 1911 design for a garage is similar in size to a small carriage barn of the period.

Another important stylistic feature of both carriage barns and old garages is the windows. Early garages and carriage barns were fairly generously fitted with either double-hung windows, like those used in the houses of the day, or non-openable, multiple pane, so-called "barn sash," which are still available today. Modern style windows such as the jalousie, awning, hopper and slide-by are not recommended for use on a historically styled garage or carriage barn nor are the small octagonal ornamental wooden windows commonly mass produced today. It would be

A circa 1920 garage.

appropriate, however, to install a diamond-shaped, half-round, or round window in the gable of a reproduction carriage barn. The windows and doors should be framed with surrounds composed of flat, wide boards instead of the narrow "brick molding" which comes factory applied to most standard, new pre-hung window units. Before installing a new pre-hung window or door unit in a reproduction garage or carriage barn, the brick molding can be removed and replaced with board trim better suited to the design of a period style garage or carriage barn.

Most frame carriage barns or early garages were sided with one or a combination of the following materials: Narrow clapboards to match the house, drop siding (also called shiplap), wood shingles, or, in the case of carriage houses built before 1890, board and batten, which consists of wide vertical boards butted up against each other with the joints covered by narrow wooden strips called battens. Drop siding, which is still available today, can give a reconstructed carriage barn

Wood trim should be used around a window or door.

or an early garage a distinctive period appearance not possible with other siding materials. Because of its thickness, usually at least 3/4-inch, drop siding historically was not usually installed over an underlayment of sheathing boards and was instead nailed directly over the wall studs. Current building codes would still allow this practice for a garage or accessory building, but it is recommended that some type of sheathing material such as plywood or insulating board be used as an under-

layment for any siding material installed on a new outbuilding today. Early garages and carriage barns were often sided with narrow wooden clapboards (see **"Wood, Siding and Trim" chapter**). Like the houses of the era, each outside corner of a wood-sided carriage house or early garage was fitted with vertical corner trim boards. Today, it is possible to substitute smooth (non-wood grained), narrow exposure, aluminum or vinyl siding for use on a new carriage house or garage in place of wood siding, if wood trim is used around the windows and doors and for the corner boards. Wood siding, however, is still the preferred material because it allows greater freedom to reproduce an historic color scheme.

A modern carriage house style garage under construction.

Carriage barns and garages generally featured a so-called "service door" used for pedestrian access. A wooden, four-panel service door is generally appropriate for use on any style pre-1935 garage or carriage barn.

For security-minded homeowners who are concerned about the strength of the wooden panels, a 1/2 or 3/4-inch-thick plywood panel can be screwed to the inside of the door for additional strength.

The carriage or automobile access door is called, respectively, a barn door or a garage door. Before about 1920, a wooden sliding door or a side-hinged, swinging door was most likely to be used on a carriage barn or garage. These doors, which were made in a seemingly endless variety of designs, were one of the pivotal architectural features of the building. Choosing a new, appropriate looking garage or barn door can be a challenge. A sliding barn door often was mounted on a metal track on the exterior of the building. Although many carriage barns and most garages had big, hinged, swinging double doors, early twentieth century garage doors were also made in narrow hinged vertical sections that slid along top and bottom metal tracks and retracted along the inside walls of the garage. If an existing garage or carriage barn still retains its original sliding or side-hinged doors, every effort should be made to preserve them and adapt them to today's functional requirements by installing an electric opening device.

The most common type of garage door today, which is the overhead, sectional type that rolls up on a metal track attached to the garage ceiling, was apparently introduced in the 1920s, about the time that the solid panel tilt-up overhead door came into use. Overhead doors were immediately popular because they took up less space and were less likely to get stuck or be blocked by objects in their tracks than the side-hinged or sliding garage doors.

DESIGNS FOR EARLY TWENTIETH CENTURY GARAGE DOORS

CARRIAGE HOUSE AND GARAGE DOORS THAT COULD BE USED AS INSPIRATION TO DESIGN A DOOR FOR A NEW GARAGE

One of the earliest types of overhead door was made of the simple, wooden, multi-panel construction which is still available today. The frame-and-panel overhead wooden door is a good choice when restoring or recreating a post-1920 garage. You should also keep in mind that it was traditional during the early twentieth century to have a pair of seven- or eight-foot-wide overhead doors on a two-car garage rather than the single 16- or 18-foot-wide overhead door most commonly used today. It was also almost universal that carriage barn and garage doors had windows in them. Incidentally, electric garage door openers were available by the mid-1920s that operated by means of a pressure-sensitive switch in the driveway pavement or a pole-mounted key switch that a driver could reach from the car window.

Kwasniewski Collection, Univ. of WI-Milwaukee

A 1930s garage with frame and panel doors.

By applying flat, beaded wood strips and wooden moldings to the face of a standard solid, flush-panel, tilt-up or sectional roll-up overhead garage door, it is possible to successfully recreate the appearance of the side-hinged or sliding doors originally used on carriage barns and pre-1930s garages while still having the convenience of an overhead door. Most contemporary-style overhead doors are not suitable if you are seeking to recreate an early twentieth century appearance. Try to avoid using a fiberglass, imitation wood grain vinyl or metal door, or a "flush" overhead door which has the appearance when closed of a single, featureless flat panel.

SMALL ACCESSORY BUILDINGS

Some city properties that are too small for a garage will still accommodate some type of small detached storage building. Many of the nineteenth century designs for small ice houses, pump houses, and even poultry coops can be adapted for use today as charming, but useful, backyard storage buildings.

Small sheds were originally a common feature in the backyards of many pre-1910 houses, particularly those that did not have carriage houses. Small pump houses to shelter a well, for example, were necessary on many city properties in the days before all houses were hooked up to the city water system. By the 1920s, improvements in the delivery of municipal services such as sewer and water, and legal restrictions on city dwellers raising small farm animals in their backyards, did away with the need for most small backyard buildings. Many of these were detailed to

reflect the architecture of the main house. A well-detailed custom wooden storage building is a better choice than the prefabricated metal or plywood structures that are commonly sold today in kit form at building supply houses. The designs of the structures in the following plate could be adapted to use for gazebos, small guesthouses, pool houses, backyard workshops or storage buildings.

Milwaukee County Historical Society

Circa 1890 photograph of a house with an open deck.

DECKS

The raised wooden patio deck so popular today is really a product of the last 30 years. Its popularity can be traced to the widespread availability of pressure treated lumber and the trend toward a less formal, more sunworshipping lifestyle. Although not common in Victorian times, uncovered decks were not unheard of. Their popularity was limited, of course, by the extensive maintenance they required and by their limited usefulness. The Victorians were not the sun worshippers we are today since the aesthetic mores of the time highly valued a pale complexion, particularly

THREE GAZEBOS OR SUMMER HOUSES

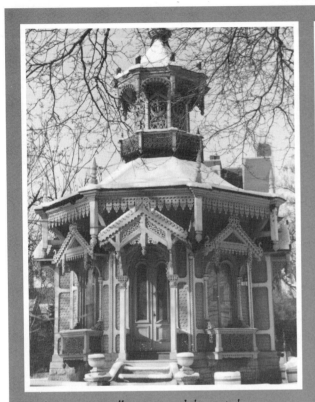

An ornate scroll-sawn wood decorated summer house dating from 1872.

An 1880s scroll-sawn gazebo.

A Neoclassical style gazebo.

in women. Sun tanned skin was often considered to be an indication of working class status, and would have been avoided by the middle classes to the greatest extent possible. Old photographs reveal that when an open deck was part of the design of a house it was detailed the same way a covered porch deck would have been, with handsome skirting and railings. The exposed parts were always painted or stained to coordinate with the colors of the house. If you are considering adding an open deck to your old house, even if it is on the rear, it is recommended you detail the skirting and railings to reflect the architecture of your house and its porches and stain or paint the wood to give it a finished look. ∎

FOOTNOTES

1 Stephen W. Sears, **The Automobile in America**, New York: American Heritage Publishing Co., 1977, p. 51.

2 William Francis Raney, **Wisconsin**. Appleton, Wisconsin: Perin Press, 1963, p. 333.

3 **American Architect**, Jan. 5, 1926, p. 121.

4 **Horseless Age**, April 11, 1906, p. 528.

5 **Ibid.**

6 Raney, p. 333.

7 **Milwaukee Journal**, April 22, 1923, Real Estate Section, p. 1.

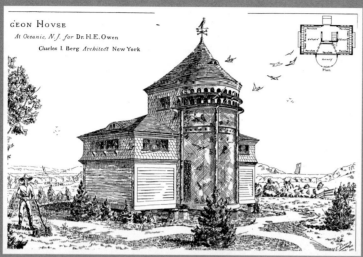

A pigeon house (1882).

A hen house (c. 1880).

NINETEENTH CENTURY DESIGNS FOR VARIOUS TYPES OF SMALL ACCESSORY BUILDINGS THAT COULD BE ADAPTED TO MODERN USE.

A dog house (1856).

A gazebo (1882).

FENCES AND RETAINING WALLS

FENCES AND RETAINING WALLS

FENCES AND RETAINING WALLS

FENCES AND RETAINING WALLS

FENCES AND RETAINING WALLS

Homeowners today face a challenge when seeking to build a new fence or retaining wall in one of the historic designs that were common features of the cityscape years ago, because historic wooden fences are virtually nonexistent, and there are relatively few surviving historic iron and masonry fences. Building a new fence or retaining wall that is compatible in design with your older house will enhance your property in a way you will be proud of. Passersby and neighbors will enjoy the fence, too. The Cleaveland and Backus Brothers, a nineteenth century team of architects, wrote, "The style and condition of a fence often indicates unmistakably the taste and habits of the owner. A fence should be adapted not only to the house, but to the location and the neighborhood."

Many restorers make the mistake of building fences and retaining walls that were designed for use on modern style houses. Do not assume that fences in pre-built sections or kit form will necessarily conform with local building codes or local preservation ordinances. Fences of stockade, basket-weave, split rail, or chain link design and retaining walls of railroad ties or interlocking concrete blocks are generally not permitted on properties designated as City of Milwaukee landmarks. Most landmark ordinances throughout the country have similar restrictions. These types of fences and walls are generally not appropriate for houses built before 1940. The over-reliance on the use of these few common fence types has obscured the fact that there is a wealth of late nineteenth and early twentieth century fence designs waiting to be rediscovered. Historic fence designs built in wood, iron, stone, brick or combinations of these

materials can be recreated today using modern materials with great success by a homeowner.

As we said, homeowners are at a disadvantage in designing or selecting a fence suitable for an older house, because there are so few original fences still in existence to serve as models. There are no known surviving pre-1900 wooden fences in the Milwaukee area because wooden fences inherently have relatively short service lives in a northern climate. Others have been removed simply because they were no longer in style. Wood has always been the most common fencing material because it is readily available, relatively inexpensive, and easily worked into an almost unlimited variety of shapes. Brick, iron, stone, and concrete fences and walls last longer, but are usually more costly to build and might not be suitable in design for all styles of houses. There are some exceptionally fine examples of old iron fences surviving in the city which should be preserved, but many others were the victims of rust, changing architectural tastes, and scrap iron drives during the two world wars.

PLANNING THE PROJECT

There are two important steps to take before beginning the actual construction of a fence or retaining wall:

- Determine the appropriate location for the fence, select or create a design, and choose the appropriate building material.

- Seek design approval from the historic preservation commission if the property is

in a city-designated historic district, and then obtain a fence permit from the Department of Building Inspection.

Selecting the design for a fence or retaining wall is a crucial step that often gets too little attention. Ultimately the design should be based on the style of the house, the functional purpose of the fence, such as keeping a dog inside the yard, the requirements of local building codes, and the limitations of your budget. Fences and retaining walls should also be constructed to be durable and to resist the destructive effects of time and weather. A good fence, regardless of its material, should blend with or complement the architecture of the house and its outbuildings. Fences or walls that are too tall, or incompatible in design, can detract from the architecture of the house behind it. Keep in mind that an expensive fence is not necessarily a good or attractive one. It may be helpful to think of a fence or retaining wall as a "frame" around the house. Careful attention to the design and construction of a fence can result in a better-looking and longer-lasting project.

The design of your fence will be partly determined by local building codes. According to the Milwaukee code, a fence built on a front or side lot line of a residential property may not be taller than four feet. A fence built along the rear lot lines may be as tall as six feet. Those restrictions change if a fence on a side or front yard is set at least three feet inside the respective lot lines, in which case a five-foot-tall fence is permissible. When set a minimum of six feet inside those lot lines, a fence up to six feet in height may be constructed.

Previous Page: Photo of a new dwelling in 1876 with a fence designed to complement the architecture of the house. (Photo courtesy of the Milw. County Historical Society)

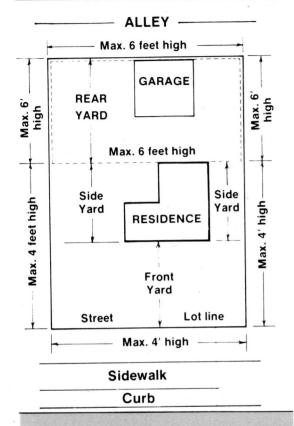

ALLEY

Max. 6 feet high

GARAGE

REAR
YARD

Max. 6'
high

Max. 6'
high

Max. 6 feet high

Side
Yard

Side
Yard

Max. 4 feet high

RESIDENCE

Max. 4' high

Front
Yard

Street

Lot line

Max. 4' high

Sidewalk

Curb

Height restrictions for fences in Milwaukee.

When you have selected your design, you must obtain a fence permit from the city's building inspection department before starting construction. City inspectors are primarily concerned about the placement and height of the fence. A survey of your lot is generally required before a permit can be granted by the building inspector. The survey marks the precise location of property lines, which must be known to keep the fence from encroaching on a neighbor's or the city's property. Never assume that the edge of the city sidewalk

marks your front yard property line. In fact, in most older residential neighborhoods in Milwaukee, front property lines typically fall one to six feet in from the edge of the city sidewalk. In other words, part of your front lawn is often actually city property, and a fence cannot be built on it. If you do not have a survey of your property, there is a chance that one might be on file with the city's Building Inspection Department or with your mortgage holder. If there is no survey in existence for your property, you may have to have a certified survey made by a licensed surveyor. If you need a survey, think of it as an investment because it is a valuable document that has a broad range of uses.

If the property is located in a city-designated historic district, you must also obtain approval of the design from the Historic Preservation Commission. A verbal description of the style of the fence may be all that is required by the Department of Building Inspection, but it is necessary to have a sketch or drawing of the fence if you need to seek the approval of the Historic Preservation Commission.

WOODEN FENCES

The majority of homeowners today choose to build wooden fences. Although a wooden fence typically needs more maintenance than its stone, brick, and iron counterparts, the wood fence has a special character that fence builders and homeowners have always found attractive. The amazing variety of designs used for nineteenth and early twentieth century wooden fences has been preserved in old photographs, pattern books, and millwork catalogs. Whether choosing a factory-made

wooden fence or designing and building a fence from scratch, it is important to realize that fence styles are, to a great extent, determined by the architecture of the house. Historic fences belong with historic houses and modern fences belong with modern houses. Historically, the designs of wooden fences have reflected the architectural tastes of the times during which they were built. Wooden fence designs can be generally divided into two categories: ornamental fences and privacy fences.

Milwaukee County Historical Society

A c. 1880 photo of a cottage with a picket fence.

ORNAMENTAL FENCES

By far the most common and widely known ornamental fence today is the picket fence with its pointed or decoratively cut pales or

boards that, from a distance, resemble the tines on a fork. The pickets are secured to horizontal members which are in turn anchored to posts in the ground. The picket fence has never really gone out of style in this country and has been used in some variation with nearly every architectural style from the eighteenth century to the present day.

Another type of ornamental wooden fence is the baluster fence. The baluster fence resembles and is constructed like a balustrade or hand rail on a porch or interior stairway. A baluster fence is composed of spindles or boards set between a top rail, which often looks like a typical handrail, and a bottom baseboard and rail. Some of the most remarkable wooden fences of the 1870s through the 1890s featured elaborately jig-sawn baluster boards, bold top rails, and a wide baseboard set between highly decorated fence posts. These fences were built to complement the richly detailed houses built during this period. Many historic designs for baluster fences also make good privacy screens and are an excellent alternative to modern stockade type fencing. Consider a baluster fence if you are looking for a unique design and a highly finished appearance. An important feature of the baluster fence is that both sides typically have the same finished appearance, unlike a typical picket fence which has a finished side and an interior side with visible horizontal and vertical structural members that must, according to the building code, face the interior of the lot on which it is erected. A baluster fence can be built to suit most architectural styles. The elaborate baluster designs featuring ornately shaped sawn boards should be reserved for houses built in Milwaukee before 1900. Designs for fences with simple, square or turned spindle-like

Fence pickets can be cut in a wide variety of shapes.

balusters are suitable for most architectural styles built through the 1930s.

Picket fence tops can also be cut to form gently rolling curvilinear patterns such as this example on N. Green Bay Avenue.

Many Victorian era wooden front yard fences were essentially ornamental and were low, often only three feet tall or less. Fence posts were usually thick, often measuring eight inches square or more. Often there was no gate with these diminutive fences.

Most of the classic wooden picket and baluster fences built in Milwaukee through the 1930s featured a continuous horizontal bottom board or baseboard, which is seldom part of modern picket fence designs today. This baseboard is a wooden imitation of a stone base, called a plinth, which is a feature of many iron and stone fences. The baseboard is an easy way to enhance the design of a simple picket fence as well as to add strength. Visually, a baseboard is desirable since it gives a fence a much more solid, architectural appearance.

Picket fence designs of the 1870s and 1880s with baseboards.

Baluster fence designs of the 1870s and 1880s.

An 1883 drawing of a house with a treillage privacy fence.

PRIVACY FENCES

Throughout history, the privacy fence has been a common feature of residential properties in American cities. These tall, view-obscuring fences were most commonly used to enclose rear yards. In the nineteenth and early twentieth centuries, rear yards of houses were often used as service areas where laundry was hung to dry, firewood was stored, vegetable gardens were grown, and other utilitarian domestic activities took place. Because these spaces were not formally landscaped pretty places, they were often enclosed with a tall fence. Today, the rear yard of a house is often thought of as a private space for outdoor family activities and as a secure domain for children and pets. As a result, it is still common to enclose it with a privacy fence.

Privacy fences in the nineteenth century were almost always constructed of vertical boards butted up against each other. This same type of fence is still common today and is an excellent choice for a privacy fence. It should not be mistaken for the ubiquitous stockade fence made of rough, half-round, cedar poles. A vertical board fence is constructed of finished boards that are painted or stained an opaque color. The tops of the boards may be notched, shaped or topped with a cap board to present a more decorative appearance. From the 1870s to the early 1900s, it was common to saw or pierce the top edge of the boards so that they would present a pattern of decorative cutouts when butted-up against each other.

A modern treillage fence.

The traditional treillage fence, which combines a course of lattice work atop a solid board fence, is a more ornamental type of privacy fence and another good alternative to the uninspiring designs of most modern privacy fences. Treillage fences were known to be in use at least from the early 1880s through the 1930s and complemented most architectural styles popular during those years. Advanced carpentry skills may be required to build the sophisticated treillage fence designs of years ago which featured graceful curves in the top rail that capped the lattice work, but a simulation of the same effect can be accomplished using pre-made lattice, and cutting the panels in an attractive curving shape.

To summarize, a vertical board fence is the best type to use around a rear yard when privacy is the goal. It is a fence that looks good with virtually all styles of houses. Stockade, basketweave, shadow box, and various other types of horizontal board fences, such as ranch and split-rail, are not appropriate for use with older urban houses. As a final note, historically wooden fences were always painted or stained an opaque color to complement the color of the house and were never left to weather or given a natural wood stain finish.

GATES

The gate can be designed to be a contrasting focal point to a fence or it can continue the design of a fence. A smoothly operating, sturdy gate has an inviting feel that makes a positive first impression on those entering your yard. The gate must be built solidly and fitted with good quality hardware because it is subject to more wear and abuse than any other part of a fence. Visually, the gate can be accented or made to look important simply by making the gate posts slightly taller and larger than the line posts and capping them with larger finials. Some builders do this by using 6" by 6" gate posts and 4" by 4" line posts. You may also choose to vary the size of the gate's

A tall picket fence.

A Victorian style board fence.

TRADITIONAL TYPES OF PRIVACY FENCES

A Craftsman style fence.

A solid board fence with a cap board.

pickets or balusters. The gate design may also reflect an architectural detail or motif on the house. Choosing a gate design that is completely different from the fence, however, can be risky in terms of the architectural effect it will produce. Keeping a fence or gate simple is usually safer than making it too elaborate.

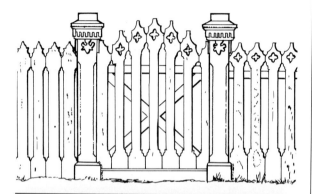

A picket fence with a matching gate design.

A fence with a contrasting gate design.

Colonial   Arts and Crafts   Spanish

English   Mission   French

Gate designs that would be appropriate for houses built between 1910 and the 1930s.

A typical gate for a picket fence can be little more than a basic wooden 2 x 4 frame stiffened with a diagonal brace that is cut to fit from the bottom corner of the hinge post side to the top corner of the latch side. The brace is vital to prevent the gate from sagging. There are many ways to join the pieces of the frame depending on your level of carpentry skill. The simplest framing method for a gate is the butt joint where the pieces are simply "butted" against each other and then nailed or screwed together. The half lap or rabbet joint is stronger. Pickets are then attached over the frame. The gate should be hung on the fence post with heavy-duty galvanized or rust-resistant hinges. There is a wide selection of gate hardware available through hardware stores.

FENCE POSTS

From Victorian times until well into the twentieth century, graceful wooden fences were constructed that featured prominent fence posts that were frequently boxed-out to dimensions as large as 12 inches square and decorated with applied moldings and sometimes topped with urn-shaped or ball finials.

Nineteenth century corner fence posts.

Posts are an important design feature of most wooden fences. In its simplest form, the top of any wooden fence post should be beveled to shed water. Fence posts with decorative tops not only look more interesting, but they also shed water which helps preserve the posts. Historic wooden fences often featured highly ornamental corner posts and gate posts, while the line posts were hidden behind the picket or baluster design. The major fence posts were important visual elements and were carefully designed.

A modern paneled boxed fence post.

For the typical flat-topped post used today, ready-made turned finials can be purchased and attached to the top of the post. A simple picket design combined with a baseboard and finial-capped posts can create a very elegant, yet affordable, fence. Many hardware and building supply stores now offer turned finials to cap fence posts, but many of these ready-made finials lack the character of historic designs. Let the post caps and finials illustrated in old millwork catalogs be your guide in selecting the proper finial for your fence.

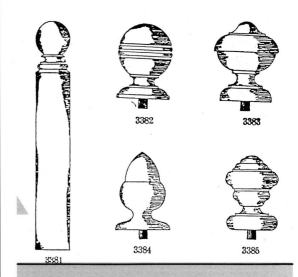

Turn-of-the-century fence post caps.

Some millwork manufacturers are now trying to more faithfully duplicate the profiles of authentic period finials. The best quality finials for exterior use manufactured today are made of clear-heart redwood, which is highly decay resistant and paints well. Finials made from untreated fir or pine lumber will be highly susceptible to decay unless treated first with a quality wood preservative and then primed and kept well painted or stained.

SOME BASIC DESIGNS FOR HISTORIC FENCES

Pattern books and old architectural journals often feature sketches of fences, but few give precise dimensions or working drawings to aid in actual construction. However, one experienced turn-of-the-century fence builder recommended the following dimensions for the 45-inch-tall basic picket fence illustrated in the figure on this page: "The best proportions for pickets are 7/8" thick by 2-1/2" wide by 38" long, set 3 inches apart with Gothic points 4 inches high." His fence also features a 1" x 6" baseboard capped with a 1" x 1-1/4" drip molding.

Another turn-of-the-century fence builder offered the straightforward, but elegant and sensibly-designed, baluster type fence illustrated on the next page. The moldings on this fence can be made with a router and table saw. The beveled 2" x 4" bottom block is designed to direct water away from the bottom end of the balusters, which are vulnerable to decay. The top rail, which looks much like a hand rail, is composed of three separate pieces of wood which should be put together with screws and waterproof glue or epoxy. All of the components should be primed or stained before assembly. Both of the turn-of-the-century fence builders specified lumber sizes that are not commonly stocked today, but today's builder could easily substitute standard lumber that is close in size to the originals.

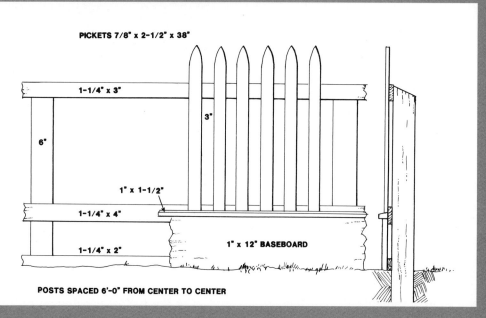

A design for a traditional picket fence (below) and a photo of a fence of this type (top).

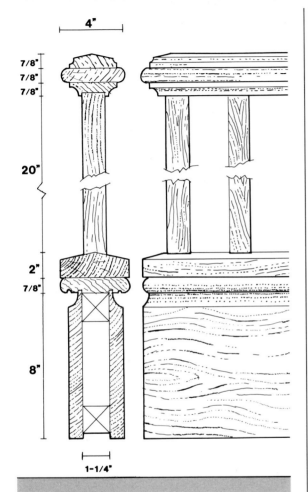

4"

7/8"
7/8"
7/8"

20"

2"
7/8"

8"

1-1/4"

A design for a baluster-type fence.

CONSTRUCTION DETAILS FOR WOODEN FENCES

Since a wooden fence can represent a substantial investment, a homeowner should carefully consider the materials used to build it. Using untreated construction grade pine or fir lumber that is primed and painted is not recommended, because of the decay-prone nature of much of today's common lumber. (See chapter on **"Wood, Siding and Trim."**) A good choice for a long-lasting fence would be pressure-treated yellow pine posts, commonly available at most building supply stores, and cedar pickets. Redwood is an excellent, highly decay resistant fencing material, but it is an endangered species of wood and should be used only for the finest projects. Pressure-treated pine could also be used for the pickets, but it does have some drawbacks, as noted in the **"Wood, Siding and Trim"** chapter, because of its tendency to warp, shrink and check, and the fact that it is difficult to paint or stain immediately.

Years ago when a wider variety of domestic wood species were commonly available, chestnut wood and black locust wood were sometimes used for fence posts because of their exceptionally high natural resistance to decay. In some cases, the fence pickets or boards may have also been made of these woods, if the budget permitted. More frequently, however, years ago fence boards were made of white pine cut from forests in northern Wisconsin, Michigan and Minnesota. As a type of preservative treatment, many fence builders in the past treated the ends of the posts coming into contact with ground by lightly charring them in a fire and then covering them with tar. Charring alone was often considered a sufficient preservative treatment. Today modern chemical preservatives are more effective and safer.

Today, the most frequently used square fence posts are called four by fours, referring to their dimension in inches before final planning at the mill. A "four by four" actually measures about 3-1/2 inches square. They are commonly sold in 8, 10, and 12 foot lengths. During the nineteenth and early twentieth centuries, when lumber was relatively inexpensive and plentiful, fences were often built with six by six posts, which would be 5-1/2 inches square in actual measurement today.

Thanks to the revival in interest in historic design, wooden fence pickets, boards and posts can be purchased with ready-cut tops in a variety of designs that suit older homes. However, a homeowner with basic power tools and plenty of patience can create a custom picket top based on designs from the past. By custom-cutting fence pickets and posts, a builder can also be more selective about the type, size, and grade of material used to build the fence.

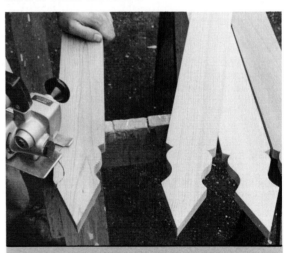

The pointed tops of these decorative pickets were cut on a table saw, and a hand-held jig saw was used for the curve cuts.

Regardless of the wood species you choose, try to select lumber with the fewest, smallest knots, and make sure the knots are sound and not cracked or loose. Lumber with numerous

knots is difficult to keep painted or stained. If you decide to buy cedar lumber board stock and cut your own fancy shaped pickets, you need to know that cedar lumber with a named thickness of one inch will actually measure about 3/4" thick and will typically have a rough side and a smooth side. For an extra charge, many lumber yards will surface plane the rough side giving a smooth appearance to both faces of the board, which is necessary if you want to construct a high quality period fence. Modern picket or baluster fences will not totally duplicate the appearance of old fences because the pickets or fence boards in old fences measured between 7/8" to 1-1/4" in actual thickness rather than the 3/4" thickness standard today. The thicker lumber of the past undoubtedly gave those fences a decidedly more substantial appearance and helped them last longer.

A modern picket fence of traditional design.

The enemy of all wood is water. On a wooden fence, it is standing water that leads to rot. When building a wooden fence, try to visualize where water or moisture could be trapped because these "wet spots" create the conditions that lead to the premature decay of the fence. Construction methods that eliminate wet spots can greatly lengthen the service life of the fence.

The typical wooden picket fence tends to trap moisture at the points where the pickets or boards lap the horizontal cross members. These areas consequently tend to decay quickly. There are at least three ways to deal with wet spots. The easiest, and probably least effective over time, is to caulk the tops of all the overlaps to try to seal out the water. Eventually, the joints will open, however, and water will get in no matter how good a caulk you use. A better method is to gap all the overlap points that can catch water by using galvanized metal or hard nylon washers when attaching the pickets to the horizontal support members. The resulting thin space or gap between the connecting boards would allow water to drain through the gap rather than getting trapped between the pickets and the rail creating the conditions that lead to decay. The quicker wood can dry out and thus be protected from prolonged contact with moisture, the longer the wood will last.

A third method of dealing with moisture-related decay in a fence is to recess horizontal members of the fence such as the baseboard and rails into wide grooves, called rabbets, cut into the fence pickets or boards. This construction, called joinery, will deflect water down the face of the fence to the ground

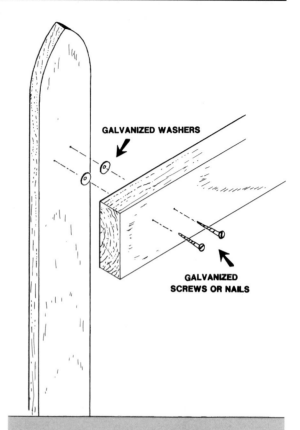

GALVANIZED WASHERS

GALVANIZED SCREWS OR NAILS

The washer gap method of building a picket fence.

instead of trapping it where the boards lap. The recessed lap joint is more difficult to construct and requires a few more woodworking tools and skills than the average homeowner may have. A carpenter, however, should be able to do the joinery. Considering the cost of quality wood today and the amount of labor it takes to design and build any fence, the cost of the special joinery may pay for itself in the long run with a longer-lasting, easier to maintain fence.

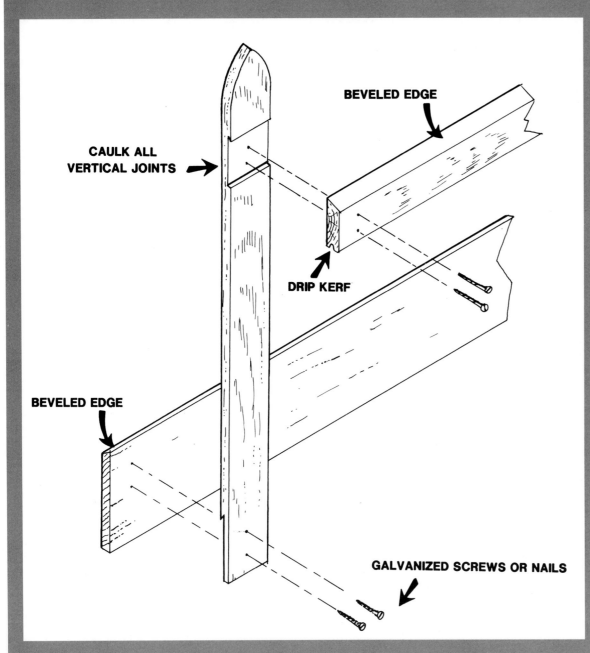

CAULK ALL
VERTICAL JOINTS

BEVELED EDGE

DRIP KERF

BEVELED EDGE

GALVANIZED SCREWS OR NAILS

The joinery method of building a picket fence.

PAINTING

A lack of periodic repainting can be one of the major factors contributing to the premature deterioration of a wooden fence. It is often easier to maintain the finish on a new fence if the bare wood is stained with a so-called "solid-hide" exterior stain which is now available in many colors including white. Many users of solid-hide stains report that little or no scraping is required when the finish needs to be renewed, although the stains tend to fade quicker than regular paints. Many carpenters recommend priming and painting or staining all of the individual pickets of the fence before assembly in order to better seal out moisture.

CONSTRUCTION

Digging holes for fence posts is hard work and if your fence will have a large number of posts, you may choose to hire the labor of a commercial post hole digging service. Posts should be set a minimum of 30 inches below grade and usually no more than eight feet apart from center to center. Holes can also be dug with a traditional manually operated clam-shell type post hole digger or you can rent an auger type gas-powered post hole digger. Regardless of the digging tool you use, expect your work to be slowed considerably if the site is rocky or contains buried debris. It is also helpful to have a long bar to help clear obstructions from the bottom of the hole.

To align the posts, you can stretch a string along the path of the fence, anchoring it to

wooden stakes. Make sure you use a level to "plumb" the posts so they are set perfectly vertical. To lay out long stretches of fence, some builders use an optical tool called a sight level or transit, both of which resemble a small telescope on a tripod. Once the post is set in the hole, you have the option of backfilling the post hole with either compacted earth or concrete. Before backfilling, some builders recommend setting the end of the post in about six inches of compacted stone to help drain water away from the bottom of the post. Posts that support a gate are ordinarily set in concrete, since the weight of the gate can easily pull a post out of line if it is set only in soil.

CONTRACTORS

Homeowners are often capable of designing and building a fence of excellent quality, but many people choose to have a contractor do the work. A contractor may have an advantage over a homeowner because he has better tools and a skilled work force. A detailed contract is important to protect both the homeowner and the contractor. The homeowner should feel free to specify in the contract exactly how the fence should look and be constructed. A typical fencing contract may include a scale drawing or sketch of the proposed fence along with additional written details such as dimensions, precise location, the type and grade of materials used, applicable building codes that must be followed, method and time of payment, approximate starting and finishing dates, and who is responsible for obtaining the necessary building permits.

ORNAMENTAL IRON FENCING

Because iron is a long-lived material, there are still some historic iron fences in existence, although many need restoration. Even if your property never had an iron fence, or if it has been removed, you may be interested to know that there are craftsmen around today capable of recreating the ornamental iron designs of the late nineteenth and early twentieth centuries. In addition, today, there has been a resurgence in interest in ornamental metal fencing and numerous manufacturers are recreating historic fence designs in stamped and tubular steel and aluminum as well as traditional cast iron and wrought iron.

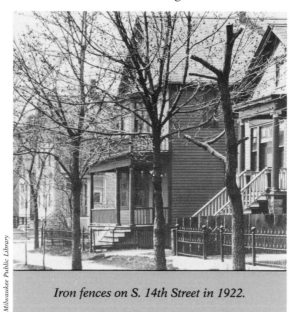

Iron fences on S. 14th Street in 1922.

Milwaukee Public Library

Historically, there were two major types of metal fencing, wrought iron and cast iron, each possessing its own unique qualities. Ornamental cast iron is made from molten metal poured into molds. Many designs that can be carved or fabricated in wood can be cast in iron. Cast iron fencing was typically mass-produced in a foundry. In contrast, wrought iron was made from iron bars that were heated yellow hot to a pliable state and then pounded, cut, pulled and twisted into the desired shape by a process called hand-forging. Hand-forged wrought iron is truly custom work. Cast iron, although very durable, is more brittle than wrought iron, which has been known to last for centuries.

Historic wrought iron, its beauty aside, is also worth preserving because the material is no longer made. Ornamental iron works today use mild steel for hand-forged work. True wrought iron, manufactured up until about 1960 in this country, is pure iron (not steel) containing about three percent, by weight, of impurities called slag. The slag gives historic wrought iron a graininess and character that is lacking in the relatively smooth mild steel iron workers use today. This is not to say, however, that today's best ornamental iron work is any less attractive than that of years ago. Historic wrought iron was also much more corrosion resistant than mild steel because of the manufacturing process. The last known commercial manufacturer of genuine wrought iron went out of business in Sweden about 1970.

It is becoming increasingly difficult to find salvaged iron fencing, particularly if numerous matching sections are needed, but some restorers still manage to find salvaged fencing from antique dealers and demolition contractors. Often the fencing will be found in a very rusted and damaged condition, but it can usually be restored. It is also possible to have new iron fencing sections or pieces made to match old or existing iron fencing.

An 1880s photograph of the Hornbach and Wagner plant on North Water Street, one of several companies in Milwaukee that made wrought iron fences in the 19th century.

Rust and bent or broken metal are the two most prevalent conditions to be dealt with in restoring ornamental iron work. The only way to successfully fight rust is to completely remove it from the iron work. Simply using an ordinary metal paint over a rusted fence will not necessarily protect it from further deterioration. Most paints applied over a rusted surface still allow water and air to reach the metal so that the rusting process actually con-

tinues under the skin of new paint. Rusted ornamental iron work should be cleaned to bare metal and then repainted. Rust, scale, and layers of paint can be removed from old fencing by sandblasting, a process which was developed during the late nineteenth century primarily to clean iron and steel. Sandblasting is an acceptable method to restore iron and steel, but it should not be used to clean soft materials such as brass, bronze, copper, brick, stone, and wood, which can be seriously damaged by the blasting process. Sandblasting ordinarily removes only the rust and paint from iron and steel leaving the sound metal untouched. For in-shop sandblasting services, homeowners may consult one of the many local cemetery monument makers. They use sandblasting equipment in the production of monuments and many welcome the cleaning of iron items. There are also painting firms that specialize in bringing sandblasting units to the job site, but this work usually requires a permit from the City Health Department because of the health hazard caused by blowing sand. Some sandblasters will, upon request, use walnut shells or glass beads as the abrasive agent rather than sand, when a finer finish on the cleaned metal is desired. Ironwork that can be removed from the job site can also be successfully cleaned by a dip-strip process used by several local metal cleaning and de-rusting companies.

After cleaning, either by dip-stripping or sandblasting, the bare iron will be light gray in color and must immediately be primed and painted with high quality metal paint to prevent rust from forming. Two-part epoxy urethane paints are presently considered the best choice for a lasting, protective finish on clean iron fencing. The epoxy paints do an excep-

An architectural antiques company fencing department.

tional job of sealing out rust-causing air and moisture. These paints come in two parts which are mixed together just before use. They are expensive, but will last much longer than conventional metal paints if applied properly.

Craftsmen, such as blacksmiths doing hand-forged work, are capable of straightening bent wrought iron work by heating it and then pounding and bending it back into shape. Cast iron ornamental work, however, which is inherently brittle, tends to break rather than bend and, therefore, new pieces may have to be cast and then reattached by a process called "brazing." Brazing is basically a type of soldering operation using an alloy such as brass. Cast iron usually cannot be successfully welded because the intense heat generated by the process can actually make the iron too brittle for use. There are a few small foundries capable of doing short production runs or perhaps making a one-of-a-kind casting at relatively

A cast iron fence of the 1870s or 1880s.

A cast iron fence of the 1880s.

An iron fence of the 1890s or early 1900s.

HISTORIC IRON FENCE DESIGNS

A cast iron fence of the 1870s or 1880s.

An iron fence of the 1890s.

An iron picket fence of the 1880s or 1890s.

An iron picket fence of the 1890s.

An iron picket fence of the 1930s.

A Prairie Style iron fence.

HISTORIC IRON FENCE DESIGNS

An iron fence of the early 1900s with boxed iron posts

An iron picket fence of the early 1900s.

A modern iron picket fence.

reasonable prices. The quickest and cheapest way to have a cast iron replacement piece made is to carve, cut and shape a model of the needed part out of foam boards such as the type used for insulation. The foam can then be packed in foundry sand to form a mold, and when the molten metal is poured into it, the foam pattern vaporizes leaving behind the new metal casting.

The increased interest in restoration and historic design has resulted in many new sources of iron and metal fencing being put on the market in a wide range of quality and prices. New cast iron fencing, made like the nineteenth and early twentieth century originals, is available from several firms around the country. Some of the new reproduction fences, such as some of those made of stamped and tubular aluminum, do not approach the quality and detail of the original iron fences. Compare prices carefully before buying. Quality is often not as expensive as you might think. There are many ornamental iron contractors working today, but few are capable of doing restoration work on old ironwork. Most ornamental iron companies today purchase ready-made ornamental steel shapes and then weld them together to form attractive fences suitable for use at older homes. For those devoted to quality and who also have an ample budget, the hand-forged custom work of a blacksmith is still available here in Milwaukee.

HISTORIC ESTATE TYPE FENCES IN MILWAUKEE

Many historic fences were made of two or more materials. There were combinations of stone and brick, stone and wood, iron and stone, or iron and brick. Fencing sections set between stone or brick posts or piers was considered a very fashionable combination during the late nineteenth and early twentieth centuries. The posts often featured decoratively shaped or carved tops. Decoratively-sawn tops can still be made by local stone quarries today.

Eric Moebius, a Milwaukee iron craftsman, at work in his shop.

Iron fencing sections set between brick or stone piers was common only on very expensive houses because it was such a costly fence type. For a fence of this type, the brick piers must be more than twelve inches square when working with standard-sized brick, and each pier must have a concrete footing extending below the frostline. Many early twentieth century architects specified that the concrete footing for brick fence piers be placed 4'-6" below grade to protect them from the destructive effects of the annual freeze/thaw cycle. Generally, these types of fences, sometimes known as estate fencing, are most appropriate for use on large, early twentieth century houses set on ample grounds. They would generally be out of place in front of most Victorian houses and in neighborhoods characterized by small lots.

An estate type iron fence with brick piers.

An 1870s estate fence in the Italianate style.

A 1904 estate fence in the French style.

A 1905 estate fence in the Colonial style.

EXAMPLES OF ESTATE TYPE IRON FENCES WITH MASONRY PIERS

A 1920s estate fence in the Neoclassical style.

A 1930s estate fence in the Colonial style.

A 1920s estate fence in the Mediterranean style.

RETAINING WALLS

The foundation of this new brick and dressed stone retaining wall extends four feet below the grade level to ensure a quality job that will resist the potentially damaging effects of the annual freeze-thaw cycle.

Building a retaining wall is a labor-intensive project, and, because such walls are invariably very bulky and massive, careful consideration should be given to the visual impact the wall will have not only on your property but also on your neighbors'. Many homeowners want to build retaining walls to eliminate the hill, called a berm, where their front lawns slope down to the sidewalk. Admittedly, it may be difficult to push a lawn mower up some of the more steeply bermed lawns to cut the grass, but building a retaining wall to eliminate the hill and hold back the earth behind it is even more difficult and generally very, very expensive. A grassy berm is also a more historically correct treatment for most houses, since retaining walls were not a common feature of nineteenth and early twentieth century neighborhoods in Milwaukee.

Some homeowners use landscape timbers or railroad ties to build retaining walls because they are relatively inexpensive and it is much easier to construct a timber wall than a masonry wall. In the long run, however, wooden retaining walls, as commonly built today, do not have sufficient weight and mass to hold back the earth behind them. After a few years of service, it is common to find a wooden retaining wall leaning out of shape, very weathered, and appearing shabby rather than rustic, much to the disappointment of the homeowner. Wooden retaining walls are, at best, a quick fix, and not a long-term solution to landscaping problems. Also, timber retaining walls are a relatively recent invention and are not appropriate for use in an older neighborhood. For these reasons, wooden retaining walls are not recommended for use in front yards if you want to complement the architecture of your older house. Wooden retaining walls are generally not allowed in city-designated historic districts. A traditional masonry retaining wall made of dressed stone or brick is considered a much better investment and is much more complementary to the architecture of older buildings. Retaining walls made of hollow or solid interlocking concrete block are not recommended for some of the same reasons that landscape timbers and railroad ties are not and because these relatively recent inventions present a starkly modern appearance that is not compatible with most older houses.

Building a retaining wall has always been an expensive and risky undertaking. As a result, in the past, most homeowners, unless they were very affluent, avoided building them, preferring natural landscape solutions instead. A masonry wall that rests on soil sub-ject to freezing during the winter literally rides a roller coaster of churning earth that can easily crack a wall apart at the mortar joints. Moist soil that freezes in winter will expand and push up everything above it, including a heavy masonry wall. The opposite effect happens during the spring thaw as the soil contracts. To minimize the effects of the freeze-thaw cycle, the foundation for a masonry wall, called a footing, should ideally be set about four feet below grade, which is several inches below the level of maximum frost penetration. This is very costly, however, particularly when the desired height of the retaining wall or fence above ground may only be two or three feet. Brick retaining walls, which are generally the most historically and aesthetically correct choice, must be built with footings.

An impressive battered retaining wall made of random-cut, rock-faced ashlars.

To eliminate the need for expensive foundations, one possible choice is a stone retaining wall that is laid up "dry," that is, without mortar in the joints. Such a wall stays in place by

the weight of the stones themselves. This type of wall, however, is not appropriate for all types of houses, because of its rustic appearance. It would look inappropriate in front of most Victorian houses and many very formal twentieth century dwellings, although it might be all right for use in a side or rear yard.

The dry-laid stone wall is said by some to be the easiest masonry wall to construct. Homeowners with basic building skills and a strong back should be able to build a dry laid stone wall with excellent results. Typically, large stones are selected for the base and laid just below grade on undisturbed, leveled soil. On top of these stones are placed the regular wall stones. According to one old rule of thumb, a dry masonry wall should not be less than two feet in thickness at the base for a wall up to three feet in height. For every six inches of additional height, the width should be increased by four inches. Although many stone walls are built perfectly vertical or "plumb," many builders choose to "batter" the wall, which means it slopes inward from the base to the top.

Stone walls can be built in many different patterns and textures, but the four most basic types of stone walls that can be dry-laid are: random rubble, coursed rubble, random ashlar, and coursed ashlar. The simplest of these, random rubble, is made of irregular, random-dimensioned, natural stone that cannot be laid with continuous horizontal joints. Random rubble walls have a rustic, informal appearance and are laid with as little cutting or splitting of the stone as possible. Coursed rubble walls are made from irregular stone, but laid in recognizable horizontal courses or layers. An ashlar is a squared, or dressed,

building stone. Random ashlar walls are made of dressed stones of various sizes that permit close fitting joints. Coursed ashlar walls are generally formal-looking and are made of regularly-shaped, block-like stones that can be laid in precise patterns with continuous horizontal joints.

A dry laid stone wall at 2601 N. Wahl Avenue.

Limestone is a common type of building stone, and it is readily available from local sources. It was, and still is, the most common choice for stone retaining walls. Limestone ashlars and rubble can also be salvaged from demolition sites. Salvaged stone makes a fine retaining wall and can be relatively inexpensive to acquire, although moving it to the construction site can be back-breaking work. ∎

COURSED ASHLAR

RANDOM ASHLAR

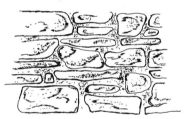

COURSED RUBBLE

RANDOM RUBBLE

Types of stone masonry.

A good example of a traditional stone retaining wall.

A good example of a traditional brick retaining wall.

RETAINING WALLS

A timber retaining wall should not be used at an old house if it will be visible from the street.

An interlocking concrete block retaining wall should not be used at an old house if it will be visible from the street.

GLOSSARY

GLOSSARY

GLOSSARY

GLOSSARY

GLOSSARY

GLOSSARY

GLOSSARY

GLOSSARY

GLOSSARY

GLOSSARY

ANNULAR NAILS — Nail with circular ridges on the shank to give it greater holding power.

ARCHITRAVE — The bottommost member of a 3 part, classical entablature. Also refers to a molded window or door enframement.

ASHLAR — A squared or rectangular building stone.

BACK PLASTERING — Plastering that is applied within wall cavities or rafters to make the building warmer and keep out the cold. (See Energy Conservation and Insulation chapter for illustration.)

BACK-SET — Distance from the outside edge of a lock to the center of the door knob.

BALLOON FRAME — Type of wood frame construction with wall studs extending in uninterrupted lengths from the foundation to the top of a wall. (See Wood, Siding and Trim chapter for illustration.)

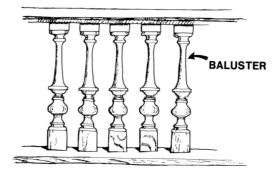

BALUSTER — An upright member supporting a railing or banister.

BALUSTRADE — A railing composed of a handrail supported by balusters.

BARGEBOARD — A wide ornamented fascia board hung from the eaves or in a gable.

BATTEN — A narrow vertical wooden strip installed to cover the joint between two larger boards. Used in "board and batten" exterior siding.

BAY WINDOW — A polygonal window unit that projects from of an exterior wall and extends to the ground level. A rectangular-shaped bay window is called a "box bay window."

BELT COURSE — A continuous horizontal band on an exterior wall. Also called a "string course," it can be made of brick, stone or wood.

Previous Page: Detail of 1201 N. Prospect Avenue

BEVEL SIDING — A traditional wooden siding material made of overlapping horizontal wedge-shaped boards. Commonly called clapboard siding.

BOWER-BARFF PROCESS — Named after its two English inventors, it is a heat and chemical surface treatment used on iron hardware that produced a blue-black finish without paint or stain.

BRACKETS — Supporting members of wood, stone or metal often used for both decorative and structural purposes and generally found under projecting features such as eaves or cornices. Also, the supports for a balcony.

CAME — Channel-like strips of lead or zinc that are used to join the individual pieces of glass in a leaded glass window.

CAPITAL — The decorative head or top of a column or pilaster.

CASEMENT — A window that is hinged on one side and swings open like a door. (See Wooden Windows chapter for illustration.)

CHAMFER — A beveled edge

CLAPBOARDS — See "Bevel siding."

CORBELING — A series of stepped or overlapping pieces of brick or stone, often forming a support.

CORINTHIAN — A classical style of architecture characterized by columns with capitals that are adorned with acanthus leaf ornament.

CORNER BOARDS — Vertical trim boards installed at the outside and inside corners of a wall covered with wooden siding.

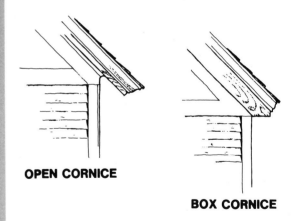

OPEN CORNICE

BOX CORNICE

CORNICE — Generally refers to the horizontal, projecting molding that crowns the top of a wall. In classical architecture, it is the uppermost part of the entablature.

CRESTING — Wood or metal ornament used to trim the ridge on a roof.

CRICKET — See "Saddle."

CUPOLA — A small, domed or pointed-roof structure located at the top of a roof; it often has louvered sides and may be used to ventilate the interior of a structure.

CUT NAIL — The correct name for an old-fashioned, "square" nail.

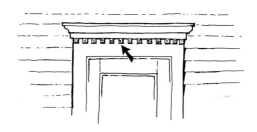

DENTIL BLOCKS — A molding composed of a series of regularly spaced small blocks usually placed under a cornice or overhang.

DORIC — A style of classical architecture characterized by columns with simple round capitals without carving.

DORMER — A window projecting from a roof.

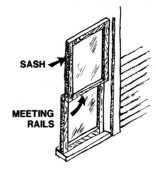

SASH

MEETING RAILS

DOUBLE HUNG WINDOW — Most common type of wooden window in older houses. Composed of two glazed units, each called a sash, that slide vertically by each other in separate channels.

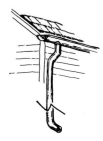

DOWNSPOUT — Vertical pipe that carries run-off water from a gutter.

DROP SIDING — Sometimes called "shiplap," it is a type of interlocking, horizontal board siding, usually at least 3/4" thick, with a decoratively machined edge. (See Wood, Siding and Trim chapter for illustration.)

DRY ROT — Traditionally refers to a type of wood decay caused by moisture. Today the term is often used to describe rotted wood in a soft, dry, crumbly condition.

EAVE — The part of a roof that projects beyond the side walls of a building.

EAVES TROUGH — A half-round gutter.

EFFLORESCENCE — White, powdery substance sometimes found on mortar joints and brick.

ENTASIS — A very slight bulging or convex curve incorporated into the shaft of a column that serves as a visual correction to make the column appear straight.

EPOXY — A modern plastic-like material used to repair wood or stone that results from the chemical reaction caused by mixing a catalyst with a resin or paste.

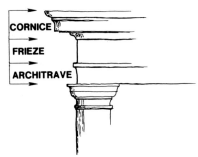

ENTABLATURE — The horizontal architectural component at the top of a wall in classical architecture. The architrave is the bottom-most part, the frieze is located in the middle, and the cornice is at the top.

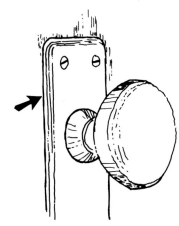

ESCUTCHEON — Decorative metal plate on which a door knob is mounted.

EYEBROW DORMER — A low curvilinear dormer window that has no distinct side-walls because the roofing material gently curves over the window. Common to Queen Anne, Shingle and Craftsman style houses.

FACADE — The main elevation or entrance front of a building.

FANLIGHT — A curving window over a door, usually semicircular or semi-elliptical in shape with radiating spokes or muntins that give it the appearance of a fan.

FASCIA BOARD — A finish board attached to the ends of roof rafters.

FENESTRATION — The arrangement of windows and doors on a wall

FINIAL — A carved, turned, or sawn ornament made of wood, metal, or stone that crowns a gable, gatepost, or some other peaked element.

FISHSCALE SHINGLES — Wood or terra cotta shingles with rounded butts.

FLASHING — Strips of metal or other material installed on architectural features that project from walls or roofs to prevent water leakage. Typically found at dormers, valleys on roofs, around chimneys, and at the top of belt courses, window and door openings.

FLUE — Hollow shaft in a chimney that conducts fumes, heat, and other products of combustion from heating equipment out of a building.

GLOSSARY

FOOTING — The lowest part of a foundation system that rests directly on the soil and serves as a base for the foundation wall. Footings are usually made of concrete or limestone and are located several feet underground.

FRIEZE — The middle element of a classical entablature. It is usually plain, but sometimes features decorative carving. See "Entablature" for illustration.

GABLE — The triangular upper portion of a wall beneath a peaked roof.

GABLE ROOF — A roof composed of two sloping planes that meet at a ridge.

GABLE ORNAMENT — Ornamental trim beneath the peak of a gable.

GALVANIC ACTION — Chemical corrosion caused by the meeting of two dissimilar metals in a moist or wet environment.

GALVANIZING — A coating of zinc to prevent iron or steel from rusting.

GAMBREL ROOF — Roof composed of two sloping planes of differing pitches on either side of a ridge; the lower plain is the steeper one.

GLAZING — The transparent or semi-transparent glass or plastic in a window.

GRADE — Surface level of the ground.

GUTTER — Horizontal metal trough at the edge of a roof used for conducting water to downspouts.

HEMACITE — A type of composition material used for making door hardware invented during the late nineteenth century that is made from a tightly compressed mixture of sawdust and animal blood.

HIGH-BACK GUTTER — A traditional type of rain gutter that is attached to the roof by means of a continuous, integral metal flange that extends up the roof a few inches beneath the first row of roofing shingles.

HIP ROOF — A roof with sloping planes on all four sides that meet at a central ridge or point.

HOOD — A small, projecting roof often supported by brackets that shelters a door or window.

HOOD MOLD — A projecting molding made of wood, brick or stone above an arch, door, or window.

INSULATING GLASS — A factory-prepared "sandwich" of two sheets of glass with a sealed air space in between that reduces heat loss.

IONIC — A style of classical architecture characterized by columns with capitals ornamented with large spiral scrolls, called volutes.

JAMB — The top and side members of a door or window frame.

JOIST — A structural member which supports a floor.

KEYSTONE — The topmost or center brick or stone in an arch.

LATH — Perforated expanded metal sheets or thin strips of wood that serve as a base for plaster or stucco. (See Brick, Mortar, Stone and Stucco chapter for illustration.)

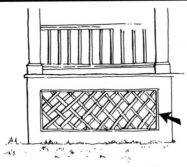

LATTICE — An openwork grille produced by lapping or weaving strips of wood.

LEXAN® — The brand name of a popular, break resistant, clear, polycarbonate (plastic) glazing material that is sometimes used in place of glass.

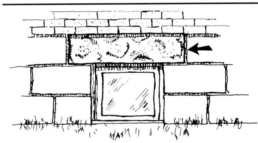

LINTEL — A horizontal beam bridging a window or door opening to carry the weight of the wall above the opening.

LUNETTE — A crescent shaped window opening or panel.

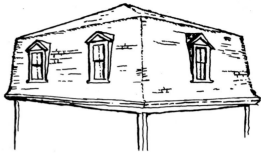

MANSARD ROOF — A type of roof with a steeply pitched, nearly vertical, lower plane topped by a low sloping or flat deck.

MARGARD® — The brand name of a special type of Lexan® (plastic) glazing material that is scratch-resistant.

MEETING RAIL — The bottom horizontal member of the outer sash and top horizontal member of the inner sash of a double-hung window. (See "Double Hung Window" for illustration.)

MINERAL FIBER — Formerly called cement asbestos, it is roof and siding material made from Portland cement, and asbestos or another mineral fiber which is molded under intense pressure to make thin, slate-like shingles or sheets.

MINERAL WOOL — Term used to collectively describe insulation materials made of fiberglass, rock wool or slag wool, all of which have a soft, wool-like texture and composition.

MITER BOX — A tool for cutting precise angles in wood.

MITER CUT — A bevel cut used to join two pieces of wood together at an angle.

MORTAR — Mixture of sand, cement, water and, usually, lime used for bonding together brick or stone.

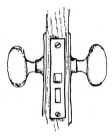

MORTISE LOCK — A metal locking mechanism that is made to fit into a pocket, called a "mortise," cut into the edge of a door. Mortise locks were used for most interior and exterior doors made before 1935.

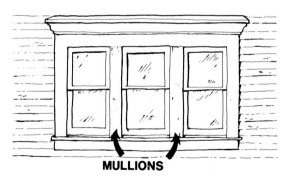

MULLIONS

MULLION — The vertical dividing members between multiple grouped windows. Sometimes used to describe vertical muntin bars.

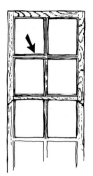

MUNTIN — The strips that separate panes of glass in a sash.

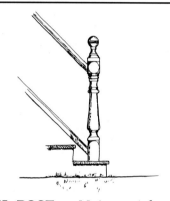

NEWEL POST — Main upright member that supports the handrails of a staircase, especially the post found at the foot of a staircase handrail.

OCULUS — A round or oval window without tracery or muntins, sometimes called a bull's eye window.

OLD GROWTH — Refers to mature virgin timber that was very old when it was harvested and has superior durability and working qualities.

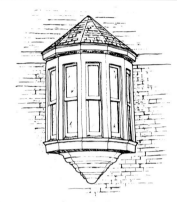

ORIEL — A multi-sided window unit that projects from the surface of an exterior wall that does not extend to the ground level, but rather is supported by means of brackets or corbeling.

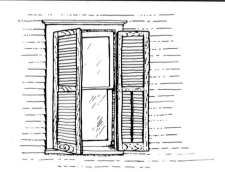

OUTSIDE BLINDS — A frame with movable or fixed horizontal wooden slats called louvers that is installed on hinges at either side of a window and that closes over the window opening to regulate the flow of light and air. See also "Shutters."

PALLADIAN WINDOW — An ornamental window unit composed of a central, round-head window flanked on either side by a separate, smaller, rectangular window.

PARTING STRIP — The thin vertical piece of wood that separates the tracks that the upper and lower sash of a double-hung window move in. (See Wooden Windows chapter for illustration.)

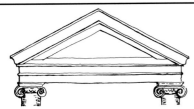

PEDIMENT — The enclosed triangular space in the gable of a classical style building or any similar form above a door, window, or portico.

PENNY — A measure of nail size that is abbreviated by the letter "d."

PILASTER — A shallow rectangular pier articulated like a column that is mounted on a wall surface.

PLATES — Horizontal pieces of framing lumber at the top and bottom of wood-framed walls to which the studs are fastened.

PLATFORM FRAMING — Wood framing method in which each story of the building is framed as a unit with the wall studs only extending the height of one-story. The floor of each story serves as a "platform" for the construction of the story above it. (See Wood, Siding and Trim chapter for illustration.)

PLEXIGLAS® — The brand name of a popular clear acrylic (plastic) sheet material often used as a substitute for glass. Although many times stronger than glass, it is breakable. See "Lexan®".

PLUMB — Term used to describe an object, such as a post or wall, is perfectly vertical and stands at a 90 degree angle to a level surface.

PORTICO — A projecting, classical style porch supported by columns.

PRIME WINDOW — Refers to a built-in window that is permanently attached to a house as opposed to a storm window.

PUTTY — A mixture of calcium carbonate, linseed oil, and other ingredients historically used for filling holes and installing window glass. This material is not the same as modern glazing compound which is often called putty.

QUATREFOIL — A circular ornamental shape or window with four intersecting lobes also called "foils." Associated with Gothic Revival, Victorian Gothic, and Italianate style architecture.

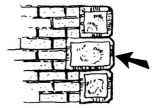

QUOINS — Slightly projecting ornamental stone blocks, sometimes simulated in brick or wood, used to accentuate the corners of buildings.

RABBET — A lip or groove cut into the edge of a piece of wood.

RAFTER — Usually the sloping or horizontal structural framing member to which the roof sheathing and roofing materials are attached.

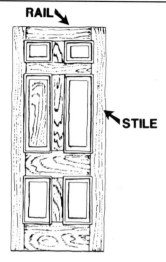

RAIL — A horizontal member in a door or window.

RAKING MOLDING — Exterior trim or molding on a wall or fascia that is applied parallel to the roof slope. See "Ridge Cap" for illustration.

REHABILITATION — Renewing old buildings for modern living while preserving original architectural features and character.

REMODELING — Rehabilitating an old building by removing or destroying its original features and substituting new features to give it a new appearance unlike its original look.

RESTORATION — The rejuvenation and/or replication of historic architectural features to match exactly the original appearance.

RETAINING WALL — A wall built to hold back a bank of earth.

RETURN — A molding or cornice carried around a corner and then stopped. Typically found on the gable end of a building.

RIDGE — The peak of a roof. Also the horizontal framing member at the peak to which the rafters are attached.

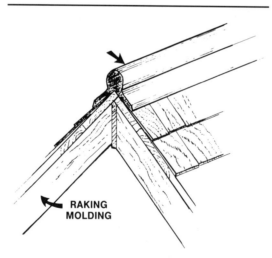

RIDGE CAP — A metal or wood cap that tops the ridge of a roof.

RIM LOCK — A surface-mounted, boxlike door locking and latching mechanism popular in the 18th and early 19th centuries. (See Doors and Hardware for illustration.)

RISER — The vertical face of a step.

R-VALUE — Measure of a building material's ability to resist heat transmission. The greater the R-value, the better a material will insulate.

ROUND HEAD WINDOW — A window with a semicircular top.

SADDLE — Small, inverted, V-shaped assembly placed at the back side of a chimney rising from a sloping roof to divert water away from the chimney. Also called a "cricket." (See Roofing Systems chapter for illustration.)

SASH — Wood or metal frame composed of rails and stiles into which glass window panes are set. See Double Hung Window for an illustration.

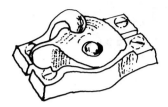

SASH LOCK — Hardware used to lock two window sash together.

SASH WEIGHT — An iron weight used to balance a sash so that it can be opened to any desired extent. (See Wooden Windows chapter for illustration.)

SCAFFOLDING — Temporary work platform, usually made of steel, set up in, or around, a building to reach work areas high above the ground or floor level.

SEGMENTAL ARCH — A shallow curved arch formed by the segment of a circle.

SHAKE — A thick, rustic-looking wooden roofing material made by splitting, rather than sawing, a log. Not suitable for use on Milwaukee's existing historic housing stock.

SHEATHING — Boards applied over the wall studs or rafters to which the finish wall or roofing material, such as bevel wood siding, brick, stucco or roofing shingles, is applied.

SHED ROOF — A roof type composed of a single sloping plane.

SHUTTERS — Solid wooden panels installed on hinges at each side of a window that cover the window openings when closed. Shutters should not be confused with outside blinds that feature movable or fixed slats called louvers. See "Outside blinds."

SILL — The bottom member of a window frame. Also the heavy timber member resting on the foundation to which the wall studs are attached.

SOFFIT — Refers to the exposed and finished underside of a roof overhang, staircase, arch, or box beam.

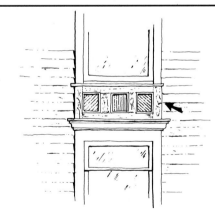

SPANDREL — The triangular space between the curve of an arch and an enclosing right angle. Also commonly used to describe a panel below a window.

STANDING GUTTER — See "Yankee gutter."

STILE — The vertical side member of a door or window sash. See "Rail" for illustration.

STOP — A strip on a window frame against which the sash slides.

STORY POLE — A stick marked off in carefully calculated units that is used to properly align courses of siding or masonry.

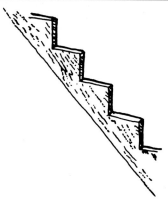

STRINGER — Sloping wooden structural members that provide the main support for a staircase.

STUCCO — An exterior finish plaster material that is rich in Portland cement.

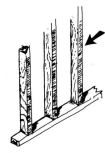

STUDS — Vertical framing members in a wood-framed building.

SURROUND — An enframement, as around a window or door.

SWALE — A small depression in the earth designed to divert surface run-off water.

TERRA COTTA — A fired clay building material.

THRESHOLD — The bottom member of a door frame.

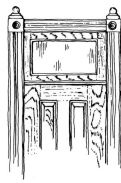

TRANSOM — Small window, sometimes movable, located over a door or another window.

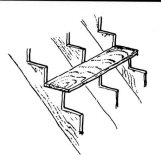

TREAD — Often called a step, it is the horizontal part of a staircase.

TREILLAGE FENCE — A traditional style of fence that features a band of lattice work atop a solid, vertical board base.

TUCKPOINTING — Refilling deteriorated mortar joints with fresh mortar.

VAPOR BARRIER — Moisture-resistant material installed in a wall or on the ground to retard the passage of moisture.

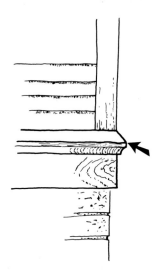

WATER TABLE — A molding or projecting sloping shelf located at the bottom of a wall that is designed to divert run-off water away from the masonry foundation below it.

WINDOW CAP — Decorative element that trims the top of a window surround.

WYTHE — One unit thickness of a masonry wall.

YANKEE GUTTER — Also called a standing gutter. A surface mounted V-shaped trough located about a foot above the edge of a roof to conduct run-off water to a downspout. A Yankee gutter allowed an unobstructed view of decorative or ornamental woodwork mounted on a fascia. (See Roofing Systems chapter for illustration.)

ZINC — A silver gray, rust-resistant metal. Sheet zinc was a popular building material for ornamental metal work 100 years ago. Zinc is also used as a thin coating or plating over steel nails or thin sheet steel to prevent rust. See "Galvanizing."

BOOKS

Blake, Ernest G., <u>Roof Coverings: Their Manufacture and Application</u> (London: Chapman and Hall Ltd., 1925).

Brown, Robert W., <u>Residential Foundations</u> (New York: Van Nostrand Reinhold Co., 1984).

Buckley, Ernest R., <u>Wisconsin Geological and Natural History Survey</u>, Bulletin No. IV on the Building and Ornamental Stones of Wisconsin, (Madison, WI: State of Wisconsin, 1898).

Cleaveland, Henry W., et al., <u>Village and Farm Cottages</u> (New York: D. Appleton and Co., 1856).

<u>Cyclopedia of Architecture, Carpentry and Building</u> (Chicago: American School of Correspondence, 1909).

Davey, Norman, <u>A History of Building Materials</u> (London: Phoenix House, 1961).

Ellis, Raymond, <u>Making a Garage</u> (New York: McBride, Nast & Co., 1913).

Ericson, Emanuel E., <u>Glass and Glazing</u> (Peoria, IL: The Manual Arts Press, 1926).

Faloon, Dalton B., <u>Zinc Oxide: History, Manufacture and Properties as a Pigment</u> (New York: D. Van Nostrand Co., 1925).

Flower, Frank A., ed., <u>History of Milwaukee</u> (Chicago: Western Historical Publishing Co., 1881).

<u>Garages: Country and Suburban</u> (New York: The American Architect, 1911).

<u>Glass, Paints, Varnishes and Brushes</u> (Pittsburgh: Pittsburgh Plate Glass Co., 1923).

Graham, Frank D., <u>Audels Carpenters and Builders Guide #3</u> (New York: Theo. Audel and Co., 1949).

Hampton, Taylor, <u>The Nickel Plate Road</u> (Cleveland: The World Publishing Co., 1947).

Hickin, Norman E., <u>The Dry Rot Problem</u> (London: Hutchinson of London, 1972).

Hodgson, Fred T., <u>Modern Carpentry: A Practical Manual</u> (Chicago: Frederick J. Drake and Co., c. 1916).

Hunt, George M., and George A. Garratt, <u>Wood Preservation</u> (New York: McGraw-Hill Book Co., 1967).

<u>International Library of Technology</u>, Stair building, ornamental ironwork, roofing, sheet-metal work, building superintendence, contracts and permits. (Scranton, PA: International Textbook Co., 1909).

<u>International Library of Technology</u>, Excavating, shoring, stone masonry, carpentry, etc. (Scranton, PA: International Textbook Co., 1909).

Kidder, Frank E., Building Construction and Superintendence: Carpenters' Work (New York: William T. Comstock Co., 1922).

Kidder, Frank E., Kidder-Parker Architects' and Builders' Handbook (New York: John Wiley and Sons, Inc., 1931).

King, Charles A., Inside Finishing (Chicago: American Book Co., 1912).

Koel, Leonard, Carpentry (Homewood, IL: American Technical Publishers, Inc., 1985).

Kouba, Theodore F., Wisconsin's Amazing Woods Then and Now (Madison, WI: Wisconsin House Ltd., 1974).

Lloyd, William B., Millwork: Principles and Practices (Chicago: Cahners Publishing Co., 1966).

London, Mark, Masonry: How to Care for Old and Historic Brick and Stone (Washington, DC: The Preservation Press, 1986).

Milwaukee Builders' and Traders' Exchange. Souvenir and Hand Book (Milwaukee: Commercial Printing and Publishing Co., 1893).

Olin, Harold B., et al., Construction: Principles, Materials and Methods (Chicago: The Institute of Financial Education, 1983).

Raney, William Francis, Wisconsin (Appleton, WI: Perin Press, 1963).

Ries, H. and F. L. Gallup, Wisconsin Geological and Natural History Survey, Bulletin No. XV on the Clays of Wisconsin and Their Uses (Madison, WI: State of Wisconsin, 1906).

Sabin, Alvah Horton, House Painting (New York: John Wiley & Sons, Inc., 1924).

Sears, Stephen W., The Automobile in America (New York: American Heritage Publishing Co., 1977).

Standard Practice in Sheet Metal Work (Pittsburgh, PA: National Association of Sheet Metal Contractors, 1929).

The Painter, Gilder and Varnisher's Companion (Philadelphia: Henry Carey Baird, 1860).

Towne, Henry R., Locks and Builders Hardware: A Hand Book for Architects (New York: John Wiley & Sons, 1904).

Van Den Branden, F., and Thomas L. Hartsell, Plastering Skills (Homewood, IL: American Technical Publishers, Inc., 1984).

Walker's Insulation Techniques and Estimating Handbook (Chicago: Frank R. Walker Co., 1983).

Wells, Robert, Daylight in the Swamp (Garden City, NY: Doubleday & Co., 1978).

Wood Engineering Handbook, Prentice-Hall, Inc. (Englewood Cliffs, NJ: Prentice-Hall, Inc., 1982).

MISCELLANEOUS SOURCES

Architectural specification sheets used by architects Rau and Kirsch.

General Ordinances of the City of Milwaukee up to January 1, 1896 (Milwaukee: Milwaukee Common Council, 1896).

Milwaukee City Directories

Steer, Henry B., Lumber Production in the United States 1799-1946, Miscellaneous Publication No. 669 (United States Dept. of Agriculture).

Wisconsin Administrative Code (Uniform Dwelling Code).

NEWSPAPERS AND PERIODICALS

American Architect and Building News

American Preservation Technology Bulletin, Vol. XX, No. 3, 1988, p. 29.

Architectural Era, The

Brickbuilder

Building Age

Carpentry and Building

Fine Homebuilding

Horseless Age

House Beautiful

Journal of Light Construction

Milwaukee Journal, Apr. 22, 1923, Real Estate Section, p. 1.

Milwaukee Sentinel, Oct. 6, 1875, p. 8, col. 2.

New England Builder

Old House Journal

Scientific American

Scientific American Supplement

Traditional Building

SUGGESTED READING

ARCHITECTURAL REFERENCE AND DESIGN

American Victoriana (New York: Van Nostrand Reinhold Co., 1983).

Classic Houses of the Twenties (New York: Dover Publications, Inc., 1992).

Comstock, William T., Country Houses and Seaside Cottages of the Victorian Era (New York: Dover Publications, Inc., 1989).

Grow, Lawrence, The Old House Book of Cottages and Bungalows (Pittstown, NJ: The Main Street Press, 1987).

Karp, Ben, Ornamental Carpentry on Nineteenth-century American Houses (New York: Dover Publications, Inc., 1981).

Phillips, Steven J., Old-House Dictionary (Lakewood, CO: American Source Books, 1989).

The Victorian Design Book (Ottawa, Ontario: Lee Valley Tools, Ltd., 1984).

CARPENTRY

Kahn, Renee and Ellen Meagher, Preserving Porches (New York: Henry Holt and Co., Inc., 1990).

Koel, Leonard, Carpentry (Homewood, IL: American Technical Publishers, Inc., 1985).

Meers, Gary D., The Carpenter's Toolbox Manual (New York: Simon and Schuster, Inc., 1989).

MASONRY

Bricklaying: Brick and Block Masonry (Reston, VA: Brick Institute of America, 1988).

Clifton, James R., ed., Cleaning Stone & Masonry (Philadelphia: American Society for Testing and Materials, 1986).

Concrete, Masonry and Brickwork (New York: Dover Publications, Inc., 1975 Reprint).

London, Mark, How to Care for Old and Historic Brick and Stone (Washington, DC: The Preservation Press, 1988).

PAINTING

Moss, Roger, <u>Century of Color</u> (Watkins Glen, NY: American Life Foundation, 1981).

Pomada, Elizabeth, and Michael Larson, <u>America's Painted Ladies</u> (New York: Dutton Studio Books, 1992).

Pomada, Elizabeth, and Michael Larson, <u>Daughters of Painted Ladies</u> (New York: E. P. Dutton, 1987).

Pomada, Elizabeth, and Michael Larson, <u>Painted Ladies</u> (New York: E. P. Dutton, 1978).

Pomada, Elizabeth, and Michael Larson, <u>The Painted Ladies Revisited</u> (New York: E. P. Dutton, 1989).

ROOFING

Johnson, William E., <u>Roofers Handbook</u> (Solana Beach, CA: Craftsman Book Co., 1976).

PERIODICALS

<u>American Bungalow</u>

<u>American Preservation Technology Journal</u>

<u>Fine Homebuilding</u>

<u>Fine Woodworking</u>

<u>Historic Preservation</u>

<u>Journal of Light Construction</u>

<u>Journal of the Society of Architectural Historians</u>

<u>Preservation News</u>

<u>The Old House Journal</u>

<u>The Old House Journal Catalog</u> (annual)

<u>Traditional Building</u>

<u>Victorian Homes</u>